TILE
INDOORS & OUT

TILE

INDOORS & OUT
EVERY KIND & USE

MONTE BURCH

CREATIVE HOMEOWNER PRESS®

A DIVISION OF FEDERAL MARKETING CORPORATION,
24 PARK WAY, UPPER SADDLE RIVER, NEW JERSEY 07458

Manufactured in United States of America

Current Printing (last digit)
11 12 13 14 15 16 17 18

Editorial Director: Shirley M. Horowitz
Editor: Gail Kummings
Art Director: Léone Lewensohn
Designers: Léone Lewensohn, Paul Sochacki
Illustrator: Norman Nuding

We wish to extend our thanks to the many designers, companies, and other contributors who
allowed us to use their materials and gave us
advice. Their names, addresses, and individual
identifications of their contributions can be
found on *page 141.*

LC: 81-65569
ISBN: 0-932944-28-0 (paper)
      0-932944-27-2 (hardcover)

CREATIVE HOMEOWNER PRESS®
BOOK SERIES

A DIVISION OF FEDERAL
MARKETING CORPORATION
24 PARK WAY,
UPPER SADDLE RIVER, NJ 07458

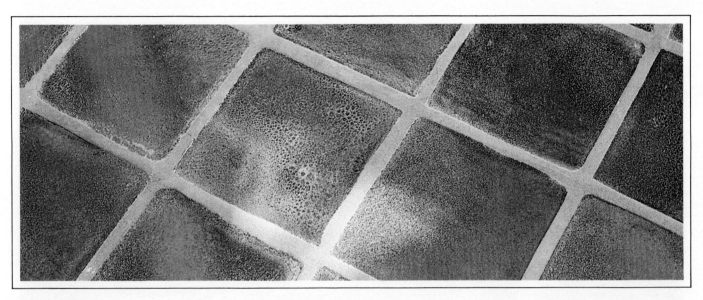

FOREWORD

Today, tile installations of all types are seen more frequently than ever before. In the past, whether on walls, floors, fountains or patios, tile was considered the province only of the wealthy or the exotic. Ceramic tile contributed to the beauty of Egyptian pyramids, Moslem mosques, and Spanish murals. Tile mosaics on Roman villa floors bespoke gracious living and vibrant architecture. Parquet wood floors, inlaid piece by piece by craftsmen, graced the mansions of the landed gentry. Resilient tile, on the other hand, was for a long time considered appropriate only for institutions such as schools or hospitals, because it lacked the beauty and charm desired in a home. With the wider range of tiles now available, all of these conceptions have changed.

Tile no longer is thought of as strictly an expensive or a regional design option. This change is partly due to its increased availability through distribution outlets. Another factor is the invention of thin-set adhesives, which require fewer masonry skills for application. Tile is gaining nationwide popularity as a surfacing for counters, floors, tubs and walls. New materials and new techniques also have resulted in additional designs for resilient

tile. In addition, homeowner demands have resulted in products that never existed before — carpet tile, mirror tile, beveled glass tile — to name a few. Carpet tiles are suitable for a family room floor, or the walls, ceiling or floor of a van. Designer ceramic tiles or glass tiles can surface the top of a coffee table, and wood parquet tiles may cover a plywood cube or end tables to match a floor installation.

New mastics that form strong, instant bonds have led to the creation of self-stick products that are quick to install and easy to maintain. Moreover, new materials have expanded the areas in which tile can be installed. Special adhesives enable the homeowner to consider outdoor as well as indoor projects.

However, for all the advances in design and adhesives, when a homeowner considers any tile installation, he or she is not contemplating a simple task. There are a number of reasons for the complexity of the task. In the first place, the tile you select is rarely made of the same substance as the surface upon which it is laid. Adhesives must bond to both surfaces. The planning of an installation requires care, for you are breaking one long visual expanse into small units that may or may not be of uniform size. Compounding the

problem is the variety of manufacturers involved in the creation of tile materials.

The instructions in this book, if carefully followed, lead the amateur through the steps necessary to result in a finished project that looks like a professional installation. If any steps are omitted — such as properly preparing a surface, or establishing correct working lines — the finished product will have a very short life or a far from satisfactory appearance.

The chapters in this book refer again and again to the role of the tile dealer in the planning process of any tile installation. There are many companies that produce tile, adhesives and (for ceramic tile) grout. The information given here applies generally to all products. However, the characteristics vary somewhat from manufacturer to manufacturer. For instance, quarry tile, a strong, naturally-colored ceramic tile, is often applied to floors. However, quarry tile comes in many varieties. Your tile dealer is·your best source concerning the characteristics of your particular choice. For instance, he will know whether it is water-resistant, or strong enough for use on a floor. Do not fail to take advantage of the dealer's expertise, or to read the instructions that the manufacturer supplies with the materials.

CONTENTS

TILE CHOICES

Tile is one of the most versatile building materials available. It can come in brightly colored ceramic, soft cushioning shag carpet, glittery mirrors, polished wood and marble, vinyl flooring; tiles can be of metal, cork or wallpaper. One of tile's main advantages is its ease of application. Of course, some types are more difficult to install than others; however, the average homeowner can easily install nearly any type of tile, including ceramic and marble, without a large investment in tools. In fact, a tile dealer will rent almost all of the specialized tools that you need for tile installation. For instance, about $20.00 is the usual rental for the tile cutter needed to cut ceramic tile. When you return the tool, the dealer usually will refund the entire amount. Ceramic tile kits made expressly for the do-it-yourselfer are readily available, but actually a homeowner can install almost any ceramic tile product without buying a kit.

Because so many different kinds of tile exist, there are best uses for each size, shape and material. Choosing and installing the correct tile for each situation is very important. Within the various categories of tile, such as ceramic or resilient, there are also different types for specific jobs — such as for floors, walls, edgings and specialized trim. A good tile dealer will help you decide which specific types

Water-resistant ceramic mosaic tiles come in sheets — plastic or thread binds the tile backs together. The sheets simplify the task of covering a wet bar with small tiles.

◁ A ceramic tile floor in a work room not only contributes to the room's beauty, but requires little time or effort to maintain.

Marble tile usually is applied to floors, but on a fireplace front it provides a fire-resistant covering that is often associated with elegant, expensive construction.

Ceramic tile need not be limited to inside installations. Here, a raised entryway of red brick tiles is color-coordinated with the living area to which it leads.

of tile are most suitable in a specific location or for a particular use. He (or she) can also help you select the adhesives needed and the best type of application methods for the materials chosen.

CERAMIC TILE

Ceramic tile has been a valued building material for many centuries. It was a favorite of the Egyptians and it has been used to create some of the most beautiful mosques in the world. Ceramic tile still is widely used, due to its durability, easy maintenance and, most of all, its long-lasting beauty.

General Characteristics

When installed by a professional, ceramic tile is one of the more expensive floor and wall coverings. This is obvious when you compare the cost of having a countertop-backsplash tiled to the cost of having one covered with plastic laminate. However, if you install the tile yourself, the costs diminish significantly — they will average quite a bit less than a professional laminate installation. What is more, the finished top will look much more like a professionally finished job than usually is the case with a homeowner-laminate installation — and you will have the benefit of the enduring ceramic surface that laminate lacks.

Ceramic tile is made by hardening a mixture of clays at extremely high temperatures. The different clays that are used and the temperatures at which they are baked determine the surfaces of the tiles, as well as to some extent their smoothness and color. Ceramic tile comes glazed and unglazed. Glazed tile is the common wall tile. The glazed color is applied after the tile has been cured in the kiln. Then the tile is baked a second time. On the other hand, unglazed tile (for instance, pavers or quarry stones) has coloring mixed in with the clay before the initial baking. The color runs throughout the tile. Quarry and paver tiles utilize natural, earth-tone coloring agents, such as clays; these are not processed but used in the state that they are mined. Ceramic moasics utilize manufactured pigments made from chemicals mixed together.

There is almost no limit to the different types of ceramic tile. Its colors cover the rainbow, from light tints to shockingly brilliant colors. In addition to all the different colors, ceramic tile also is available imprinted with hundreds of different patterns. The surface of the tile may resemble glass or a soft mattelike suede finish. The texture of the surface may range from ultra-smooth to coarse, or even sculptured. Each type of tile also has standard trim pieces available for finishing the work at joints around floors, around windows, on counter edges, and so on. Self-sticking ceramic tile also is now available. You peel off a paper backing and press the tile in place. A powerful adhesive already on the tile back forms a permanent bond with the wall. Then apply grout to the spaces between the tiles, just as with dry-back ceramic tiles.

Ceramic tile comes in many shapes and sizes. Choose the usual square or rectangular configuration, or one such as this ogee-shaped unit.

Ceramic tile sizes range from tiny mosaics to 10-inch-square quarry tiles. The shapes vary; they are available in the traditional squares, as well as rectangular, cloverleaf mosaics, hexagons, octagons and the moorish curve.

One of the chief advantages of ceramic tile is its durability. It withstands scuffing, and also is extremely popular as a kitchen countertop material since it cannot be cut with a knife or easily scratched. It cleans well with soap and water. Another important feature is that ceramic tile is fireproof, which makes it suitable for the safety-conscious (as we all should be) on surfaces near fireplaces and wood stoves. Since it

Because of its water-resistance and durability, ceramic tile is a logical and desirable choice for a tub surround and nearby walls.

Because of the thread backing, mosaic ceramic sheets can cover counter edges to create a continuous, smooth surface.

is a traditional, classic material, ceramic tile fits into any decorating style or period whether it is Early American, Court French, Oriental or contemporary.

Types of Ceramic Tile

Choosing the correct tile for the job is extremely important in terms of appearance, the long life of the tile, easy maintenance, fire-protection and safety. Wall tiles are usually not as thick as the quarry, paver or floor tiles; thicker tiles should be used for flooring. Thin tiles will not hold up well under normal household foot traffic and heavy counter use. The resulting breakage will entail expense for replacement. Unglazed tiles are subject to moisture damage; glazed, glassy surfaces are not suitable to areas where people can slip — on shower floors or around pools.

Quarry tile. Quarry tile is an unglazed tile available in several rich-looking, natural earth-tone colors. Primarily used as a floor covering, it may be used inside and outside. Usually quarry tile is large — from 6x6 inches up to 8 or 10 inches square — and its thickness ranges from ⅜ to ½ inch. There are a number of different shapes from which to choose: square, hexagon, rectangle, moorish and octagon. Some tiles also come glazed.

Pavers. Paver tile resembles quarry tile in composition, style and use. Rustic and durable, it is designed for high traffic areas, such as walkways, terraces and pa-

The coloring of quarry and paver tile comes from the natural tones of the clays from which they are made. Both types come glazed or unglazed. They are commonly used on floors.

◊ Antique Persian tiles cover this fireplace opening and hearth. The simplicity of surrounding paneling highlights the tiles' ornateness.

Colored grout in a hallway offers obvious design advantages. Its second advantage is less obvious — it hides the dirt and discoloration that often are problems with white grout.

Light-colored grout accents the darker octagonal quarry tiles.

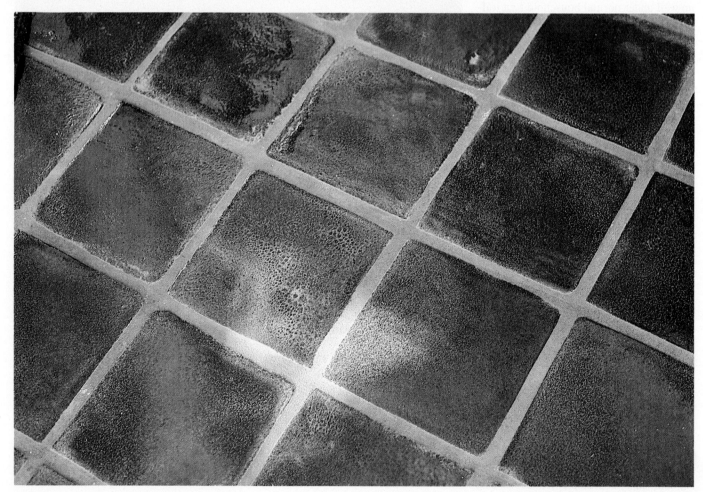

Glazed ceramic tile was chosen for a morning room (see p. 2) because the tile withstands changes in temperature and humidity levels.

Entryways and other high-traffic areas require a floor covering that can withstand wear and tear. Quarry tile is especially appropriate because of its thickness and strength.

Glazed ceramic floor tile comes in a color range unavailable in quarry or paver tiles.

To the beige walls and rattan furniture of this kitchen, the rich earth-brown of glazed quarry tile brings a contrasting texture and color. Quarry covers the floor, table and countertop.

Grout color that contrasts with the tile is integral to the design scheme of this room.

tios, and is quite commonly used in shopping malls. It also is suitable for such surfaces as interior floors and walls, and fireplace facings. When proper installation methods are followed, paver may also be used on exterior floors and walls — but only if they are not subject to freezing. The tile is usually finished with a slip-resistant surface to provide safe walking under wet conditions. Available in a number of different earth tones, this tile is most often thick and comes in sizes ranging from 4x8 to 8x8 inches. A number of different trim pieces are sold with it, as with quarry tile.

Floor brick. Floor brick is an extremely heavy-duty flooring material. It is most commonly used in industrial applications, although it sometimes is used in residential patios and driveways subject to heavy use. Available in three or four different earthtones, it is made of high-quality shale and is designed with several different surfaces, including scored diamond-tread for safety. A number of trim units can be purchased to handle various shape requirements.

Swimming pool tile. Swimming pool tile is a rugged quarry tile, which is glazed to provide an excellent surface for pool interior applications. It comes colored only in Olympic blue. It is most commonly manufactured in ½x6x6 inch squares with either smooth or abrasive surfaces. There are also depth-marker tiles available, as well as cap units, to complement the blue field tiles.

Glazed wall tile. This is the most frequently used type of ceramic tile. Although it is commonly called wall tile, some varieties can also be used as flooring. It is excellent for use on interior walls, kitchen countertops and vanities. Some types can also be used on exterior walls. Check the manufacturer's recommendations regarding uses of a specific tile.

Glazed wall tile is available in a number of sizes, colors and surfaces. Usually it is ¼ to ⅜ inches thick and from 2x4 and 4x4 inches to 8x8 inches square. It comes in many shapes, including square, rectangular, hexagonal, moorish, and octagonal.

Even swimming pool tile has changed in recent years. The extra touch of designer trim tiles personalizes an installation that otherwise could have had an almost institutional appearance.

When you lay out a countertop, leave openings that correspond to the tile size. Then sink small metal pans into the openings for a place to start seedlings and houseplants.

◁ Quarry tile is durable and long-lasting, even in an outside location. Quarry's natural coloring blends with nearly any landscaping.

This ceramic tile countertop holds up under the high heat of wok cooking. Special "keystone" shaped tiles curve around the built-in burner and provide ample working room for the cook.

Water and stain-resistant, ceramic tile is a safe, easy-to-clean surface for a wet bar.

Stove burner units often come in sizes that are a multiple of the tile dimensions. Proper spacing allows for simple installation.

◁ In this bathroom, diagonal layout and alternated tile sizes create a striking room. Advanced planning and careful layout are the keys.

Instructions for countertop tile installation around a corner sink are in Chapter 3.

Ceramic tile, installed on water-resistant backing and with water-resistant adhesive and grout, covers both the shower stall walls and the adjacent tub.

An unusual project involves tiling a range hood. For instructions, see Chapter 3.

These designer tiles feature figures. The tiles come with or without the months of the year.

Designer tiles offer attractive custom effects. Here special tiles by Summetville are randomly interspersed with gray field tiles. Wide grout lines enhance the appearance of the tiles.

Colors range from hospital white to brilliant orange-red and a deep blue. Some varieties are speckled or flecked, others imprinted to resemble Dutch, Spanish or other types of hand-decorated "native" tile.

Some types of glazed ceramic tile have a high gloss finish; others are textured or matte. Still others have a crazed finish (as on the cover): glaze is applied to the tile; the tile is heated and then quickly cooled, which causes the glaze to develop fine cracks that are darker than the tile's original color. Special wall tile for kitchen countertops has a heavy-duty glaze. Other special tiles have a slip-resistant finish for safety in bathrooms or around pools.

The clay of wall tile is usually more porous than that of quarry or paver tile, but the glazing prevents water penetration. However, the glaze can be scratched, so do not use a wall tile for floors in high traffic areas unless the manufacturer so specifies.

A number of trim tiles are available. These are discussed at length in the next chapter. You can often match the tile color and finish with glazed ceramic bathroom accessories. These include towel bar brackets and bars, soap dishes and roll paper holders. For finishing the edges of countertops there is a special contoured countertop trim designed to prevent drips.

Pregrouted sheets. Ceramic wall tiles are also available in sheet form. As many as 8, 12, or 64 tiles are held together with a special white silicone grout to provide quick, easy application. The tile size in a given sheet can run from 1x1 inch mosaics to 4x4 inch conventional size. Because the grout has been treated with a special mildew and fungus inhibitor, pregrouted sheets are excellent for shower and tub enclosures. On the other hand, because of this special treatment, the FDA does not recommend installing the sheets on kitchen countertops or in other food preparation areas. (Many people use sheets of the small tiles for tabletops. However, you probably should not use them on serving tables, given the FDA recommendations.) The grout, which is water-repellent and stain-resistant, cleans easily with a damp cloth. The sheets are flexible enough to bend and stretch with normal building movement. A number of standard trim

Pregrouted sheets, like mosaic sheets, are easy to install and follow curved surfaces with an ease that larger tiles cannot imitate.

It is easy to cover a bath area with pregrouted sheets because silicone grout is already inserted between the tiles.

An old island becomes brighter and easier to clean with the application of ceramic tile to several of its surfaces.

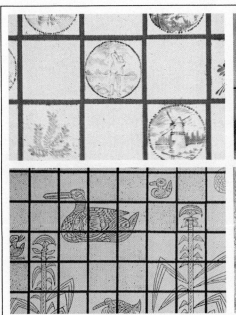

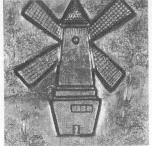

Designer tiles come in many styles. Some imitate regional tiles, such as the blue Delft pattern seen here. Others include designs that are not regionally defined. For recreational areas, consider including tiles whose patterns are etched into or raised above the body of the tile, such as the windmill shown. Especially unusual are large, mural-style patterns that utilize the grid pattern of ceramic tile and grout, but do not necessarily confine the designs to a single tile.

sets are also available. After installation, a special rubber silicone grout is applied to match that in the sheets. Thus, grouting time is substantially reduced.

These pregrouted sheets also come in kit form, including special rounded corner strips to finish tiled tub and shower surrounds. The sheets are self-trimming, since not only the surfaces but also two edges are glazed. Internal corner strips and tile leg strips are used to finish at the vertical edges of the tub and the corners. The internal corner strips allow for variance in the straightness of the walls and provide a curved, easy-to-clean corner.

Ceramic mosaic tile. Ceramic mosaic tile is small, fine-grained porcelain tile made of clay that has been thoroughly mixed with colored pigments. It can be found as tiny, round, pebble-shaped tile, 2x2 inch squares, and many other shapes and sizes in between. This includes standard shapes, as well as some that are not so standard, including "teardrop" and "cloverleaf." Most are ¼ inch thick. Quite impervious to water, ceramic mosaic also is stainproof, dentproof and frostproof. Finishes range from very high gloss for walls and counters to textured for slip-resistant floors. With proper installation, ceramic mosaics make excellent surfaces for counter and vanity tops, interior walls, exterior walls and floors, swimming pool linings and all types of buildings.

In addition to all this, ceramic mosaic tile has another characteristic that gives it even greater design potential. The tiles are commonly adhered to a backing sheet of rubber, plastic, paper or heavy thread. This makes them a versatile surfacing ma-

terial available for both indoor and outdoor installation, because the large panels can be used to cover rounded surfaces such as curved counters, swimming pools, fountains and columns.

Custom stones. One of the chief advantages of ceramic tile is that its use and appearance have almost no limitations. Several tile manufacturers will make custom-designed tiles, allowing you to create hand-painted tiles to suit your particular decor. Most often, as with wall tile, the custom design is added at the time of the glazing process. You also can order custom-shaped tiles made to fit the specific shape of a free-form bathtub, swimming pool or fountain.

Of course, free-form and hand-painted and glazed tiles are quite expensive. Still, it takes very few hand-painted accent tiles inserted on, above or behind the kitchen

countertop, in a table or on a bathroom wall to personalize a room design. Specially shaped tiles add both unusual freedom of structural design and form and the convenience and beauty of ceramics. Together, these attributes can result in a unique architectural feature.

Outdoor Use

Ceramic tile is not just for indoor use. In fact, it is probably as important as an outdoor building material as it is indoors. Ceramic mosaics can add underwater artwork to a swimming pool or cover a beautiful backyard fountain. Ceramics can even "pave" a courtyard, as well as the front stoop or the walks around your home. Some people apply it to patios, walls and outdoor tables and seats. Others use it to cover barbecues, planters, stairs and steps.

Lay ceramic tile on a concrete patio or walkway. Choose tile that is appropriate for outdoor use. Take advantage of unusual forms and special trim tiles.

Porcelain ceramic tile sheets were laid over a poured concrete planter. The trim tiles along the edge were individually set.

In this outdoor setting, the geometric forms of tile and bricks set off a large, formal series of pools surrounded by natural growth and trimmed formal plantings and planters.

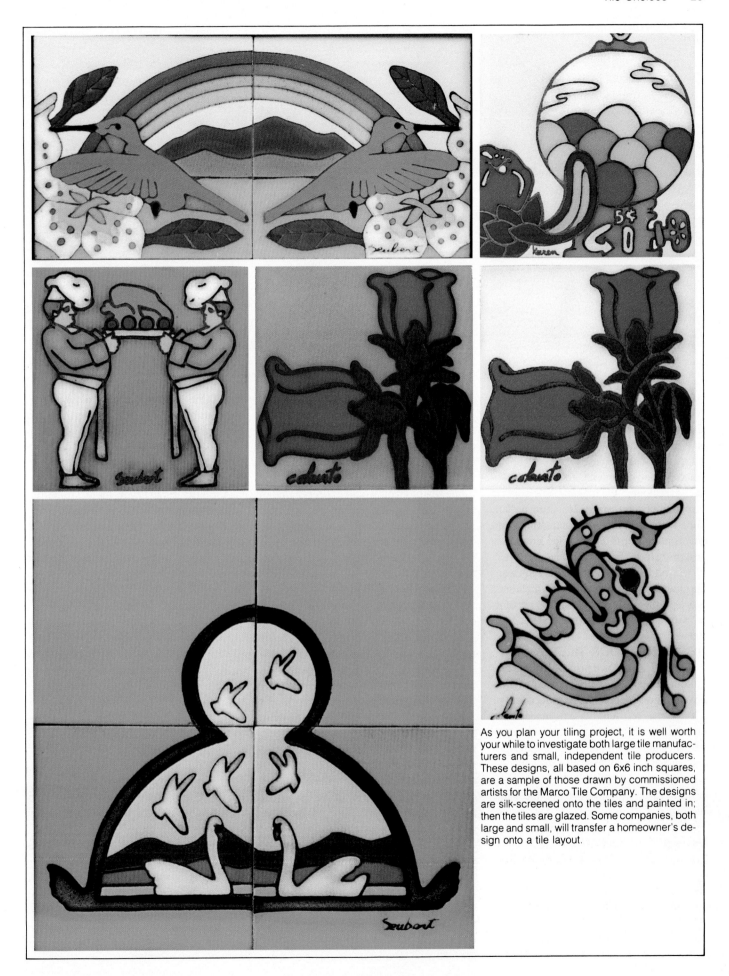

As you plan your tiling project, it is well worth your while to investigate both large tile manufacturers and small, independent tile producers. These designs, all based on 6x6 inch squares, are a sample of those drawn by commissioned artists for the Marco Tile Company. The designs are silk-screened onto the tiles and painted in; then the tiles are glazed. Some companies, both large and small, will transfer a homeowner's design onto a tile layout.

Apply tile to a tabletop with organic adhesive. Then nail on a wood strip border.

The ceramic tile on this patio is a continuation of the tile used in the sitting room inside the house. The patterned strips come as an accessory to sheets of field tile.

Grout

When ceramic tile is installed, thin spaces are left between each tile in the tile expanse. These spaces (joints) are filled with a special grouting material that comes in several colors and with different properties. Grout and tile color can be either matching or contrasting. Matching or dark grout will help hide dirt. Contrasting grout enables the user to employ the grout as a design feature. Today's grouts are waterproof, mildew-resistant and easy to clean. Dirt buildup in the grout line, which once was a problem, can now easily be prevented with a spray-on silicone sealer.

RESILIENT FLOOR TILES

Resilient floor tile is a prime example of a building material that has evolved and improved a great deal in the past decade. For a long time, resilient tile was made of asphalt. Then vinyl asbestos tile was introduced. It offered more appealing designs and easier upkeep than did asphalt tile. Now vinyl composition floor tile may eclipse vinyl asbestos tile for the same reasons.

General Characteristics

Today's resilient floor tile is a far cry from the old style institutional asphalt flooring. Resilient flooring can simulate the appearance of almost any material, from brick to flagstone to marble. There are hundreds of designs and colors — as well as textures — that can be used to create flooring designs and effects, including natural-looking patterns that duplicate substances such as butcher block parquet. You can choose the look of moorish ceramic tile or flagstone. There even is a used-brick pattern, complete with the imperfections and subtle shading you would expect to find in the real thing. Some resilient tile so closely resembles ceramic tile that it appears to have come right out of the kiln. Resilient tile also offers decorative colors and patterns unique to its type.

You can install resilient tile over any surface in the house, including over wood, concrete or old resilient or ceramic tile — as long as the original surface is smooth, uncushioned and solidly laid. Installed on a wall resilient tile creates an unusual and durable wall covering or room accent.

There are several advantages to resilient tile. It is one of the more economical flooring materials and is relatively easy to install. Resilient tile is easy to maintain and is durable, although it will not hold up as long as ceramic tile. It comes either with a hard-textured ("slick") finish or with a cushioned, soft surface.

Resilient floor tile is usually installed with adhesive. It also comes with adhesive already applied to the tile backing. The tile comes in two sizes, 9x9 and 12x12. Also available are contrasting features — narrow strips of resilient material that you can lay in with square tile to create borders, geometric patterns or unusual personal designs. (Full-sized tile of contrasting colors also can be used for these effects). Vinyl base molding matches or contrasts with the vinyl flooring materials.

Types of Resilient Tile

Asphalt. Pioneer of the resilient-tile field, asphalt tile is the most economical of the flooring tiles. It is available only in a limited number of colors and patterns and requires more maintenance than do the more modern tiles. Another disadvantage is that it is more rigid than the newer tiles, so it cracks more readily. However, asphalt tile is good for utility areas or for other places demanding economical tile.

Vinyl asbestos. One of the most popular resilient flooring materials consists of modern vinyl resins fortified with strong asbestos fibers. This type of tile is greaseproof, long-wearing, and easy to maintain. Vinyl asbestos tile is quite durable and resistant to indentation. It can be installed almost anywhere in your home. Fairly economical and available in a number of different styles and colors, it is probably the most popular and commonly used tile today.

Vinyl asbestos tile is available with a no-wax feature, providing a crystal-clear, glossy surface that shines without waxing. Normal cleaning will maintain the shine for a long time. (Eventually, no-wax tile requires special polish sold by the manufacturer.) Vinyl asbestos comes in self-sticking and adhesive-installed styles.

This resilient tile looks like wood, is self-stick, and never needs waxing. The result is an attractive, easy-to-install, easy-to-clean floor.

Solid vinyl tiles. This is the aristocrat of the resilient tile field; it is fast gaining in popularity, even though it is expensive. Manufactured from vinyl resins to withstand pressures up to 25 pounds per square inch, it practically never suffers from indentation problems. The high vinyl content in solid vinyl tile provides a very dense material noted for its true whites and clear, brilliant, rich-looking colors. Since the vinyl surface is nonporous, it is more resistant to dirt, stains and grease than is vinyl asbestos tile. Finally, it is easier to install than vinyl asbestos tile. Solid vinyl is more flexible, and it can be cut more easily. Trimming this tile to fit around an intricate molding does not require a tremendous amount of skill.

Combinations. Manufacturers also have created tiles by sealing material such as cork, or even wood veneer, with a vinyl layer. These combinations will work as floor coverings, but they are hard to find and usually are not as popular as the other, more common, resilient flooring materials.

Vinyl wall tile. Also on the market is a special self-sticking vinyl wall tile that resembles ceramic tile. The classic, 17th century painted design looks like that of a hand-painted, hand-fired ceramic tile. Its water-resistance permits application on kitchen backsplashes. However, it should not be used for the countertops or tub or shower areas because the tile adhesive cannot hold up to that amount of water

exposure. Although it resists grease, do not install vinyl wall tile over a range because it withstands heat only up to 140 degrees. These tiles can be cut with a knife or bent around corners. They are approximately four inches square and come in sheets of four each. The mortar line spacing is usually ⅛ inch wide, to which a special grout is applied.

WOOD TILES

Parquet or inlaid wood tiles traditionally have been used to create elegant and long-lasting floors in the finest homes. Creating these beautiful floors used to be a difficult, time-consuming, task. An artisan would fashion the chosen floor design by carefully cutting and fitting the pieces of wood right at the site. Today, parquet comes in preassembled squares, or tile, that are installed easily either by adhering them to the floor or by nailing them down in the traditional manner.

The tile comes in two forms. The first has the flat edges found on all tile. These butt together, and installation is simple. The second comes with special tongue-and-groove joints, which fit together as you lay the tile. Installing this version requires more care. However, the process creates a strong, long-lasting joint that will not shrink or pull apart, resulting in a continuous and beautiful floor surface.

Parquet tiles are finished in a variety of wood tones, or they can be purchased in unfinished style. Finished tile normally is the easiest for the average do-it-yourselfer to install, because it requires no special skill in floor finishing. On the other hand, unfinished tile allows the homeowner the option of matching the stain in the floor to the room's decor and existing flooring.

Laid square by square, wood parquet floors are easier to install than they once were. Hold the tiles in place with adhesive or small nails.

Here wood tiles are used to cover a tub enclosure. Then the tub is set on top of the tiles. Cover such an installation with a waterproofing varnish such as marine spar varnish.

To create an attractive end table, design a cube that corresponds to the size of the wood tiles you will use. (See Chapter 6).

An alternative table design is shown here. The edges of wood squares are finished.

Most wood tile is $5/16$ to $3/4$ inches thick. Sizes range from 6x6 to 13x13 inches square. Also available are 3x6 inch blocks and random-length plank strips that are 3, 5, and 7 inches wide. Manufacturers have inserted small circular wooden insets at each end of many of the plank strip styles. The insets are colored differently than the planks themselves, so that the planks appear to have been fastened down with wood pegs.

Solid wood tile is durable, long wearing and easy to maintain. The prefinished blocks have a factory finish that preserves the natural beauty of the wood. Traffic marks do not show, and normal care requires only vacuum cleaning.

Both the flat-edge and tongue-and groove types can be laid quickly. Wood parquet may be applied directly over a concrete, resilient tile, plywood, or solid wood surface. The tile may also be nailed to a wooden subfloor. It should not be installed over rubber tile because the adhesive for wood tile is not compatible with the rubber.

Wooden tile can also be used to create an accent wall. One unusual design combines it in rows with rows of mirror tile. Leftover tile from one job can be used to produce matching accessories or elegant table tops for cocktail tables or end tables.

SPECIALTY TILES

In addition to the usual materials meant by the term ''tile,'' there are a host of specialty tiles, most of which are designed for covering interior walls. Some come with self-stick backings, so they provide an easy method for highlighting small or large areas of a room, adding variety to its decor, or solving the problems presented by particular or difficult areas such as behind a stove. Others are adhered with double-faced tape. The most expensive — marble and beveled glass — require adhesives. The tiles listed below range from inexpensive wallpaper squares to costly marble and beveled glass. All add design options and decorator effects worth consideration when you are thinking of and planning the tiling of a room or surface.

Self-Stick Options

Wallpaper tile. Wallpaper is now available in square tiles, which are much less awkward to put up than long strips of wallpaper. The preglued squares are presoaked and pressed to the wall. The key to good application is practice at aligning the squares. If you spend too much time aligning the papers, the edges will dry a little too much before they adhere, and they will curl. In such cases, apply wheat or vinyl paste (depending upon type of paper and location) for a smooth, professional-looking result.

Cork tile. Cork tile is not only easy to install, it is easily cleaned with a vacuum cleaner brush. Cork tile comes in a num-

ber of different designs and colors, and it definitely has good insulating value. The usual size is 12x12 inches and $3/8$ inch thick. Most is self-sticking, although some require a special adhesive. Either type can be trimmed with a knife or scissors to suit the application. When cork tile is laid in strips or in a checkerboard with mirror tile, or with light wood tile, the results can be striking.

Special cork sealers are available in spray or brush form. These cut down on the cork smell, and help prevent the cork from crumbling. Their use is not required — just recommended.

Cork tile can be installed over any clean, dry surface. However, because of the way cork is formed it breaks apart quite easily, so it is not recommended for floor installation. If you do lay it on a floor, you will have to seal it with many coats of varnish before the surface will be secure. If you truly want a cork floor, investigate the vinyl composition tiles that have cork sealed into the vinyl.

◁ Wood tile also comes in plank style. The wood's richness is the same as that of a normal hardwood floor — a more difficult installation.

Tape or Adhesive Mounting

Mirror tile. Mirror tile installation requires no experience or special tools. With a box or two of tile you can quickly turn a wall into a bright decorative accent. Since mirror tile creates the illusion of more space, it not only enlarges any room, it also lightens up a dark area, such as an interior hallway. A wall of mirror tile in a bedroom is both decorative and functional.

Mirror tile can be laid on any clean, level wall surface. However, although mirror tile can be used in almost every room of the house, I would not suggest it for a small child's room. Moreover, for safety reasons, you should not attempt to place mirror tile on a ceiling. This installation should only be done by a professional.

Mirror tile is traditionally made of glass, but some also is available in acrylic. The size of both is usually about ⅛ inch thick and 12x12 inches square. This simplifies figuring the amount you will need for a room's square footage. The tile usually comes six to a package, along with the mounting tape needed for installation. Do not attempt to get a stronger bond by substituting adhesive for mounting tape. Most adhesives dissolve the mirror backing and ruin the tile. A special mastic will be available as of Spring, 1981; check in your local area. Also available is special metal edging, which encloses the tile within its frame. It takes about an hour to cover an average wall.

Mirror tile today is made with almost any type of design or pattern you can imagine imprinted on it. Along with standard clear tile there are gold veins, gold veins on smoked glass, black veins, silver

Available in clear, and as here, veined styles, mirror tile adds light and space to any room. The tile's beveled edges add an elegant touch.

swirls, gold foil and red or brown foil veining. Imprinted on some varieties are geometric patterns such as circles, chevrons or arrows. The tile also comes tinted in several different colors. Imprinted edges on some create the illusion of beveled mirror tile. These variations enable you to create a highly personalized room decor.

Carpet tile. Carpet tile turns the messy, awkward job of carpet installation into a quick and easy one. Placement requires less time and few special tools. Carpet tile can be chosen for any room. The pile is not as dense as that in rolled carpet, but it can serve well in both high- and low-traffic areas.

Carpet tile (or "carpet squares") normally comes in one size: 12x12 inches. Varying thicknesses and patterns are available, as well as hundreds of different colors. Carpet tile can be purchased either dry-backed or self-sticking. Dry-backed carpet tile needs a special adhesive or, for less permanent jobs, double-faced tape. Carpet tile can go over almost any surface, as long as it is clean and dry. However, it is not highly recommended for use in below-ground areas, such as a basement, because it could mildew.

Shag. Shag carpet tile greatly resembles its counterpart in roll carpeting. Because of its high loop and thick pile, no seams show once it is installed. Heavy, dense foam-rubber backs provide a cushioning effect. Shag carpet tile is available in a number of pile thicknesses, lengths

and colors. Most types come with self-adhering backs, so the installer need only peel off the backing paper and press the tile in place.

Cut shag. Cut shag tile is less expensive than the loop and pile shag. It is an excellent choice for family rooms and other areas that receive moderately hard use. It is shorter than shag and has a foam backing.

Kitchen squares. This decorated printed carpet tile has a short fiber on a foam-rubber backing. Spot and spill-resistant, it is excellent for kitchens, play rooms and other hard-use areas.

Outdoor-indoor carpet tiles. Made from materials such as olefin, this soil-repellent flooring is excellent for porches and breezeways and for hard-wear areas such as family rooms and kitchens. It has a very short, dense fiber on a foam-rubber backing. The interior variety can be found with adhesive backing. The types used for exterior or wet-damp settings come dry-backed and require a special adhesive. Some outdoor-indoor tile is water-resistant. Check the manufacturer's label if you need a water-resistant surface, such as in a bathroom.

Metal tile. Metal tile is made of aluminum. Its surface is then finished to resemble metal finishes or imprinted with decorative designs to resemble hand-painted ceramic tile. The common metal colors are brushed aluminum, copper and stainless steel. Some metal tiles have a baked epoxy finish. These come in metal

finishes, such as copper and a natural aluminum, as well as white, blue, brown, gold and green. They also are sometimes imprinted with a number of different designs. The tiles are normally 4¼ x 4¼ inches square. They can be installed with self-sticking tape on any wall surface. If they are installed in an area of high heat — for instance, behind a stove — use adhesive for the necessary bond.

Metal tile is especially suited for use behind stoves or next to ovens because of its heat-resistant qualities. It can also be used on backsplashes in the kitchen, as well as for decorative colorful accents in any room in the house. However, metal tile requires frequent cleaning in areas that are exposed to moisture, grease or dirt.

Tin wall and ceiling pieces. Tin ceilings are made from sheets of steel that are fed through huge, old drop presses — the same presses that were used when tin ceilings were common, some seventy-five years ago. Because the presses are so old and because of the techniques are "less technologically advanced" than those of modern presses, each panel produced is slightly different than the next. As a result, any installation of tin ceiling and wall pieces will have its own unique character. Two companies — the Barney Brainum-Shaker Steel Company of Glendale, New York, and the W. F. Norman Company of Nevada, Missouri — are manufacturing the tin panels with the same dies their companies used years ago.

Most of the panels are large: they average between 2x4 and 2x8 feet in size. However, their designs often resemble a set of tiles — a 2x4 panel, for instance, may resemble four 12x12 inch tiles. As a result, the panels provide an easy way to "tile" a wall or a ceiling. Even more appropriately called "tile" are the small sections available from the Norman Company. Pieces come in 12x12 and 12x24 inch sizes. As such, they can be used in the same manner as other decorative tile. The tin tiles are relatively inexpensive and are easily installed. The units attach to furring strips placed over an existing surface. As a result, you do not have to prepare the surface, as you do with other tiles. In fact, one reason that tin ceilings and walls were so popular was that they could be fastened over old ceilings of broken and cracked plaster without necessitating repair of the original surface.

Metal tile is set with adhesive or double-faced tape. The tile is noted for its heat-resistance, making it popular for backsplashes behind stoves.

Finally, tin tiles create a durable protective surface. They can be painted with oil-based paint, but they can also be left in their original matte metal finish. (In cooking areas or any other which are more prone to collect grease buildup, some installers cover the tin with protective clear acrylic layers.) Do not use water-based paint; it will cause the metal to rust. Tin tiles work well in areas subject to high heat; once they were widely used in public buildings because they were an extremely efficient firestop. Thus they are appropriate for installation on or around fireplaces or stoves.

Once installed, the tin pieces require only the normal cleaning for a metal or a painted surface. Both companies offer sheets of steel; the Norman Company also stamps panels and tiles of solid brass and solid copper.

Beveled glass. Beveled glass tile comes in two different forms: large sheets of tile-size squares and small squares manufactured primarily for inclusion in stained glass projects. The large sheets come in 10x10 foot panels. Such a panel creates an unusual wall. Beveled glass above a fireplace or above a wainscoting contributes to the formality of a room. A wall of beveled tile in a bedroom can dress up the room and enlarge it. However, such an installation is as difficult as it is beautiful. The sheets require special fasteners. The panel size makes the sheets unwieldy and dangerous for the amateur. Any installation of this kind requires a professional's services.

Small beveled glass tile come in a number of sizes, from 2x8 inch strips to 3x3 inch squares. If you attempt a project involving glass tile, you must pay attention to the surface under the tile, since the tile is transparent. Beveled glass tile cannot be secured with any type of adhesive; nor should you attempt to drill holes in the tiles. However, the beveled glass tile can be set into special frames to create unusual coffeetable tops. It can also be soldered together in the same manner as stained glass pieces, and used to create room dividers, windows or wall hangings.

Stone and slate. Two unusual sources of tile are stone and slate. They are more available in some areas of the country than others, and availability directly affects cost. In spite of their possible expense, however, both create a striking surface, either inside or out.

Stone and slate come in natural earth colors, ranging from blacks and grays to pinks and reds. Some come in shades of blue and green. Slate can be purchased in boxed sets, but stone is more difficult to find. Most boxed slate comes in batches of mixed colors, but, since a floor made from these sets will be very distracting to the eye, select variations on a single shade and texture. If necessary, insist that your dealer special order the slate you have chosen.

Inside, slate and stone create very hard floors. Because of their weight, the joist support in the floor often must be doubled or bridges added before the tile can be laid on top. Outside, they are a desirable patio choice. It should be noted, however, that slate does not hold up as well as other

A special metal tile that has been recently reintroduced is one that used to make up tin ceiling and walls. Some tin sheets come in small enough pieces to qualify as tiles.

Sturdy enough to qualify as firestops, tin ceiling pieces are easy to install (the panels are nailed to furring strips). They can be painted to match the existing decor or left plain.

stone in outside installations. Inside installations are laid in the same way as ceramic tile. Outside installations, however, require a thick bed of mortar.

Marble tile. No other tile equals the luxury of marble tile. Due to its durability and beauty, it has traditionally been used to create impressive and long-lasting entryways. It can be installed on walls, floors, and even on furniture, such as Italian Provincial. Use it as an elegant accent or indulge yourself with a wall-to-wall treatment. Available at most leading tile stores are special marble sealers that help protect the marble surface from serious stains. Even with sealer, however, marble is not recommended for kitchen floors. Once installed, marble tile requires only simple rules of care and maintenance. See Chapter 8 for information on maintenance and repair.

Polished marble tile is available in several different solid colors — including white, black, red and several tones of brown — as well as veined and travertine (pitted). The tile is 6x6 inches square and ¼ inch thick. You can, of course, quite often have it custom cut to specific sizes at local marble companies.

Marble tile is excellent choice for the facing on a fireplace or for a fireproof base for a free-standing stove or fireplace. In fact, major flooring stores and leading mail order houses such as Sears offer kits for the latter two projects. Each kit contains the required materials, including adhesive and grout, and tools for installing the tile as a fireplace facer or as a hearth.

Synthetic marble. Synthetic marble tile can also be found. This unusual tile, which costs about half as much as authentic marble, is created by embedding marble chips in a material such as polyester resin and is available in a number of different colors and sizes. Day-to-day maintenance of synthetic marble is less of a problem than is maintenance of authentic marble. However, synthetic marble will not last as long as true marble. The synthetic mars more easily and scratches are far less easy to correct.

Both marble and synthetic marble can be installed over any surface on which you might lay ceramic tile. Their methods of installation also are the same.

TILE COST COMPARISONS*

Type	Cost
Ceramic Tile	$1.50 to $5.00 per sq. ft. for standard factory-made tile. Up to $50.00 per sq. ft. for custom tile.
Resilient Tile	$.20 to $1.00 per sq. ft.
Vinyl Wall Tile	$1.00 per sq. ft.
Wood Tile	$2.00 to $7.00 per sq. ft.
Carpet Tile	$.60 to $2.00 per sq. ft.
Cork Tiles	$1.00 per sq. ft.
Mirror Tile	$1.00 per sq. ft.
Metal Tile	$1.50 per sq. ft.
Tin Tile	$7.00 per sq. ft.
Marble Tile	$5.00 per sq. ft.

*As of June 1980. Note: although costs rise, the relative costs should remain the same.

Italian ceramic tiles cover the floors of an entryway, kitchen and dining area. The tile floor unites architecturally separated rooms.

CERAMIC TILE BASICS

Installing ceramic tile appears to be a complicated job requiring special tools and training. Indeed, not too many years ago homeowner installation was difficult because the tile had to be set in a thick bed of mortar. Today, however, with quick-set adhesives and special trim pieces, installing ceramic tile can be fast and uncomplicated, even for someone who has never done the job before. In addition, installation can be accomplished using very few special tools. Although you could probably get by with the kitchen tool drawer, using tools suited for tiling not only makes the job easier, but usually results in better workmanship.

GENERAL MATERIALS LIST
Tools

If you are a handyman, you probably already have many of the tools necessary for tile setting: a carpenter's level, tape rule, plumb line, chalk line, carborundum stone or whetstone, straight edge, scraper or putty knife, sponge and cleaning rags. In addition, you will need some specialized tools, which can be purchased from your tile dealer. You will need a notched trow-

el, a tile cutter or glass cutter, tile nippers, and a rubber float or squeegee for grout application. Do not purchase this equipment until you have finalized your plans. Then be sure you buy the kind of trowel required for application of your particular ceramic tile adhesive.

Depending on the methods used for tile application, you may also need other tools, but they will be discussed as the specific projects are covered. In addition to tile, you also need adhesive and grout.

In many cases the tile dealer will offer a special tool kit that includes those tools necessary and useful for your particular project. If you do not wish to buy your own, many dealers will loan or rent the tools when you purchase the tile. In my estimation, however, the purchase of good, quality tools is a very worthwhile investment. Not only will they last a lifetime, enabling you to use them whenever you need them, but they also appreciate in value as they get older, if they are well taken care of.

Layout stick. You can easily make up one special tool — a layout stick — that will help estimate the amount of tiles that you need. You can also use it to establish working lines on walls and floors. The

layout stick can be an old yardstick, a piece of lattice stock or a ripping from the edge of a 2x4. In any case it should be about 1/4 to 3/8 inch thick, 1 1/2 inches wide and at least 3 feet long. With a sharp pencil, mark the dimensions of your tile and joints all along the stick. (In the case of pregrouted sheets of tile, use the size of the sheets instead, leaving spaces for the joints between the sheets.) If the tiles have lugs, use them to mark the spacing on the stick. Although your tile dealer can help you decide the amount of materials you will need, you usually can do a fair job at home by using the layout stick.

Lay the stick along the length of the area you wish to tile, as if you were measuring it. If you lay the stick down twice, with half the distance of the stick left over, and there are 34 tiles per stick, then you will need 85 tiles for the length of the area to be tiled. Do the same for the width. Multiply the two sums together to get the estimated number of tiles you will need.

For example, you wish to tile a countertop 24 inches wide and 6 feet long. You have marked the layout stick for 4 inch tile with 1/4 inch spaces, so there are marks for 8 tiles on the layout stick. Place the stick across the width (front to back) of the countertop; count the number of tile spaces (there will be about 5 1/2). Then lay the stick along the length two times. Two lengths of layout stick means you will need nearly 17 tiles for the length. Round off both figures to the next highest number and multiply (17x6 = 102).

You will want to buy extra tiles to allow for breakage, of course. Your tile dealer can help you determine how many, on the basis of the number of tiles you will have to cut at the sides, back, front, and around fixtures.

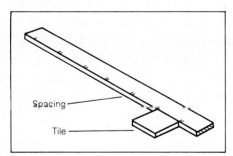

The most common tools for ceramic tile projects are as shown (left to right): tile cutter, tile nipper, notched trowel to apply adhesive and a squeegee to apply the grout.

A layout stick should be at least 36 in. long. Mark for tiles and grout lines along the stick. Use the stick to find how many tiles are needed and the positions of accessories.

Common Trim Tiles

The standard piece of ceramic tile is called a field tile. All four edges are unfinished. Field tiles do not turn corners. Special trim tiles supply smooth finished edges and corners for specific areas.

Angles: left-out, right-out, left-in, right-in. These trim tiles create sharp corners instead of rounded ones.

Apron. Half-size tiles called aprons are used to fill in narrow areas, such as along the front of a countertop.

Base. A tile designed specifically for the floor line, base trim (sometimes called a runner) has a finished top edge. It can be used in areas in which the floor has been tiled, but the wall has not.

Beads. This trim is also called quarter round. It is used to finish off corners and edges. The pieces are narrow, and they turn a rounded, 90 degree angle.

Bullnose. Bullnose trim is a regular field tile with one curved, finished edge. It finishes a course without turning a corner. Often it is paired with an apron tile; the apron tile meets the bullnose at a right angle. The result is a smoothly turned corner and edge.

Countertop trim or sink cap. This special trim piece is set on the outside edge of a countertop. Its raised lip is designed to prevent drips.

Cove. Cove pieces are used to turn corners at a right angle. The corners can turn either inward or outward. Cove base turns a corner at floor level; cove itself turns a corner in any course. Special cove pieces have a finished edge; these could turn a corner at the top row of a backsplash, for instance. Other cove pieces have no finished edges. Since the inside surface of cove is hollow, it can compensate for out-of-plumb corners.

Miter. Two miter pieces together create the look of a miter joint in a corner.

Rounds: in- and out-corners. This trim tile creates a rounded corner instead of an angular one.

Swimming pool edging. Designed to cover the coping on swimming pools, this edging requires a thick-set mortar bed.

Window sill. Window sill tile has a finished edge on one side, and a rounded corner on the other. It covers the sill itself and turns to meet the tile on the wall. Without this trim piece, you would need two tiles — a flat field tile for the sill itself and a quarter round to turn the corner. Sill trim simplifies the installation.

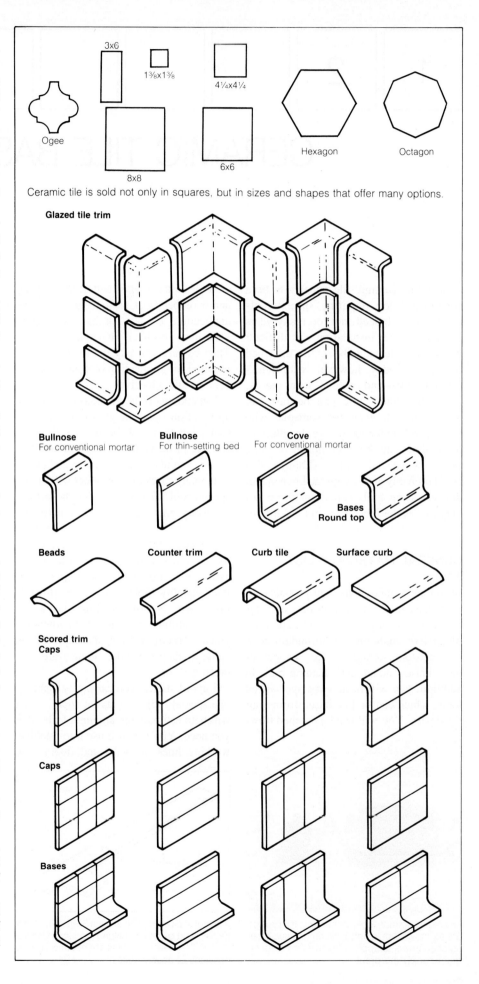

Ceramic tile is sold not only in squares, but in sizes and shapes that offer many options.

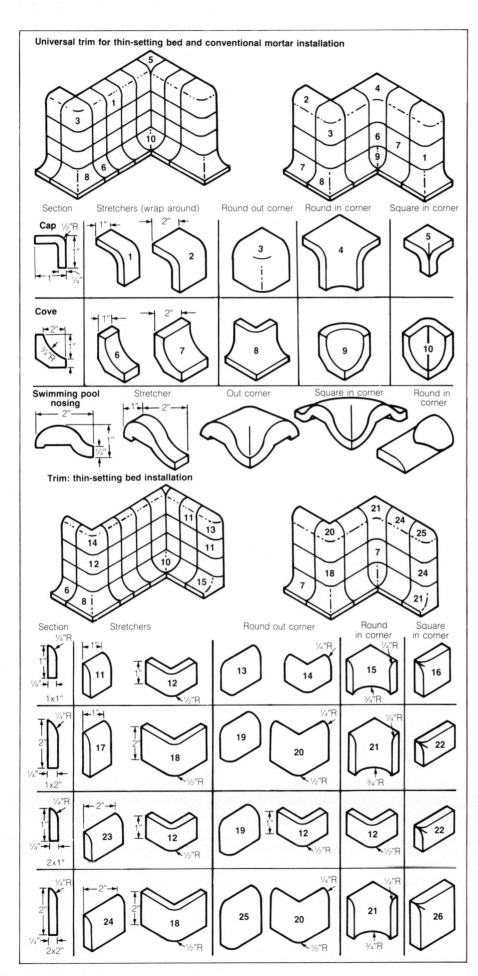

Adhesives for Ceramic Tile Application

The traditional method of setting ceramic tile has been in a bed of conventional portland cement mortar called thick bed. This is still used today by many professional tile setters and is necessary in some cases. For instance, a floor that is very uneven can be leveled with a mortar base. However, installing tile in a thick bed mortar base is complicated and requires a fair amount of skill. The creation of the new thin-bed or thin-set mastics has lessened the degree of skill required for tile installation, so that it can be mastered by a careful, interested amateur.

What has made these newer materials so popular is their ease of use. You need not apply a heavy mortar bed for application of the tile, nor must you soak the tile before you apply it to the surface, as is necessary with thick bed setting. Thin-set adhesives can be troweled onto almost any level surface to a thickness of about $3/32$ inch thick in order to form a sufficient bond with the tile. In most cases a gallon of thin-set floor tile adhesive will cover about 50 square feet. A gallon of wall adhesive covers from 45 to 50 square feet.

Thin-set adhesives come in three basic types: dry-set or cement base, organic adhesives and epoxy adhesives. Each has its own particular uses, advantages and disadvantages.

Cement base. Cement bases are actually forms of mortar base, although they should not be confused with the older, thick-set mortar. They are nonflammable

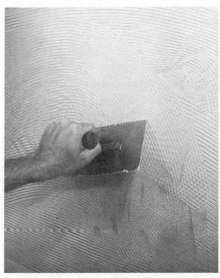

Different adhesives have varying characteristics; choose the one that suits your project's requirements. Use a notched trowel to apply it, following manufacturer's instructions.

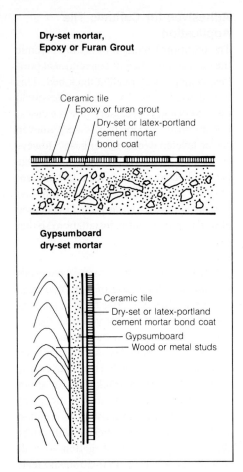

Dry-set mortar, Epoxy or Furan Grout

Ceramic tile
Epoxy or furan grout
Dry-set or latex-portland cement mortar bond coat

Gypsumboard dry-set mortar

— Ceramic tile
— Dry-set or latex-portland cement mortar bond coat
— Gypsumboard
— Wood or metal studs

Dry-set mortar or latex-portland cement mortar

Ceramic tile
Dry-set or latex-portland cement mortar bond coat

Dry-set mortar or latex-portland cement mortar

— Ceramic tile
— Dry-set or latex-portland cement mortar bond coat
— Masonry

and are mixed with water. They are excellent for use on surfaces that are not quite perfectly smooth, such as swimming pools. There are two types of cement-based adhesives: dry-set mortars and latex-portland-cement mortar.

Dry-set mortar. Dry-set mortar is so called because even though it has a cement base, there is no need to presoak the tiles before installation. Highly resistant to water and impact, dry-set mortar is water-washable, nonflammable, and is good for exterior work. Although this type of adhesive is not affected by prolonged contact with water, it does not form a water barrier. Commonly applied in a layer as thin as $3/32$ inches, dry-set is not a setting bed, nor is it intended to be used in trueing (or leveling) a surface.

Dry-set mortar is suitable for use over a variety of surfaces. These backings include plumb and true masonry, concrete, styrofoam, insulation board, gypsumboard, reinforced backer board, cured portland cement mortar beds, brick, ceramic tile and marble. Dry-set mortar is a good choice for use on sunken tubs. It comes in dry powder form and is mixed with the proper amount of water according to the manufacturer's directions.

Latex-portland-cement mortar. A mixture of portland cement, sand and a special latex additive, this mortar is used as a bond coat for setting the tile. The uses for latex-portland cement mortar are similar to those of dry-set mortar. However, it is less rigid than portland cement mortar. Just as with dry-set, latex-portland can be chosen for ceramic tile installation in areas that may not thoroughly dry out in use, such as in swimming pools or sunken tubs. However, in these projects the completed installation must be given at least 14 days to "cure" — that is, given time to set up or strengthen — before exposure to water. This is called a "dry cure." Early exposure to water prevents full development of the strength of the latex mortar and increases its water sensitivity. Mortar that has not cured properly will absorb the moisture and finally deteriorate.

Latex-portland-cement mortar is mixed by adding a given amount of the dry powder to liquid latex, carefully following the manufacturer's instructions. Stir until the mixture is the consistency of heavy cream. In most cases, let the adhesive sit for about 10 to 15 minutes to homogenize it. Then restir, to make sure it has been mixed thoroughly. One of the problems with latex

portland cement mortar is achieving the proper consistency. It should not be so thin or runny that the ridges left by the trowel will not stay up, yet it should not be so stiff that you have difficulty troweling it in place. This mortar sets fairly fast, so if it starts to film over, scrape it away and apply a fresh layer.

Latex-mixed adhesives are good for use in hearths and fireplace installations as well as for countertops. Neither water nor latex-mixed adhesives should be used on wooden floors because they can cause moisture problems and warping.

Organic adhesive (mastic). Also commonly called mastics, organically based adhesives are prepared materials that require no further addition of liquid or powder. They cure or set by evaporation. Organic adhesives are suitable for tile installed on floors, walls and counters over properly prepared surfaces such as concrete, gypsumboard, backer board, plaster, cement-asbestos board, wood, plywood, brick, ceramic tile, marble, plastic laminate, or terrazzo.

Apply organic adhesives in a thin layer with a notched trowel. The tiles do not need to be soaked before you lay them. As is the case with portland-cement-based adhesives, if the surface that you intend to cover requires leveling or trueing, mastics will not serve that purpose. Instead, you must first install an underlayment of ¼ inch tempered hardboard or particleboard. Such an underlayment is especially useful on hardwood floors that have cupped or very warped boards. Unlike cement-based adhesives, mastics supply some flexibility to the tile facing. This is useful if you intend to tile surfaces such as walls covered with sheetrock. (The wall can be pushed in with your hand; if the adhesive is too rigid it will crack away from the tile.) The bond strength varies among the many brands available.

Organic adhesives come in two types. It is a good idea to be aware of their differences before deciding which will best serve your project.

Type I. Type I mastics have solvent bases and are suggested for use in areas that may face prolonged exposure to water, such as showers or countertops. If you do use a solvent-based adhesive, make sure you extinguish all flames when working with it since some of the solvents are flammable. The fumes also can be irritating, so provide plenty of ventilation.

Type II. Mastics of this type utilize a latex base and are not as irritating or nearly as flammable as the solvent-based adhesives. However, they are recommended only for areas of intermittent water exposure, such as for walls and floors in dry areas of bathrooms.

Heat affects Type II mastics, so if you use one for fireplace installation, allow the adhesive to cure for at least 24 hours before use. The same is true when the mastic is applied to a concrete floor that has inlaid heating cables. Turn off the cables during adhesive application and installation of the tiles, and keep the cables off for at least 24 hours.

Epoxy base. Epoxies are not used as much by do-it-yourselfers because they are not only more expensive than the other adhesives, but are considerably more complicated to apply. They must be mixed just right to achieve the right setting time or pot life, and they must be applied at the correct temperature. When they are used, they are usually paired with epoxy grout.

Epoxy mortar system. This type of adhesive employs an epoxy resin and an epoxy hardener. The portions must be mixed just before application according to directions on the label. Installers use epoxy mortar when they need a high degree of bond strength, or when the surface on which they are working will receive a high degree of physical or chemical wear and tear. Acceptable subfloors include properly prepared concrete, wood, plywood, steel plate and ceramic tile. Application is made in one thin layer. Pot life, adhesion, water cleanability before cure, and chemical resistance vary with the manufacturer.

Epoxy mortar is used primarily by professionals for commercial jobs, but it also can be used for really difficult jobs around the home, such as a driveway. This material produces a more flexible surface during application than does epoxy adhesive.

Epoxy adhesive. This is an adhesive formulated for thin-setting of tile on floors, walls and counters; epoxy is the major binder. It is designed primarily for economical, high-bond strength and ease of application, but not for optimum chemical resistance. However, its chemical and solvent resistance tends to be better than that of organic adhesives. Epoxy adhesives are a little easier to apply than the epoxy mortars but they will sag, which means they present problems when applied to walls.

Spacers. When ceramic tiles are set into adhesive, they do not butt against each other. Instead, spaces are left above, below and between them. Once the adhesive has set, the spaces are filled with grout, creating a "grout line." There are several methods of ensuring that the grout lines are of uniform size. Some tiles, especially wall tiles, come with built-in spacers attached to the sides of each unit. If there are no built-in spacers, you may purchase spacers from your tile dealer. Some of these stay in place only until the adhesive has set and the tiles will no longer slide in the adhesive. Others need not be removed at all; the installer simply applies the grout right over the spacers.

You need not always use especially manufactured products, however. If your grout line is fairly narrow, from between ⅛ to ¼ inch wide (as is the case with much wall tile), use toothpicks to hold the

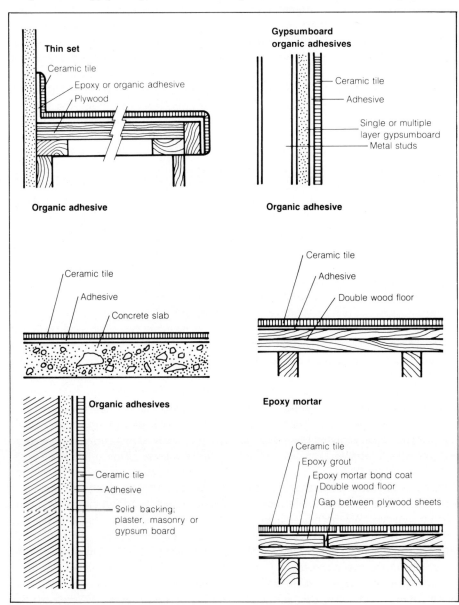

Some tiles come with built-in spacers to ensure straight grout lines. If your tiles have no spacers, purchase specially manufactured spacers of the required size.

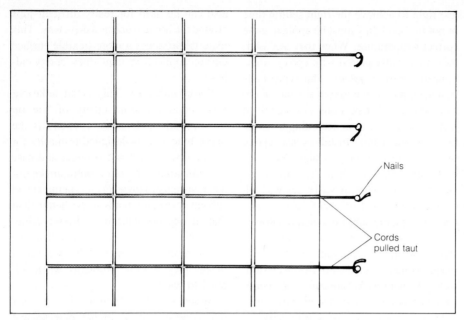

One way to space the tiles is to draw a dampened cord between nails along the grout line.

Grout color is no longer limited to white or gray. You can find colored grout that contrasts with or complements your tile. Grout color must be part of your overall design plan.

lines even. For wider lines, which usually occur with tiles larger than 4x4 inches, some installers use cotton cord as a spacer. To do this, nail in 6 inch finishing nails, one on each side of the prospective line, along the surface you are tiling. Then dampen cotton cord that is of the width that you desire and pull it straight between a given pair of nails. Install the tiles along the line (do not forget to allow for the grout lines between the tiles, running perpendicular to the cords). Remove the cord before the adhesive has a chance to set for very long. Otherwise you will disturb both the adhesive and the set tiles, and you may have to begin again.

If the grout line is relatively wide, another alternative is to install the tiles next to thin plywood strips or battens. These must be removed before the adhesive has a chance to set.

Grout

After the ceramic tile has been set in the mastic, the spaces between the tiles are filled with grout. Years ago, grout was available only in white or gray, but today it is available in many colors so that it offers design opportunities for unusual contrasts in colors and patterns. However, grout is more that just decorative; it prevents water and other foreign material such as grease or dirt from getting down between, and even under, the tiles. It also helps bind tile to tile. Therefore, proper application of the grout is an important step in a tile project.

As with adhesives, grout is available in

a number of materials for different types of situations. Choose the grout best suited for your project on the basis of the following considerations: the type of tile used, the area in which the tile will be set, and the size of the grout line. Choosing the proper grout for a specific job is extremely important. Your tile dealer can help with your decision.

There are three basic kinds of grouts preferred for most residential installations. They are cement-based grout, epoxy-based grout, and silicone rubber grout.

Cement-based grout. Portland cement is the base for the cement-based grouts. You may add coloring agents, available from your tile dealer, to these grouts. However, since the agents may stain some unglazed tiles, test the grout's effect on a few tiles before applying it to the whole job. Spread the grout on some pieces of scrap tile, wipe it off and see if it leaves a stain.

Make sure you follow specific manufacturer's directions for each specific type of grout. In addition, remember to use a rubber trowel when applying sanded grout to glazed tiles. Otherwise, you can permanently scratch the tiles.

If you store cement-based grouts for some time, they all have a tendency to pick up moisture and become hardened and useless. If you have a sack of old grout with a few lumps in it, remove the lumps before adding the water or latex.

Commercial portland-cement grout. This mixture of portland cement and other

ingredients produces a water-resistant, dense, uniformly colored material. The variety chosen for walls usually is white in color and is designed for thick-bed mortar installation for which the installer must soak the wall tile in water for 15 to 20 minutes before application. The formula for floors usually is gray. It has been designed for use with ceramic mosaics, quarry and paver tiles on both walls and floors. Commercial portland-cement grout is most commonly paired with portland cement mortar and requires damp curing for both walls and floors.

Sand-portland cement grout. You can mix this grout on the job. The proportions of portland cement to fine-grade sand depend upon the widths of the spaces between the tiles. Use one part cement to one part sand for joints up to $1/8$ inch wide, one part cement and two parts sand for joints up to $1/2$ inch wide, and a ratio of one to three for joints over $1/2$ inch wide. You may also add up to $1/5$ part lime to provide elasticity and strength. This sand-portland cement grout can be used when applying ceramic mosaic tile, quarry or paver tile to floors or walls. Damp curing is necessary.

Dry-set grout. This mixture of portland cement and additives offers water retentiveness. Dry-set grout has the same characteristics as dry-set mortar. It is suitable for grouting all walls and floors that are subject to ordinary use. This grout can be used without first soaking the wall tile. However, if you go through a hot, dry-weather spell, the grout might dry out so quickly it would shrink. Wetting the tile and damp-curing may develop greater grout strength under these conditions.

Latex-portland cement grout. This is a mixture of any of the three preceding grouts, plus a special latex additive. To create it, mix portland cement and sand together; then add liquid latex. Suitable for all installations subject to ordinary use and for most commercial installations, latex-portland cement grout is less rigid and less permeable than is regular cement grout. It needs no damp curing if you follow the manufacturer's specific instructions.

Epoxy grout. Epoxy grout is made of portions of epoxy resin and a hardener. Because of the grout's high degree of chemical resistance, it is often used for industrial and commercial applications. In a home, epoxy grout's chemical-resistant properties would be valuable in a home darkroom or other work area. As with epoxy mortar, epoxy grout provides high bond strength and impact resistance.

Together, the mortar and grout impart structural strength to the finished floor, especially wood subfloors. Their use, however, involves extra costs, as well as practice and attention to detail. Epoxy grout has a consistency somewhat like heavy syrup and it is not easy to apply. For instance, if your tiles are more than ½ inch thick, and you lay them less than ¼ inch apart, the joint will be too narrow for the epoxy grout to fully penetrate the space during the grouting operation. However, if you decide your project requires epoxy grout — such as on a hood over a stove — it can be used with quarry tile, glazed ceramic tile, and mosaic and paver tiles. It comes in gray, black or dark brown.

Silicone rubber grout. This elastomeric grout system is made of a single component — unslumping silicone rubber. After curing, it is resistant to staining, moisture, mildew, cracking, crazing and shrinking. This grout adheres tenaciously to ceramic tile and cures rapidly. For interior use only, it withstands exposure to hot cooking oils and free steam, as well as prolonged subfreezing or hot, humid conditions. If your project entails pregrouted tile sheets, you will use silicone rubber grout, applying it with a caulking gun. Silicone rubber grout is also used as a caulking for edges around bathtubs, showers, and so on. (However, it should not be used on kitchen countertops or other food preparation surfaces, for the same reasons that prohibit the use of pregrouted tile sheets in these areas.) Since silicone grout is very flexible, it is an excellent choice for a project in which the surfaces tend to move or shift slightly, such as sheetrock backing. This grout is a little more expensive than the cement-based grouts and is only available in white or clear.

The accompanying chart of the various grouts and their uses is based upon the suggestions of the Materials & Methods Standards Association. Ratings on Table 2 are graded from A to E, with A representing "Best Performance" and E representing "Worst Performance".

Epoxy grout and mortar

Ceramic tile
Epoxy grout
Epoxy mortar
Bond coat
Mortar bed ¾" to 1¼"
Cement

Apply silicone rubber grout with a caulking gun. Follow instructions regarding hole size to be cut in the grout container; this can determine the grouting procedure's success.

GROUT CHECKLIST

		Grout Type						
		Commercial Portland Cement Wall Use	Floor Use	Sand-Portland Cement Wall-Floor Use	Dry-set Wall-Floor Use	Latex Portland Cement (3)	Epoxy (1) (5)	Silicone (2)
Tile Type	Glazed Wall Tile	x				x	x	x
	Ceramic Mosaics	x	x	x	x	x	x	x
	Quarry, Paver and Packing House	x	x	x		x	x	
Areas of Use	Dry and intermittently wet areas	x	x	x	x	x	x	x
	Areas subject to prolonged wetting	x	x	x	x	x	x	x
	Exteriors	x	x	x	x	x(4)	x(4)	

Notes: (1) Mainly used for chemical resistant properties.
(2) Special tools needed for proper application. Do not use in food preparation area.
(3) Special cleaning procedures and materials recommended.
(4) Follow manufacturer's directions.
(5) Epoxies are recommended for prolonged temperatures up to 140 degrees Farenheit.

GROUT: PERFORMANCE RATINGS

	Commercial Portland Cement Wall Use	Floor Use	Sand-Portland Cement Wall-Floor Use	Dry-set Wall-Floor Use	Latex Portland Cement	Epoxy	Silicone
Stain Resistance	D	C	E	D	B	A	A
Crack Resistance	D	D	E	D	C	B	A (Flexible)
Colorability	B	B	C	B	B	B	Restricted

BASIC TILING PROCEDURES

Ceramic tile can be installed over almost any type of surface including walls, floors, countertops, swimming pools, and even old ceramic tile. The following basic tiling steps are used for most projects, especially for walls and floors. Later we will discuss the special steps involved in each type of application.

There are several stages to any tiling project. You must estimate the amount of tile you will need and prepare the surfaces before you can actually lay the tile and apply the grout. The early steps are as important as the final ones. Accurate measurements can save you time later. A poorly prepared surface will result in a very short-lived finished product.

TILING WALLS
Preparation

Estimate the amount of tile. Tile needs are figured in terms of square feet. First decide upon the height of your project. (For instance, you may want to extend a shower stall only a foot or so above the shower head, rather than cover the wall all the way to the ceiling.) Multiply the height of the surface by its width. That will give the square footage of the area you need to cover. Do the same for all of the walls on which you will be working. (If the numbers are in both feet and inches, convert them to inches only; multiply height by width; then divide by 144 to find the square footage.) Finally, add the figures for all the walls together to get your final total. To allow for waste due to cut tiles, as well as errors in judgment, add 5 percent to your total. Most dealers will accept the return of any extra tile that you have. Some extras come in handy for repairs you may have later on.

Under most circumstances, do not worry about spaces such as windows or doors when you figure the square footage. The footage that they consume can be included as your waste factor. (If you do this, do not add in that extra 5 percent.) However, if the area you are covering has a large number of open areas, such as windows, make allowances for them. To do so, divide the wall into sections. Figure the square footage of the rectangles on the two sides of a window, the rectangle below (and the one above, if it will be covered), and then add the totals together.

Measure and list those edges and corners that will require specially formed tiles. Pieces such as inner and outer corner pieces and edge trims give a finished project smooth corners and finished edges, protecting those who use the area from scrapes and bruises, as well as adding a professional look to the job.

Once you have your measurements, take the list to your tile dealer, who will help you determine the amount of tile you require. You should also tell him the type of surface you intend to tile — such as plaster or wallboard with a finish coat — and the type of covering that is already there, whether it is paint, wallpaper or some other material. Your dealer can then advise you whether any special problems exist and suggest what specific adhesives, grout — or even tile — should be used for your particular situation. It is a good idea to take along a snapshot of the room.

Level and plumb surfaces. Any ceramic tile job is only as good as the surface backing to which it is applied. First, remove all fixtures, wood stripping, nails, screws, and other protruding objects. If necessary, also remove the baseboards.

To find the number of tiles needed for a wall, multiply its height times its width. Here, the area of each wall was computed; the three figures then were added together. No tiles were added for wastage because the exhaust opening area made up for cut or broken tiles.

Then smooth out all irregularities in the surface or backing, since ceramic tile is not flexible and cannot follow contours. All walls must be sound, flat and free from loose or protruding objects and holes. All corners should be as square and plumb as possible. Correct any problems in the wall surface before you apply the adhesive.

To check for flatness, run the edge of a straightedge or level along the wall. Any gaps between the wall and the edge of your tool will indicate depressions in the wall surface. Most adhesive manufacturers will state on the can the amount of varience that is allowed when using their products. To correct any depressions that are greater than those tolerances, use spackling compound, patching plaster or the repair substance recommended by the manufacturer.

To check for plumb — that is, whether or not the wall is straight up and down — you again use the level. Hold the level up and down against the wall. Look at the

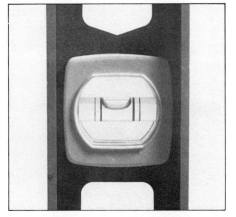

Walls must be plumb — straight up and down. Check with a carpenter's level. Lay one edge vertically along the wall. If the bubble is between the two markings, the wall is plumb.

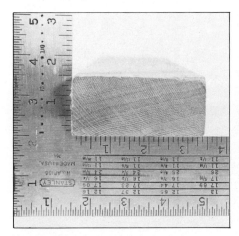

Use a carpenter's square to be sure the corners in the room are square. Check at several points along the corner joint, as well as where the wall meets the floor.

bubble tube that is in the level. If the bubble inside is between the indicator lines, the wall is plumb. All corners also should be square. Use a carpenter's square to determine this. Be sure to check several heights on all corners involved in the tiling project. If you find that the corners are not square, you will have to make allowances for that in your preparation. For instance, when installing a new backing for a shower, you can correct the corners by inserting shims — small, thin strips of wood — between the old wall and the new backing. This technique is also used to correct surfaces that are not plumb.

Preparing gypsum wallboard. Repair all holes and defects in the backing. Then clean any oil, grease or other dirt from the surface with a regular detergent; rinse thoroughly.

Small nail holes. These repairs will require only a mixture of spackling compound and water, the consistency of which resembles putty or thick mud. You also need a broad wall scraper and medium or fine sandpaper. Simply press the spackling into the hole, level, and let dry for at least an hour. Then sand.

Larger holes. To repair holes slightly larger than a nail hole you need mineral wool insulation and spackling compound.

Use a utility knife to clean out the hole. Do not enlarge it, however. Fill the hole with the insulation. Its fibers will catch on the edges of the wallboard and keep the insulation from falling inside the wall. Then fill the hole with spackling compound. (Do this carefully, so as not to push the insulation through.) Let this application dry thoroughly for at least a day. Then apply another layer of spackling. Smooth with the wall scraper. The compound should be almost level with the wall surface. This will allow for some shrinkage when the compound dries. Then sand to smooth the edges.

Very large holes. Holes of a substantial size are more difficult to repair. You have two options: you can patch with a piece of gypsum or you can remove the entire damaged gypsum panel and replace it with a new one. Often the second option is less complicated than the first.

If you feel the hole is small enough to patch, you will need these materials: utility knife, pencil, straightedge or carpenter's square, spackling compound, a piece of wallboard that is as thick as that in the wall, a pencil or a 1x3 dowel whose length is greater than the width of the hole, wire, a nail, hammer, glue, pliers, a wide-blade wall scraper, and sandpaper.

Repair small holes in wallboard and in plaster walls with spackling compound. Mix the compound with water to the consistency of thick mud. Apply compound with a putty knife.

First, prepare the hole. Draw and score a square around the opening. Include all of the hole, but no more than that. With the utility knife, cut along the outline. Press hard; try to cut through the wallboard at this time. If you cannot, keep cutting along the lines until you break through. The result should be a smooth-edged square or rectangular hole.

Measure the hole and, adding 2 inches to each side, draw a square or rectangle that size on the piece of gypsumboard to create your patch. (The extra size allows for a surface for gluing.) The wire and dowel will form a handle for the patch. To attach the handle, use the nail to punch two aligned holes 1 inch apart at the center of the patch. From the front of the patch, string the wire through both holes; the wire will tie around the dowel once the patch has been placed inside the wall.

To hold the patch in place, cover all but the center of the front of the patch with an ample amount of glue. Angle the patch through the hole and use the wires to pull it firmly against the inside of the wall. Be sure that the hole is completely sealed and that you have a good glue bond. When you are certain that the patch is in secure contact, wrap the wire around the dowel and twist the ends tightly together. Tighten the twist with pliers to ensure a good anchor that holds the patch tightly against the wall; do not tighten it so much that you damage the patch.

Let the patch sit for at least 24 hours. Then, when you are sure that the glue is dry, remove the dowel and test the patch. If it is not dry, let it sit another half day. Once it is dry, very carefully apply spackling compound all around the inside edges of the hole, sealing the line where the hole meets the patch. Let the compound dry for a day.

You may now choose one of two methods. The first is to use the wide-blade scraper to fill the hole opening with spackling compound, feathering the spackling to meet the surface of the wallboard around it. Smooth the compound until its surface is only slightly rounded above the surrounding wall. Give the spackling three days to dry thoroughly; then sand.

The second method involves cutting a piece of wallboard to fit the exact size of the original opening. This new piece will be fastened on top of the first patch. Before you apply any glue, moisten the paper cover on one side of the patch and remove that cover with the utility knife. You want to expose the rough surface of the core to provide a good bonding surface for spackling compound. Now cover the paper side of the patch with glue and place the patch in the hole. The two patches will meet, paper to paper. Give the glue at least a day to dry. Then apply spackling compound to the joints between the patch and the wall. This should dry for at least three days before you sand it smooth.

Removing a wallboard panel. If you feel that the hole is too large to patch, you

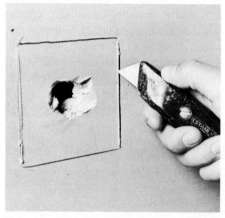

Draw a square or rectangle around the damage; score the lines with a utility knife. Cut completely through. Remove the square. Bevel the edges toward the inside of the wall.

Spread glue around the edges of the patch. Insert wire through holes in the center of the patch. Ease the patch through the hole and hold in place until glue has begun to set.

Glue must dry at least a day. Cut a dowel that is longer than the patch is wide. Hold patch in place by twisting the wire around dowel, but not so tightly that the patch is damaged.

Once the patch is dry, either fill the hole with spackling or insert a second patch. Wet one side of the patch and remove the paper covering. Apply glue to the other side.

Place the second patch in the hole, so that its paper side meets the paper side of the first patch. Allow to dry for a day. Then apply spackling to the joint and over the patch.

Let the spackling dry for several days. Then smooth the patch with fine sandpaper. The joint between the compound and the surrounding wall should be level and even.

can remove the entire damaged panel fairly easily. The degree of success will depend very much upon the amount of care and patience you exercise. The job requires these tools: a new sheet of wallboard that is as thick as the old wallboard, pry bar, hammer, finishing nails, nail set, utility knife, wall scraper, putty knife, gypsumboard nails, joint tape, spackling compound, and medium or fine sandpaper.

First remove the base molding below the damaged panel. Use the pry bar carefully — you will replace the molding later. Then tap out the nails in the molding and store it elsewhere.

Now, working carefully, hammer out the damaged panel, a small portion at a time. Do not try to remove the whole panel at once; if you do so, you will damage the good panels surrounding it. Once you come to the joint between the damaged panel and one next to it, use the utility knife to cut through the joint tape that binds the two together.

When replacing an entire panel, do not damage surrounding panels. Seal seams between panels with spackling; use a wide-blade scraper to press joint tape into spackling.

Cover the embedded joint tape with spackling. When it is dry, sand the seam so the compound and the wall meet smoothly. This is what is meant by the term "a feathered edge."

Once the damaged panel is removed, you will have a clean opening. The studs will be visible and the edges of the adjoining panels should be whole and undamaged. Hold the new panel up to the hole and, using the utility knife, have a helper draw in any cuts needed to fit the panel around obstructions, so the panel will slide into place. Cut to fit and place the panel into position.

Nail the new panel into place, spacing gypsumboard nails about three inches apart along the stud supports. Once each nail is in, hit it one more time to countersink it into the panel. The depression you create will be filled in with spackling compound. Check the edges of the panel to be sure that it is even with the adjoining panels. Trim back uneven spots with the utility knife, if necessary. Then fill in the joints and the ceiling line with spackling compound. Now embed the joint tape into the spackling. As you lay the tape on top of the spackling, press the tape in with the wide-blade scraper. This will ensure a good bond and a strong joint between the panels. Then fill in any dimples with spackling.

Let the spackling dry for 24 hours; sand; reapply spackling over the tape. Feather the spackling edges. In 24 hours, sand and repeat the spackling application. Wait another 24 hours (or longer); then sand. If the surface is to be covered, you may omit the last spackling application.

Preparing plaster. In gypsum wallboard walls, the wall is a layer of gypsum covered on each side with a sheet of paper. In a plaster wall, the wall is built up in solid layers upon a metal support called lath. (In some older homes the lath is made of wood strips.) Small repairs in plaster can be completed following the steps given for wallboard repair.

To repair larger holes, you will need the following tools: utility knife, spackling compound or plaster patching material, wide wall scraper, metal lath (available at hardware stores), water brush, sandpaper.

Clean the hole and cut back to the hard plaster with the utility knife. Do not enlarge the damaged area; only clear away loose plaster debris. Brush the opening with water if necessary to clean the edges. If the metal lath is intact, use spackling compound to repair the hole. Mix the compound to a fairly thick consistency. Wet down the hole so the plaster will not absorb water from the compound. Trowel

spackling into the hole to just below the surrounding surface, using the wall scraper. Let dry for several days. Place a second layer; feather the edges. Let dry; then sand.

If the lath is missing, use plaster patching material instead of spackling. Mix the patch according to the package directions. Cut a piece of lath mesh so it is slightly larger than the hole opening. Tie a 5-inch piece of string to the center of the mesh. Curve the mesh and insert the patch into the hole. Release the string and flatten out the mesh. To hold the mesh in place during the plastering, tie the string to a pencil and twist until it holds against the wall.

If the hole is fairly small, fill with patching plaster to 1/4 inch from the top. Let this dry. Then cut the string and remove. Apply a second layer to meet the wall surface; let dry; then sand. If the hole is fairly large, you will need a third layer. The first layer bonds the lath to the wall; the second fills the hole to within 1/4 inch of the wall surface, and the third finishes off at the surface level. Each layer needs ample drying time. When the third is fully dry, sand smooth.

Once the wall has been repaired, clean thoroughly with detergent and rinse with clear water. Let dry completely.

Preparing paneling and plywood. To apply ceramic tile over paneling or plywood walls, first clean the surface thoroughly. Remove any slick or smooth wax. Roughen the surface using carborundum stone or heavy flint sandpaper. Fill all holes and cracks with the mastic suggested by the adhesive manufacturer.

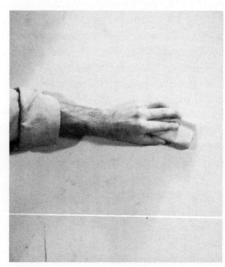

Use spackling compound or plaster patching material to repair small holes in plaster walls. Level the patch with a wide wall scraper or with the flat side of an adhesive trowel.

Preparing old ceramic tile. In some instances you may wish to tile over existing ceramic tile. This can be done only if the old tile is soundly fastened to the wall. If any tiles are loose, there will not be a strong bond. Remove all loose tile and check the wallboard for evidence of water damage. The bond between damaged backing and the tile upon it will be loose. Since you cannot lay new tile over a weak surface, remove the old tile and then the damaged backing. Replace it with new backing. If water marks are evident on the wall studs themselves, leave the entire area open for a few days to be sure that the studs are thoroughly dry before you install new wallboard or water-resistant backer board.

If the backing has not suffered from water damage, remove and re-adhere all loose tile before applying the new tiles. In cases where a majority of the tiles are loose, you would be better off to remove the old tiles and repair or replace the backing before you install the new tiles. See Chapter 8 for instructions for removing broken tile.

If the old wall is sound, the first step is to use tile cleaner to clean the old tiles. Then, using the carborundum stone or an abrasive disc in a disc sander, remove all old dirt and scum buildup. The sanding will roughen the surfaces of the tiles so the new adhesive will stick better. The sanding is a mandatory preparation step. Use clean, clear water to rinse off the sanding debris.

Preparing wallpaper. Because the weight of ceramic tile will cause wallpaper to sag and become loose, you must remove all wallpaper before installing a ceramic tile wall. Rent a steamer from a home supply store for this task, or use commercial wallpaper remover.

Preparing paint. Scrape away any loose paint. If the remaining paint is glossy, sand it just a little to roughen the surface. Remove all grease and dirt.

Preparing plastic laminate. Gently roughen the surface with sandpaper; rinse off dust from sanding.

New wallboard backing. In some instances the old backing is not solid enough for tile placement, in which case you must install a new backing. At one time, this meant applying a mortar bed. Today the best course is to install a new wallboard or backer board (for moisture-laden areas), nailing it securely to the studs or existing

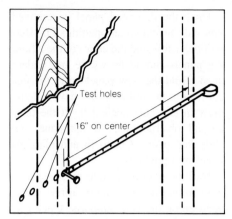

Securely nail new wallboard to studs. Usually studs are 16 inches apart, measured from center to center. Find one with a nail. Measure out to find the other studs.

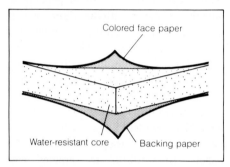

For protection in high-moisture areas install water-resistant gypsum wallboard that has a waterproof face and core.

walls. You may also use special adhesives designed to bond wallboard to wallboard.

The first step is to find the wall studs. In most homes these will be 16 inches apart, measured from center to center. Measure 16 inches out from the corner of the wall; this should bring you close to a stud. Tap a small finishing nail through the old surface to check. Then move 16 inches to find the next stud. Once you find the studs you can nail the new wallboard to the old surface with glued Sheetrock nails long enough to reach through the new and the old surfaces and then extend into the stud. Usually, 1½ inch nails will be long enough for this job. If you must adhere the wallboard in an area where you cannot find the studs, use panel or wallboard adhesive applied with a caulking gun. The sheets can be applied right next to each other, with no gaps.

If wallboard will be entirely covered, do not bother taping and spackling. If part of the wallboard will be visible, however, the seams must be finished. For instructions, see the earlier section on replacing a gypsum wallboard panel.

In kitchens and baths. If you are tiling an area around a tub or sink — or any

other spot that will be high in moisture — install a backing of special water-resistant gypsum wallboard. Water-resistant gypsum wallboard normally has a blue or green "face," instead of the usual white of standard wallboard panels. Treat the edges of the panels with a special sealer; it can be purchased with the panels. Install the panels with 1½ inch nails or adhesive and cover the nail heads with the sealer. Do not tape joints that will be covered with ceramic tile. Type I mastics are preferred.

Backer board is made of a lightweight concrete core that is encased in a glass fiber mesh. It is unaffected by water, so it is an ideal surface for tiling projects in bathrooms or on kitchen countertops. Use one of the cement-based mortars — either dry-set or latex-portland — if you have installed a backer board surface. Use 1½ inch galvanized roofing nails to fasten the backer board to wallboard or to wallstuds. Use the mortar to seal all joints; use fiberglass tape to seal exposed edges.

Priming the surface. The primer coat is important because it seals out moisture and provides a stronger bonding coat between the backing and the tile. If the surface is in a wet area, such as around a tub, cover the entire wall with a thin prime coat of adhesive. Make sure you pack the adhesive in around the pipes and other wall openings. In the case of a dry area, you should prime the wall with the primer suggested by the adhesive manufacturer. In some cases this will be a skim coating of adhesive, and in others the manufacturer may require a special primer.

A gallon of wall primer usually will cover from 225 to 250 square feet. Make

A prime coat is a moisture seal. It keeps the wall surface from absorbing moisture from the adhesive and thus weakening the bond. Sand the prime coat after it has dried.

sure you read all the manufacturer's directions before applying the coat. Then apply with a brush or roller. Most primers are flammable, so never use them near an open flame. Shut off all appliances, including gas pilot lights in furnaces and kitchen stoves, before you begin. Then provide for plenty of ventilation — and above all, do not smoke! No matter what prime coat is required, carefully follow the manufacturer's directions. A solid prime coat can be one of the most important steps to ensure that a wall of ceramic tile will remain in place for a long time.

Laying out working lines. Once the wall surface has been properly prepared, the next step is to lay out working lines so you will have a nice, neat, ''level-appearing'' job. Do not just start sticking tiles in place, although I admit that at this point it is tempting. A few basic guidelines will ensure a desirable final appearance.

(1) Plan the entire room so the starting point permits one continous horizontal line across all the areas to be tiled.

(2) If possible, set the tile in such a way that none of the tile pieces will be less than 2 inches wide.

(3) Reduce the width of trim tile only if absolutely necessary.

(4) If you must cut a course of tile, make the cut on the row close to the base or bottom course.

(5) If tiles set with a thin grout line nearly fill the vertical or horizontal dimensions, try widening the grout line to avoid cutting any tiles.

First, lay out the horizontal and vertical working lines. This will require a carpenter's level, layout stick, plumb bob, chalk, heavy string, and straightedge.

Marking the horizontal base line. Ceramic wall tiles are installed starting at the bottom row and working upward. The first step is to establish a floor-level horizontal base line. Before you can do this, you have to find the lowest point of the floor where it meets the wall edge. Using a level and a straightedge, start at one corner of the area to be tiled. About six inches above the floor draw a horizontal, level line. Place the carpenter's level along the line — the bubble in the horizontal bubble tube should be centered between the line indicators on the tube. Work clockwise around the room, continuing to draw a level line, until you have included all of the wall space that you want to tile. Now find the spot where the distance between the line and the floor is the greatest. That is the lowest point in the tiling area.

At the lowest point, working at floor level, place one tile against the wall. (If you will be using a cove base, that is what you should place here.) Then, leaving space for the grout line if a spacer lug is not built into your tile, place another tile above the first. Again, leave space for the grout line above the second tile. Mark above the second tile. Using the level, draw a line from this mark, continuing it completely around the area to be tiled. This is your floor-level horizontal base line.

Establishing a horizontal base line is a more complicated task if the wall you wish to cover contains a countertop, tub or sink. A project with any of these features looks best if a full-size course of tile lies above them, rather than a cut course. The process for establishing the base line is the same for all situations of this type. Using

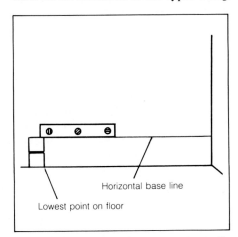

At the lowest point in the room, set one tile above another, allowing for grout lines. From the point above the second tile, extend a line through the tiling area.

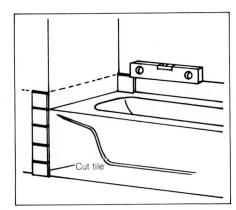

If a tub is level to within ⅛ inch, the bottom course of tile will contain full-size tiles. If the tub is not level to within ⅛ inch, cut tiles to fit the bottom course if no cove is used.

the method for finding the lowest point of the floor, find the lowest point of the top of (for example) the tub. (Do not assume that all tubs or countertops are level.) If the tub is level within ⅛ inch, merely mark the high point of the tub. Then place one full tile in that position (allow for the grout line below the tile) and use a carpenter's level to draw a level line ⅛ inch above the top edge of this tile. Continue this level line around the tub surround and the rest of the area to be tiled. Your first course of tiles will be installed below this horizontal working line.

If the tub is not level to within ⅛ inch, work from the low point of the top of the tub. Allowing for the grout line below, place one tile against the wall. Mark the spot directly above the tile, add a space for the grout line above, and draw a line. With the level, extend the line out past the tub and continue it through the area to be tiled. This is your horizontal base line. To find out whether a row of cut tile will be necessary near the floor, use your layout stick to measure down to the floor. If the distance measures out to a full tile, you are fine. If the distance measures out to less than a full tile, plan on having the cut row occur above the cove course at floor level. In some cases this row will be very narrow. If this is the case in your setting, it is better to plan to slightly cut two rows of tile rather than attempt to cut one extremely small course.

Establishing the vertical line. There are two methods for establishing the vertical line. In method one, you lay out a single row of tiles along the floor, from corner to corner. If you find that you will have to cut and lay one end tile that is smaller than half its normal size, move the tiles over so that larger cut tiles can be placed at each corner. At the approximate center, but corresponding to the nearest joint line, draw a vertical line on the wall

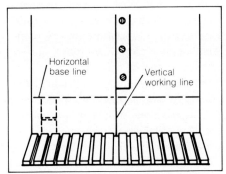

Run a dry layout of tiles along the floor. At center of layout, draw in vertical line.

from the bottom row of tile to the top row, where the tile will end. Use a carpenter's level to assure that the line is plumb. This is your vertical line.

The second method utilizes a plumb bob and a chalkline. A plumb bob is a tear-shaped metal weight that hangs at the end of a long heavy string. A chalkline is a long piece of heavy string or twine that is covered with chalk. You can purchase a commercial carpenter's chalkline or you can easily make one of your own at home.

Measure to find the center of the wall. Directly above that point, fasten the plumb bob to the ceiling about an inch out from the wall. Place two marks on the wall, directly in back of the string, one near the bottom of the wall, the other near the top. When you stand away from the wall, both marks should be obscured by the string. If one or the other is not, adjust it accordingly. Once you are satisfied, cut a piece of heavy twine the same length as the height of the wall and cover the twine with chalk. Tack one end to the top mark, the other to the bottom. When you snap the string you will leave a line of chalk on the wall. This is your vertical line.

Use the layout stick to determine whether the position of the vertical line leaves more than half a tile in each wall corner. Allow for the corner pieces you may be using (which will probably be cove tile). If there is space for half a tile, keep the line you snapped as your vertical working line. Otherwise, tack the chalkline half a tile width to the right or left and snap a new line. Repeat this for vertical line markings on each wall. If you will have two regular tiles meeting at a corner, you must make allowances for the widths of the adjoining tile edges.

In some cases, as for a kitchen backsplash, you may not want the tile to go all the way up the wall. Once the vertical lines are in, use the layout stick to determine the location of an upper horizontal working line. Be sure that you consider the dimensions of the finishing row of tile, whether you choose bullnose, quarter round or a special trim piece.

Finally, use your layout stick to plot the position of any accessories, such as grab bars, recessed paper holders or soap holders. This will minimize the number of tiles you must cut to make room for the accessory. Unless you feel particularly brave, openings for recessed fixtures need not be cut into the backing until you are ready to

lay tile in that spot and can match the sizes exactly. Most tile comes with matching accessories whose dimensions are a multiple of the tile dimensions. Careful positioning in these cases will mean that no tiles will need to be cut.

Applying Adhesives

Use the adhesive recommended by your tile dealer or manufacturer for your particular installation. As mentioned before, in most instances this will be one of the thin-set mastics applied with a notched trowel.

Read the label on the adhesive can, since adhesives do vary. A very thin initial skim coating, laid with the flat side of a trowel, is advisable for wet areas such as shower stalls. Critical water areas such as plumbing connections, joints in wall boards, corners in tub alcoves, joints between wallboard and tub, voids in back of cove base, and joints between wall tile and floor tile, should be prepacked with the water-proof ceramic tile adhesive prior to spreading the bond coat.

Allow the skim coat to dry thoroughly. Then apply the bond coat, with the notched side of the trowel. Be careful not to cover up your directional lines. Leave these visible until just prior to tiling in that area. Hold the trowel firmly against the wall at a 45 degree angle; spread the adhesive to cover from 10 to 20 square feet at a time. Do not cover a larger area; the adhesive will dry before all the tiles can be

placed. Bring the adhesive to within ½ inch of the point where the tile will end. If you are applying the adhesive with the correct amount of pressure, adhesive will appear only from the openings of the notches in the trowel. Each trail of adhesive will be called a ''bead.'' The space between any two beads will be almost bare of adhesive. To check that you have applied the proper amount, position a tile in place and twist it back and forth a little. (Set all ceramic tile in this manner.) If adhesive squeezes out from under the tile, there is too much adhesive. If no adhesive squeezes out, remove the tile and look at the back. The spaces between the beads should have filled in to completely cover the tile back. If it is not completely covered, there is not enough adhesive.

How can you tell if you applied the right amount of adhesive? If it squeezes out from behind a laid tile, there is too much. If the back does not fill in, there is too little.

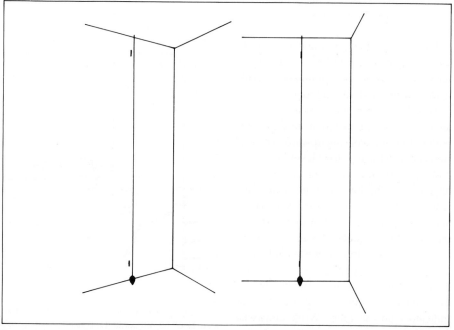

Suspend a plumb bob from the ceiling, about one inch from the wall. Mark locations near the ceiling and the floor. When the two marks are obscured by the line, snap a chalkline.

Laying the Tile

In addition to tile, adhesive and a trowel, you also need a hammer and a block of wood covered with carpet. The latter two will be used to seat the tile firmly in the adhesive once the tile has been laid. You also need a tile cutter (or a glass cutter and a metal straightedge) and a tile nipper.

Trim tiles — floor level and corners. Before you work on the overall placement, install the row of cove or other finishing tiles at the floor level. Spread adhesive along only the surface that you are going to tile at the moment. Also use adhesive to pack the backs of cove pieces.

Lay the first tile against the vertical working line at the point at which the working line intersects the floor. Work over to one corner and then to the other. Be sure to allow for grout lines. If you must cut tiles at either corner, cut the one that precedes the corner tile itself.

Once the floor level course is finished, and if you are using cove corner pieces, install the cove corners up the wall. Place the first cove corner above the point at which the horizontal base line intersects a corner. (There will be a one-course space between this and the bottom row just set.) Insert the tile that falls between the floor-level tile and the horizontal-base-line tile. This tile may have to be cut (see cutting instructions below). Then work your way partially up the wall. Do not go all the way to the top of your project, since you may have to make later adjustments to ensure straight grout lines. Just be sure that the cove corner sections are always a little ahead of the rest of the wall. Having the corners in place will simplify the job of cutting tiles later.

Cutting strategy. The row of tile above the bottom course must fit between

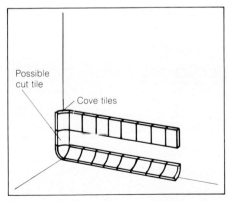

First set cove tiles along the bottom row and up the corner. Fill the horizontal-base-line course. If necessary, cut the row between the bottom row and the horizontal base line.

it and the horizontal base line. Depending upon the levelness of the floor, you may have to cut each tile individually. To determine the cutting line, you may proceed in two ways. You can immediately cut the course of tiles, or you may work on the rest of the wall and return to the cut course later.

If you decide to cut the row of tiles immediately, cut and place one tile at a time, since the exact measurements may vary a little. Begin at the vertical working line. Measure the distance between the finishing row tile and the horizontal base line. Subtract from that measurement the width of two grout lines. Mark the resulting measurement onto a loose tile, cut the tile with a cutter and insert the tile in place. Once you have filled in one half of the course, fill in the other.

If you decide to work on the cut row after you have finished the rest of the wall, use the batten method. Cut a length of 1x3 that is as long as the horizontal base line, and nail it so that the top edge of the batten lies directly on the base line. Apply adhesive above the batten. Beginning at the vertical working line, install a course of tiles directly above the batten. Do not remove the batten until you are certain that the adhesive holding the horizontal base line course has set.

How to cut tile. A good rule of thumb about cutting tile is this: if one of two adjoining tile pieces must be cut, always cut the less complicated piece (a field tile, for example, rather than a cove). The cut will be easier to make, and, in case of error or breakage, the less expensive piece will have to be replaced.

The initial step for cutting tile is to determine the cut line. The process for doing this is the same for all types of installations and tiles. A typical installation would be as follows. You are filling in the course that falls right above the horizontal base line, or the base-line course. In this particular instance you are using no corner trim tile — field tiles go straight to the corner. Work across the base line course until you can lay no more full-size tiles. Let the adhesive set. (You can continue filling in other rows during this time.)

Take two loose tiles (Tile A and Tile B) and a pencil, a felt-tip pen, or sharp, pointed tool like an ice pick or glass cutter. Place Tile A directly on top of the last full-size tile in the base line course, next to the corner. Place Tile B on top of Tile A;

then move Tile B over securely against the wall. Using the edge of Tile B as a guide, draw or scribe a line on the surface of Tile A. This is your preliminary cutting line.

Practice the technique before you actually have to cut the tile; this will help you become accustomed to shifting your hands about. Once you become acquainted with the spacing involved, you will have little difficulty adjusting to situations in which you must make allowances for trim tile. If, for example, cove corner trim had been installed up the corner, you would move Tile B over until it met the edge of the cove tile, but would not cover part of the cove corner.

To find the final cutting line, figure in the width of two grout lines. If the line is ⅛ inch wide, two will be ¼ inch. You must make allowances for the grout lines before you cut the tile. Measure in on the tile; draw the final cutting line.

Using a tile cutter. The easiest way to cut straight lines on tile is with a tile cutter, which you either buy or rent from your tile dealer. It is a good idea to practice on several scrap pieces before you start the actual tiling job. Wear safety glasses whenever you cut ceramic tile — flying clay and glaze could injure your eyes.

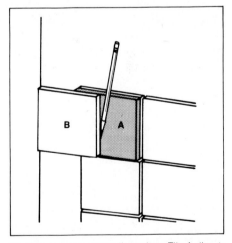

To determine the cutting line, place Tile A directly over the last full tile. Place Tile B directly over Tile A; slide Tile B over to the corner. Mark Tile A as shown.

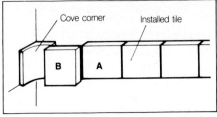

If there is a corner finishing piece, slide Tile B to the edge of the trim; mark Tile A. Allow for grout lines; then cut Tile A.

A tile cutter is a large glass cutter with a carbide tipped blade enclosed in a sliding frame. Clamp the tile into place, glaze side up. (If your tile has a ridged back, the ridges should lie parallel to the direction that the blade will cut. Re-mark the tile if this is not the case.) Score a line across the tile with the blade and remove the tile.

Tile can be cut using a rented tile cutter. Score the face of the tile as shown.

Instead of a tile cutter, you can score the tile with a conventional glass cutter.

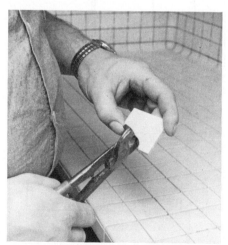

For irregular shapes use a tile nipper or a slip-joint pliers. Take only ⅛ in. bites at a time; the tile may break, otherwise.

With the glazed surface still facing up, place the scored line over a piece of wire approximately ⅛ inch in diameter. (A coat hanger is an excellent choice with wall tile — heavier floor tile may require a larger prop such as a dowel.) Place one hand on either side of the scored line and press down. The tile will snap in two.

Using a tile nipper. Cut irregular openings in a tile with a tile nipper. (You can also use an ordinary slip joint pliers.) Holding the tile with the glazed side up, take small, ⅛ inch bites with the nippers to break off tiny pieces at a time. Take your time creating the opening you need. If you take too large a bite, the tile might break. You also could destroy the cutoff line or cut too much and have to start all over again.

The nibbling method takes care of practically all irregular cuts that you may need to make. Most cutouts or holes for light fixtures or pipes will have an opening on at least one edge of the tile so that you can

Place the tile over a coat-hanger sized wire. Push down on both sides to snap tile in two.

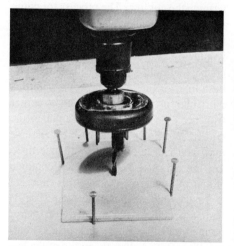

To cut a hole in a tile, secure the tile to a board with finishing nails. Cut with a hole saw in a portable electric drill.

start nibbling there. Some irregular cuts can be made with a hacksaw. You also can cut holes in ceramic tile with a hole saw. Bore small holes with a carbide-tipped masonry bit in a portable electric drill. In the event that a large opening does not intersect an edge, carefully cut through the center of the opening with the tile cutter. Then nibble out the opening and carefully fit the tile back together. The cut will hardly be noticeable.

Once the tile is cut, smooth the ragged edges with a carborundum stone or a coarse file. However, do not bother to hone down tile that will be hidden under fixtures, sink rims or tile trim.

Tile patterns. There are two layout plans for wall tile installation. The most common — and the simplest — has the tiles in each course lie directly above those in the rows below. This is called a jack-on-jack layout. In the second, called running bond, each course is staggered one-half tile over from the one above or below it. This layout requires more cut tile and is more difficult (and more expensive) to install, but the visual effect is pleasing.

Jack-on-jack. The easiest way to install a jack-on-jack layout is to fill in one row of tiles all the way from the vertical line to the corner, then continue the courses up the wall. Once one half of the wall has been completed, fill in the other. Check the straightness of your tile and grout lines often, using a carpenter's square. If a line is not straight, wiggle the tile back into place before the adhesive has set. The adhesive's setting time will vary according to brand or type; see the manufacturer's note on your particular container.

To set tile correctly, place it in the adhesive; then wiggle it gently back and forth. This assures a good bond with the adhesive.

However, although placement using this method is easy, it is difficult to keep the grout lines straight. A better installation method, because it simplifies straight lines and supports the growing weight of the wall during installation, is to place the tile in stair-step fashion. Install the entire length of the horizontal working line. Then take three tiles. Install Tile 1 in the corner created by the horizontal-base-line-course and the vertical working line. Install Tile 2 next to it and Tile 3 above Tile 1. This gives you the basic shape of your stair-step pyramid. Continue to add to the pyramid, always beginning with the bottom course and moving progressively up and over to the vertical working line. Fill in one half of the wall, and repeat for the other side.

Running bond. Begin at the vertical working line, with the vertical line running through the center of the first tile that you lay. This is in contrast to jack-on-jack, in which the line runs along the edge of the first tile. Install the horizontal baseline course for the entire wall. You may now complete one row at a time, starting at the vertical working line and filling in over to the corner, staggering the tiles by one half at the beginning of each course.

As an alternative, you may create a stair-step pyramid, as you did for jack-on-jack. However, this pyramid will stair-step up on two sides, instead of one, and will cover the entire wall in one continuous process. Begin Row 1 on the horizontal working line. Take three tiles. Lay Tile 1 so that the vertical working line runs through the tile's center. Set Tile 2 and 3 on either side of Tile 1. To build Row 2, take two tiles and place one on either side of the vertical working line. The grout lines between Tiles 1 and 2 and between

Tiles 1 and 3 will fall in the centers of Tiles 4 and 5. Cap the pyramid with a single tile — Tile 6, as shown — which is cut in half by the vertical working line.

Once you have the basic pyramid shape established, add a set of tiles to each side of each course until you complete the pyramid shape again. Always begin laying the tile at the horizontal base line and progressively work up the side and over to the vertical line. This pattern will lend support to the growing weight of the tiles.

General procedures. As the tiling progresses, check frequently both vertical and horizontal joint lines with a level. Then slide the carpet-covered board across the tiles, hammering the board firmly to ensure a good bond between the tiles and the adhesive. Remove all excess adhesive from the face of the tiles promptly with the proper solvent. Otherwise the adhesive will be almost impossible to get off.

Remember to leave openings for accessory pieces at the desired locations. If the accessories are multiples of the tile size, simply leave the appropriate number of tile spaces open. If the accessories are manufactured by another company, you may have to cut tiles to fit around the opening. In either case, adjust the positions of accessories so you will need to cut the least number of tiles.

If you are using no special corner tile, you will have to cut each tile singly to fit the space between the last full field tile in a course and the corner. Do not cut all the tile for all the courses at the same time; required sizes may change as you work upward on the wall.

How to Install Accessories

Once the tile adhesive has set (in most cases this takes at least 24 hours) you can install accessories. With the exception of grab bars, accessories can be set to a sound wall with the proper adhesives. Accessory manufacturers usually recommend using silicone cement. Some installers prefer to use floor tile adhesive because it sets up fairly quickly and gives a very strong bond. Whichever you choose, be generous with the application. Fill all voids on the back of the accessory and place it firmly. Hold the accessory in place with tape for several days, or until the adhesive has set. Do not use the accessory during this period.

Ceramic bathroom accessories come in two basic types: flush and overlay. In some instances, such as paper holders, the accessory is recessed into the wall. To install a surface-mounted accessory, cover its back with adhesive and set in place. Wiggle the accessory back and forth to get a firm bond with the adhesive. Then use

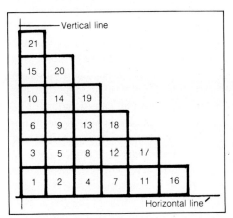

In a jack-on-jack layout, place Tile 1 in a corner of the crossed working lines. Lay Tile 2 next to Tile 1 and Tile 3 above.

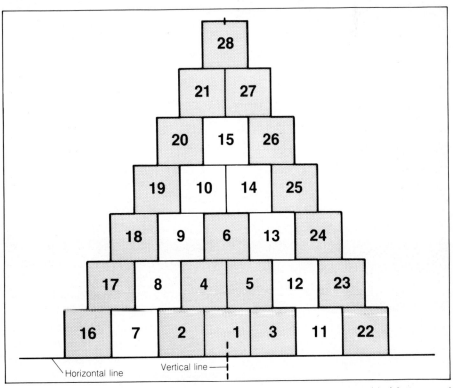

Running bond is laid upon a basic pyramid, as shown. Create the basic pyramid of 6 staggered tiles; then build layer upon layer, moving up and over to the vertical working line.

Use plenty of adhesive to set a surface-mounted accessory. The adhesive usually will hold the accessory in place. Prop heavier accessories with masking or duct tape.

Use a soft rubber squeegee to apply grout. Work the squeegee at an angle to the grout lines. This will fill the lines and leave no open air pockets.

An old toothbrush is an excellent tool for shaping grout lines. Then use a sponge to clean the tiles and to smooth, or "dress," the lines.

masking tape, or better yet, duct tape, to hold the accessory securely in place until the adhesive sets.

To install a recessed fixture, cut a hole in the wall with a utility knife. Prime the edges of the wallboard with your adhesive and let the prime coat dry. Then apply adhesive to the edges of the cavity and to the back of the accessory, and install. If any part of an accessory will contact a part of the wallboard or the inside of the wall, coat it with the adhesive. In most instances, masking tape or duct tape is all that will be required to hold the accessory in place until the adhesive sets. However, heavy accessories may need the support of a wooden prop.

While it is not uncommon for grab bars to be set with adhesive alone, they are one accessory that should be anchored studs with screws. To do so requires extra planning before you begin laying tile, but the safety benefits are worth the effort. Be sure that you purchase a grab bar that has screw openings. Then supplement the screws with extra adhesive.

Applying the Grout

The sizes of grout lines vary a great deal, depending on the project and the size of the tile. For instance in a patio installation of paver tile, the grout line might be as wide as ⅜ inch, but in a bathroom the grout line is probably from ⅛ to ¼ inch. You could, of course, have a grout line ½ inch wide in a bathroom but it would be hard to clean and would look oversized.

The color of the grout is also a factor that depends upon the project and the location of the tile. Today's colorful grouts can accentuate light, white or dark tile. A dark blue grout will emphasize the color detail of blue-on-white, Delft-like tile. There is no need to stay with traditional white grout. Grout color also helps hide soil buildup.

Wall grout, which comes in dry powder form, will usually cover about 200 to 250 square feet. Wait 24 hours or so after tiling before you begin to grout (unless the adhesive manufacturer specifies otherwise). Then mix or use the grout according to the manufacturer's instructions. Using a rubber float or squeegee, spread the grout diagonally across the joints between the tile. Make sure you pack the grout securely into every joint; watch for air bubbles. The time and type of cure will depend upon your type of grout. Some grouts require a

dry cure; others need to be dampened periodically. The length of the cure also varies. Follow the directions for your particular installation.

As soon as the grout becomes firm, use a wet sponge to wash the excess grout from the faces of the tiles. To shape the grout lines, run the handle of an old toothbrush along the joints. This process is called "striking the joints". Then clean the walls and smooth ("dress") the joints with a damp sponge. Allow the walls to dry. Then polish them with a clean cloth. It will probably take several washings to completely clean all the excess grout off the walls.

Working Out a Tile Pattern or Design

One way to individualize a room is to incorporate a design into the tiled area. The design can range from a simple line of border tiles to a supergraphic in brilliantly contrasting colors. On a kitchen wall you could place traditional designs from Early American samplers. In a hallway leading from the front door to the living room you could lay designs that reinforce the predominant decorating style of your home — subtle earth-tone designs based upon Indian motifs would complement a home that features open beams and rugged textures. A row of daisies near the bottom of a wall in a morning room or a garden room can brighten and reinforce the tone of the entire room.

Planning the layout. Incorporating a design does make determining the number of tiles you need more difficult. It also complicates the layout procedure. However, the advance planning and installation time involved are more than repaid by the results.

Once you have decided upon a design — for example a rooster on a nursery wall — sketch it to scale on onion-skin paper. Plot out the entire wall or floor plan on a piece of graph paper. Each square on the graph will represent a single tile. The amount of detail you can include will be determined in part by the size of the design and the size of the wall. Remember that you will be confined to "jerky" lines — a downward curve will proceed in stair-steps, one for every row of tile. The very nature of a tiled surface, therefore, will affect the fine-line detail for which you can reasonably hope.

On your piece of graph paper, each row

of squares equals a row of tile. (If your tile is rectangular rather than square, have a square equal the small dimension and use two for the long dimension of your tile. Thus, a 2x4 tile will be one square high and two squares long.) On the graph paper, rough-sketch the outline of the tile design. Lay the onion-skin drawing over the sketch, aligning the outlines. Once you are satisfied with the placement, pin or tape the top and the bottom of the onion-skin to the graph paper. Then slip a piece of carbon paper between the design and the graph and retrace, transferring the design to the graph paper.

Estimating quantities. Use different-colored felt-tipped pens to color in the various tile colors in the design. Then count squares to determine the number of tile of a given color that you will need. Always add 5-10 percent to the total to allow for breakage or error. Multiply the number of tile across the top of the tile area outline on the graph paper by the number of tile down the side. This is the total number of tiles you will need. Subtract the tiles that go into your design from the total number of tiles in the entire tile surface, and you will know the number of background tiles you need. You again have to add on an extra 5 or 10 percent.

Placing the tile. Laying the tile will be an involved process. You will have to fol-low each line of the graph as you go. Before you lay any row of tile, dry lay the pieces, following the graph paper carefully. That will help you avoid any errors in layout. Sometimes it helps to number the backs of the tiles as you lift them from the dry layout before applying the adhesive. This will help you remember the order in which the tiles will be set into the adhesive. Decide upon a grout color that will detract as little as possible from the overall effect of the design, especially if the design is small. (Although the process would entail a great deal of care, you might even change the grout color as needed in contrasting areas.)

Outdoor adaptations. These same steps can be used to create an outdoor design, and also can be adapted to applications of resilient, wood and other types of tiles.

TILING FLOORS

If you will tile both walls and floors, finish the walls before you do the floor. You do not want to damage the new floor, nor do you want to spill adhesive or grout onto it as you work on the wall above. In addition, cove tile is easier to place between the wall and the floor if the walls are tiled first.

Ceramic floor tile may be installed over most structurally sound and level surfaces that are free from any looseness or buckling. Since the layer of ceramic tile will add weight to a floor, check to determine if the floor is structurally sound. If the floor is over a basement or crawl space, add bridging as shown to further strengthen the floor. Use two 8d nails at the top and the bottom of each 1x4 brace.

General Room Preparation

The first step is to prepare the room and the floor surface for working. Since you will be raising the level of the floor itself, check all door bottoms to see if there is adequate clearance. If not, you will have to trim the door. To check the clearance, place two tiles, one on top of the other, against the inside door edge and mark a line above the top tile. Using a level to ensure straightness, extend this line across the bottom of the door. Remove the doors by tapping out the hinge pins. (If the hinge is an old style one, you must remove the screws holding it to the frame of the door.) Then cut along the line to provide sufficient space for the new floor.If you need to remove only a little of the door bottom, use a plane. If you must remove a fair amount, use a saw.

If you are tiling only the floor, remove the shoe molding at the base of the wall, but leave the base molding in place. To remove the shoe molding, insert a thin pry

A ceramic wall can contain a pattern — one that is very simple or, as here, one that is highly complex. Draw up a layout grid before beginning work for a patterned wall.

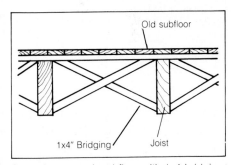

Strengthen a weak subfloor with 1x4 bridging. Fasten it to the joists with 8d nails.

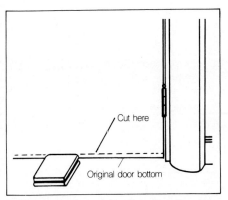

To shorten door, stack two tiles; draw line above top one; trim with a plane or saw.

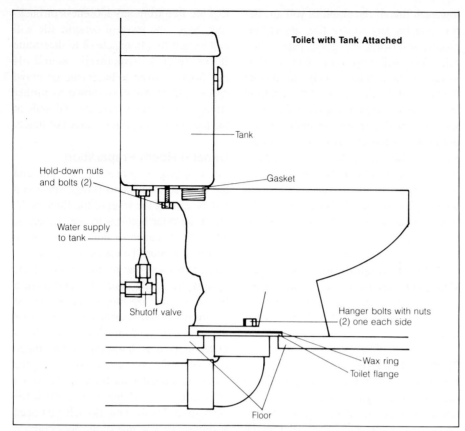

Toilet with Tank Attached

Tank

Hold-down nuts and bolts (2)

Gasket

Water supply to tank

Shutoff valve

Hanger bolts with nuts (2) one each side

Wax ring
Toilet flange

Floor

The bolts that fasten a tank and bowl together are found on both sides of and slightly behind the gasket connecting the two. Loosen these and remove the tank. Then remove the bowl by loosening the floor-level nuts that hold the hanger bolts on either side of the bowl.

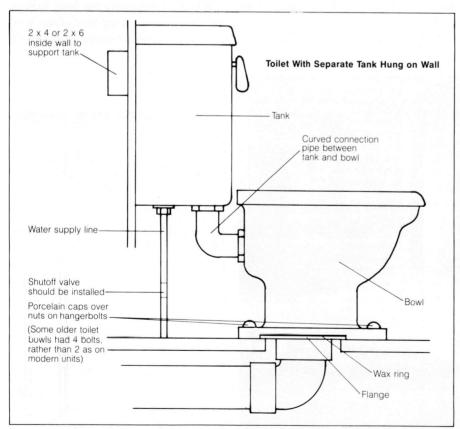

2 x 4 or 2 x 6 inside wall to support tank

Toilet With Separate Tank Hung on Wall

Tank

Curved connection pipe between tank and bowl

Water supply line

Shutoff valve should be installed

Porcelain caps over nuts on hangerbolts

(Some older toilet bowls had 4 bolts, rather than 2 as on modern units)

Bowl

Wax ring

Flange

If the tank is wall-hung and separate from the bowl, you need not remove the tank, but it must be disconnected from the bowl. Loosen the slipjoint gasket on the pipe connection leading into the stool. (If the pipe connections have become rusted, use a hacksaw to saw through the pipe. Replace the pipe later.) Then loosen the nuts on the hanger bolts.

bar under the molding and gently pry out the molding. Start about a foot from a corner; gradually work along the floor until you completely remove the molding. You will ease the job somewhat if you insert small shims between the molding and the wall as you go along. Once the molding is completely loose, store it so you can replace it when you have finished tiling.

Tiling a bathroom floor entails special problems, since you must work around the toilet stool and possibly a sink support. It is possible to cut the tile to fit around these fixtures with tile nippers and then finish off the cut line with grout. However, the finished floor will look much more professional if you remove the fixtures, extend the tile, and set the fixtures on top of the tile. You also will have to replace the bolts that fasten the fixture to the floor with bolts that are long enough to allow for the tile thickness. Holes for the bolts must be cut into the tile before it can be placed.

Remove the stool. You should have a helper for this process. First you must shut off the water. Turn off one of two supply valves, either the one in the basement or a shutoff valve in back of or under the toilet itself. Then flush the toilet so that the bowl and the tank are empty. As the water flushes, lift the lid from the tank top and hold open the assembly that forms the stopper in the tank. Remove any water remaining in the tank with a sponge and bucket; wipe down the inside of the tank. (This is important even if the tank fastens to the wall — you do not want water to drip onto the tile as you lay it.) Wipe the bowl dry. Now remove the toilet. Do not let its weight fool you: toilets are made of porcelain and can crack or even break quite easily. Use care when you lift and move the tank or bowl.

When lifting out a tank and stool that are connected, first remove the tank from the stool. Reach inside the tank and loosen the gasket that connects the tank and the stool. Then remove the two hold-down nuts located under the tank at either side of the gasket opening. Lift off the tank and store it on newspapers or old carpeting in an area away from the bathroom. Next, remove any porcelain caps over the bolts that hold the bowl to the floor (called T-Bolts or closet bolts), and remove the nuts on those bolts. Rock the toilet to dislodge it. With a helper's assistance, lift the stool. Place it carefully on newspapers.

If the tank and stool are separate, the tank fastens to the wall. A metal pipe connects the tank to the stool. Before you remove the stool, you must disconnect this pipe. Place a bucket below it to catch any water. Twist loose the slipjoint screw gasket leading into the stool. In cases where the gasket is so corroded that it cannot be loosened, cut through the pipe with a hacksaw and replace it later. Then follow the same procedure as above for removing the stool.

Sink removal. You need remove a sink only if it has a supporting ceramic pedestal. Turn off all shutoff valves or the water main. Place a bucket below the trap to catch any water or debris inside. Then loosen the slipjoint nut attaching the drain to the sink. If these are badly corroded, you will need a plumber's wrench. Then disconnect the hot and cold water supply pipes. Finally, loosen the bolts that hold the sink to the wall, and lift out the sink. Store carefully in a safe place.

Floor Surface Preparation

As with any tile job, proper surface preparation is the key to a good, long-lasting job. The surface must be clean and completely dry. Cement floors must be made level and free of holes or protrusions. Painted floors should be roughened by sanding to insure a good bond. Old tile and linoleum must be removed. If any special problems exist — such as a surface that is soaked with oil, or one that is not level because of chipped concrete or cupped and warped floor boards — consult your tile dealer. In many cases, the best course is a layer of particle board or plywood, or a new concrete over the old.

Plywood subfloor. If you are to lay the tile over a plywood subfloor, the thickness should be no less than ⅝ inch thick Exterior grade plywood. Check the thickness — and the condition — of the present subfloor in your room. If it is severely damaged, replace it. Be sure also that the present layer is thick enough. If you decide to install a new subfloor right over the floor joists, use ⅝ inch Exterior grade plywood. For expansion, allow a space of ⅛ inch between all joints and between each sheet and an adjoining wall. Stagger the sheets — that is, edges of adjoining sheets should not meet in continuous lines. To fasten, space 6d ring shank nails every 6 inches along the floor joists. Then fill the ⅛ inch expansion joints with adhesive.

Wood floor. You cannot lay ceramic tile over a springy floor. Nail down any loose flooring. If the surface still is not solid, cover the floor with Exterior grade plywood that is at least ⅜ inch thick before you begin to tile. (In fact, for older floors this is a very good idea — it helps strengthen the old floor.) Before you nail the subfloor sheets in place, cover the sheets and edges with primer; then install.

If the wood floor needs only to be leveled before the subfloor is laid, trowel on special plastic underlayment to grade the surface. This underlayment can be applied in thicknesses running from a feathered edge to ⁵⁄₁₆ inch thick in a single coat. Apply as many coats as necessary to reach a level surface.

Concrete floors. Because of its strength, concrete makes an excellent base for a ceramic tile installation. Use a chemical floor cleaner to remove grease or other stains that may prevent a strong adhesive bond. The cleaner can be found at auto supply stores. Chip away excess irregularities in the concrete or paint with a wide, flat masonry chisel. Wear safety glasses when doing this.

Some concrete floors have been painted or have an extremely slick finish. These should be sanded to roughen the surface in order to ensure a good bond between the old floor and the tile adhesive. For this job, use No. 4 open-coat sandpaper on a rented floor sander. Wear a dust mask so you do not breathe in the dust produced by the sanding.) Vacuum to remove all loose material and wash thoroughly with a stiff bristle brush and clear water.

Fill all cracks and holes with the filler appropriate for the type of installation you are planning. If you will use a thick mortar bed, use ordinary concrete patching compound to fill and level. However, if you

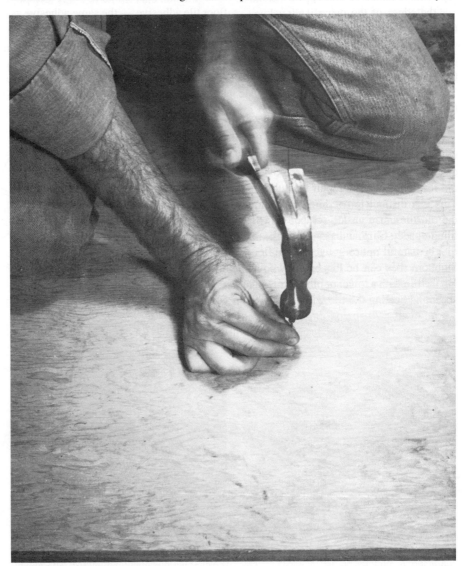

If the condition of a subfloor is such that its repair is too costly to be worthwhile, apply an additional underlayment layer of Exterior plywood or of tempered hardboard.

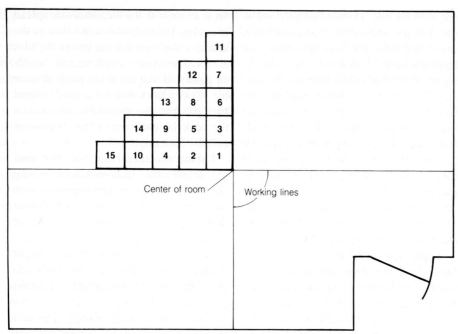

Jack-on-jack is a common layout for floor tile. Set Tile 1 in one of the corners created by the crossed working lines. Lay Tile 2 next to Tile 1; set Tile 3 above Tile 1. Tiles 4, 5 and 6 follow the stair-step pattern, moving up and over to the centerline.

Laying a jack-on-jack plan. Take three tiles. Place Tile 1 in the corner created at the room center by the crossed working lines. Place Tile 2 next to Tile 1, and Tile 3 above Tile 1. These three tiles form the basis of the stair-step layout that will fan out to cover the quarter of the room on which you are working. Fill in, beginning at one working line and moving up and over to the other working line. When you come to the wall edge, leave the space open for cut tile. After completing one quarter of the room, repeat the process for each quarter. Make sure you keep the adhesive cleaned off the tiles as you go, because it is extremely hard to remove once it has set up.

Laying a running bond plan. Follow the stairstep pattern discussed in the earlier section on walls. You will fill half of the floor at a time. In every other course, the working line will run through the center tile.

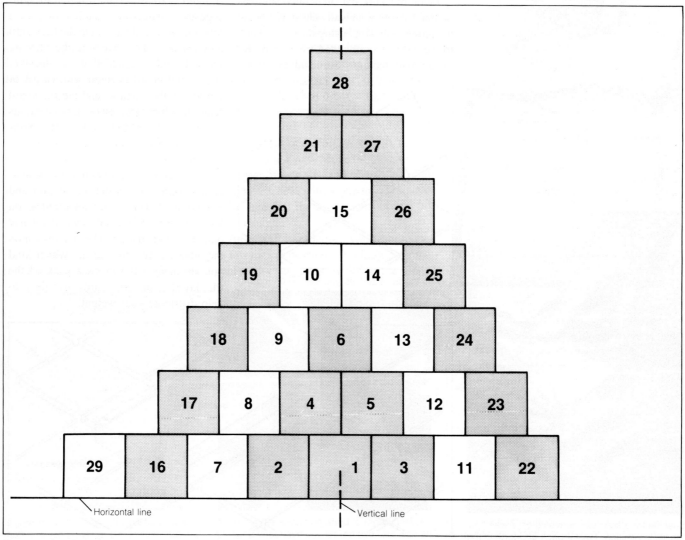

Six staggered tiles comprise the basic pyramid of running bond. Lay Tile 1 against the bottom working line so it is bisected by the other working line. Tiles 2 and 3 fit on either side of Tile 1. In the second row, Tiles 4 and 5 fall flush with each side of the working line. Tile 6 caps off the pyramid; aligning directly with Tile 1. Stair-step the next rows up and over, as shown.

Using mosaic tiles on floors. Mosaics are quite frequently used on floors. If ceramic mosaic tiles with perforated mountings are used, dry lay the sheets from the center point of the floor out to all walls. Adjust slightly for the minimum number of cut tiles, and, as always, avoid excessively small cut tiles. You may lay in the jack-on-jack method described above; however, the following layout is also quite common. Begin with the wall farthest from the door and work toward the door, a row at a time, in straight lines. Fill in all cut tiles as they occur. Check each sheet to maintain straight lines.

Applying the grout. You may prefer gray grout on the floor, since gray hides dirt better than white grout. You can buy the grout premixed, or you can mix it yourself. Allow the floor to set in place for 24 hours (or follow the directions of the adhesive manufacturer). Then clean all debris from the joints and, if necessary, remove any spacers. Apply the grout, using the techniques outlined in the section on wall tile. Work the grout between the tiles with the flat side of a rubber trowel or squeegee. Make sure you follow the manufacturer's recommendations. When the joints are firm, wipe the tiles with a damp sponge. Then polish with a soft cloth.

You will probably wish to allow the grout to dry for another day or so. Then wash the floor with a clean mop and household detergent and water. Polish with a soft cloth and add a grout sealer to the floor.

Stay off the floor for the time recommended by the adhesive manufacturer. Then replace any molding, doors or fixtures.

Re-installing Bathroom Fixtures

Before re-installing a toilet base, you must replace the wax ring which acts as a sealer between the base and the soil pipe. Wax rings are available in most hardware stores. Turn the base upside down. Around the opening in the base will be either an old wax ring or a coat of plumber's putty. Remove this and replace it with a new ring. Place the toilet base and press gently into place. Add and tighten the closet bolts carefully so you do not crack the porcelain.

Your fixture may sit on a plastic flange instead of an iron pipe. If so, install the ring; then seat the base over the hold-down bolts and replace the hold-down nuts. Tighten these gently but firmly.

If you also have removed the toilet tank, you must replace its sealer too. This will either be around the tank drain of the tank itself or around the tank drain opening on the base. Remove the old sealer — either ring or putty. Place the new ring around the tank drain opening on the base. Then fasten the hold-down nuts.

Gently reposition toilet with longer bolts to hold firmly over thicker surface of new tile.

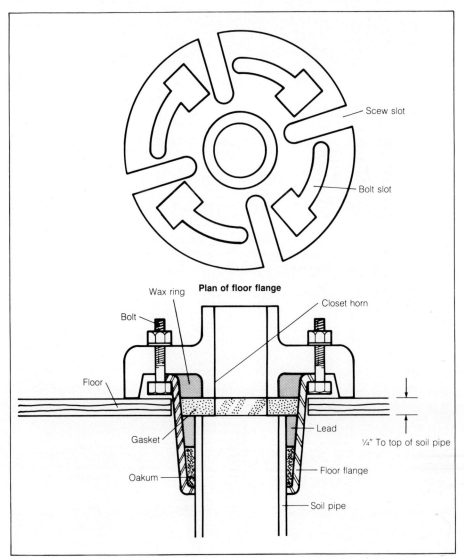

Scew slot

Bolt slot

Plan of floor flange

Wax ring

Bolt

Closet horn

Floor

Gasket

Oakum

Lead

Floor flange

¼" To top of soil pipe

Soil pipe

Insert wax ring in the lip of the toilet's floor flange; fasten fixture with bolts.

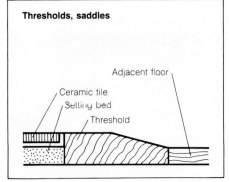

Thresholds, saddles

Adjacent floor

Ceramic tile

Setting bed

Threshold

New tile raises the floor. For a smooth transition to untiled areas, add a threshold.

INDOOR
CERAMIC TILE PROJECTS

In addition to standard floor and wall treatments, ceramic tile can also be used for a number of other projects. Because of its beauty and distinctive style, it is a unique addition to all areas of a home. Small broken pieces can be used in craft projects as well. As you become accustomed to working with tile, you will probably come up with other projects of your own design.

FIREPROOF SURFACES

Because of the growing concern about energy supply, home fireplaces and wood stoves are becoming increasingly common sights. Ceramic tile is an elegant covering for a hearth, a fireplace front or a floor beneath a wood stove. In addition, ceramic tile is a logical and sensible covering, due to its fireproof nature.

Hearth Covering

Set immediately in front of the fireplace firebox, a hearth's main purpose is to prevent sparks from burning holes in the sur-

A tile design requires careful planning — tiles, pattern and surroundings must blend. In this Victorian fireplace, the designs and textures — wood, glass and tile — complement each other.

Impervious to high heat, ceramic tile can cover both hearth and firebox floor.

rounding combustible floor. If you are installing a new fireplace, the hearth and foundation must be up to code. According to standard building code requirements, the slab forming the base of the hearth must be made of brick, concrete, stone, or other approved noncombustible materials. The slab should be at least 4 inches thick and extend at least 16 inches out and 8 inches to either side of the fireplace opening. If the opening is larger than 6 feet square, the last two dimensions increase to 20 and 12 inches. The floor itself must be reinforced with 1x4 bridging to carry the additional weight. (Since codes vary, check with your local city or county building inspector for your area's specific requirements.)

Although you can use a concrete slab as the finished surface of the hearth — it is highly functional and easily cleaned — this option is not particularly attractive. Ceramic tile is an excellent material for covering a hearth of concrete or other material in front of a fireplace. You can use it not only to cover a new hearth, but to extend an old one that isn't quite large enough to catch all the sparks.

Subflooring. The ease of extending a fireplace hearth depends upon whether it is at or above floor level. In either project you must add subflooring, but an above-floor hearth also requires some construction work.

Floor-level hearth. A "floor-level hearth" actually is about ¼ to ½ inch higher than the surrounding wood floor. First decide how much farther you want the hearth to extend into the room.

If the old hearth is covered with tile that you wish to save, remember that the extension is not likely to be covered with tiles having the same design, since the pattern will be hard to match. Instead, plan a border that will complement and highlight the old tile. To determine the proper thickness of the subflooring for the hearth extension, measure to the top of the old tile. Then substract the thickness of the new tiles from the figure. In that way the new and the old tiles will create an even, level surface.

If you do not want to retain the old hearth cover, measure the distance from the floor to the top of the old hearth. That is the thickness required for the subflooring extension.

Cut ¼ inch Exterior plywood (or the thickness necessary to match the height of the current hearth) to create a subfloor that surrounds the existing hearth and extends out to fill the area you desire to cover. Be very accurate as you fit the pieces to the edges of the existing hearth, and be sure that all corners of the new hearth are square and true. Smear the backs of the plywood pieces with latex glue and then nail them with ring shank flooring nails to the existing floor. Then "dimple" the nails (set them slightly under the wood surface with a hammer and a nail set). Fill all cracks with water putty or wood dough. Use latex concrete patching cement to seal the joint between the old hearth and the new wood subfloor.

Above-floor-level hearth. If the exist-ing hearth is higher than ¼ inch, such as two inches, use a stack of plywood pieces to extend the hearth a short distance. Build the extension flush with the existing hearth; anchor the extension securely to the floor with nails long enough to reach through the plywood and into the floor. If the extension is very large, however, this method will involve too much expense. Instead, build a frame of 2x4s laid flat. Then cover the frame with a thickness of Exterior grade plywood that will give the height required.

Preparing the surface. If only the new subfloor will be covered with tile, sand it down using a belt sander with a coarse belt. Vacuum the sanding dust. Then begin your tiling plans.

However, if you are to cover the old hearth and the new subfloor, prepare both the new area and the old. Your major concern is to provide a good solid surface for the tiles to rest on. Otherwise, the new cover will crack or break from the pressure of normal household traffic. Thoroughly patch any large defects or holes with the patching material recommended by the tile dealer for your particular surface. (For detailed information on making repairs, see Chapters 2 and 8.) If repair of the old hearth requires too much work to be a reasonable task, apply an underlayment of ¼ to ½ inch thick Exterior plywood over the entire hearth area. It is advisable to select specially treated, fire-resistant wood, such as Koppers Company's Non-Com. Once installed, this too must be sanded smooth before the tile is laid.

Install a plywood underlayment whose height is equal to that of the old hearth.

Cover nailheads and seal between plywood sheets and the hearth and underlayment.

Once the sealer has dried, sand the surface smooth with a belt sander.

Laying the tile. Select a heavy-duty floor tile such as quarry or paver tiles; check with the tile dealer to be certain that the tile you want is recommended for such

Spread a cement-based adhesive with a square-notched trowel. For best results, hold the trowel at about a 45 degree angle.

Lay the tile carefully to ensure straight courses and grout lines. Place any cut tiles at the joint between the hearth and fireplace.

Circular or oval hearths require planning on heavy paper. Lay edge tiles; adjust grout lines to avoid cut tiles. Then fill from the center of the pad out. Cut tiles with cutter and nippers; complete and smooth curves with a carborundum disc in an electric drill.

use. Install the tile with a non-flammable adhesive such as dry-set mortar or latex-portland cement mortar. These cement-based adhesives are spread with a square-notched trowel. Their consistency is such that they fill in minor cracks in the surface on which they are spread. This is particularly important in this installation. Follow the tile installation with latex-portland cement grout. Other adhesives and grout are not recommended for this installation.

Lay out working lines to ensure straight tile courses and grout lines. Plan for any cut tile to fall at the back of the hearth — either where the old and new hearths meet or where the new hearth meets the fireplace itself. Apply the adhesive and lay the tile from front to back.

Once the adhesive has set (this usually takes overnight), apply the grout. If appropriate to your color scheme, consider using a dark grout, since it will suffer less from discoloration due to exposure to ash and soot.

Adding a circular hearth. You need not confine yourself to a square-shaped hearth, but be aware that a circular one is difficult to lay. The number of cut tiles would be large and, even more serious, it would be very difficult to produce the desired smooth finished edge.

Covering a Fireplace Front or Mantel

An old, outdated fireplace or one that has broken bricks or a damaged front can be turned into a beautiful, unusual fireplace with the addition of a colorful ceramic tile front. You can cover the entire front of an old or new fireplace with ceramic tile, or set off a wood mantel and trim with decorative, handpainted or sculptured tiles around the lip edges of the fireplace or across the mantel. You can choose from many patterns, colors, and shapes. If budget is a concern, mix a few expensive tiles with plainer ones; the effect of the prized tiles will carry into and disguise the more modest ones.

Preparing the surface. If you are building a new home with a fireplace — or adding one to an existing home during a remodeling — cover the surface around the opening with a smooth coat of plaster. Once this is dry, you may apply tile without difficulty. If you are renovating an old fireplace, you probably will have to apply a smooth coat of some mate-

rial, such as epoxy plaster, to the brick or stone to create a surface that is level enough for tile application.

One way to renew the appearance of an old fireplace is to cover the entire surround with wood and edge the opening itself with a single row of decorative tiles. For this project, as with the hearth covering, you should use ½-¾ inch fire-resistant wood. Use a masonry bit to drill holes in the fireplace front. The drill hole should extend at least ¾ inch into the front. However never drill all the way through; the nails will heat when the fireplace is being used and create a fire hazard. Sink lead expansion shields into the holes. Then, using masonry nails, nail the wood front to the fireplace surround. If you wish to stain the wood, do it before you begin tiling. If you wait until the tiling is completed, the stain might discolor the grout between the tiles. Prepare the surface for tiling as you would any new wood surface (see Chapter 2). Protect the wood finish during tiling by applying strips of masking tape.

Laying the tile. Determine the layout of the tile. If the spacing does not work out exactly as you wish, make adjustments with grout line spacing, or cut filler tiles to complete your pattern. Experiment with grout line size, especially if installing a border of tiles rather than an entire facing. Wide grout lines will not look out of place in such a project — in fact, they add particular emphasis to specially chosen designer tiles.

Apply a non-flammable mortar to the area in which you want to install the tile. If you are using an organic adhesive, be certain it is non-flammable. (Some are not.) If you are using an epoxy, remember that it needs good ventilation but dries quickly, so do not apply more mortar than you can cover with tile in 30 minutes. Set each tile firmly in the mortar base with a slight twisting motion. If there are no spacer tabs on the tiles, use toothpicks or paper matchsticks to make small joints. Use purchased spacers, or even a ruler, to establish wider grout lines. If the mortar is soft and the tiles are heavy, you may have to hold the tiles in place with props or strong tape. Choose a tile grout that will accent the color and pattern of the tiles.

Floor Covering for a Wood Stove

One way to protect the floor beneath a wood stove from the sparks, hot ashes and heat of the stove is to install a ceramic tile floor covering. The shape of this pad can be anything from a half circle to a rectangle jutting out into the room.

One word of warning: if you do install a wood-burning stove, check with the local building codes before you begin. You may find that you need a building permit before you can install the flue or make other structural changes in your home. Check local fire department to be sure that your setup and dimensions are in compliance with its regulations. Consult your insurance company, both before and after you have installed the stove. Your homeowner's insurance rates may be affected by installation. Finally, once the stove is in, have both a building inspector and insurance representative inspect it. You will need their written approval in order to protect you from later fines or insurance cancellation in case of a fire.

The dimensions of the floor pad depend upon the kind, size and amount of protective backing that you install on the walls around the wood stove. (The safest procedure is to add protective backing such as asbestos millboard or 28 gauge sheet metal — or both — and then follow the clearances for an installation with no backing at all.)

CLEARANCES FOR WOOD STOVES[2] WITH NO ADDED PROTECTION[1]

Orientation	Distance
Ceiling	36"
Front	48
Side	24-36
Rear	36

[1] Information adapted from NFPA bulletin No. 89M, 1976 edition.
[2] A radiant stove is one with a single layer of metal enclosing the fire, such as a Franklin stove.

The accompanying chart is fairly general for a typical wood stove such as a Franklin or a pot-belly. They are called "radiant stoves"; all radiant stoves are so constructed that they enclose the fire with a single layer of metal. No dimensions are set for the extension in front of the stove. Plan to cover at least a space large enough to load and unload the stove with comfort. That distance will also protect that part of the floor most likely to suffer damage from dropped ashes or flying sparks. You cannot exercise too much care about placement of your wood stove. Therefore, check the requirements of your particular

manufacturer and of your individual community.

A floor pad can lie flush with the floor, or it can be raised. If raised, build a framework of 2x4s set on edge. Cover the frame with ¾ inch Exterior plywood. If it is available, use fire-resistant wood. The sheets do not have to be staggered. Sand carefully. If the stove is a large one, or if you are installing a free-standing fireplace, use two layers of plywood, one that is ¾ and one that is ⅜ inch thick. Use 8d nails to toe-nail the frame to the floor. Then sand the wood.

Laying the tile. Plan your tile layout so that any cut tiles will appear at the back rather than at the front of the pad. If you must cut tiles on the sides, arrange for cuts of equal dimensions on either side, so that the appearance of the layout will be uniform.

Select a tile that is certain to tolerate both the heat and weight of the stove. Paver or quarry tile are the most suitable. However, glazed ceramic tiles strong enough for floor application are appropriate. Check with your tile dealer about your specific choice. Handle the actual tiling as you would for a new plywood floor. Use only cement-based or epoxy-based adhesives and grouts, because of their fire-resistant characteristics.

Raised Entryways

Changing a floor level by means of a raised entryway not only creates more visual interest, it also forms boundaries that delineate traffic patterns and living spaces. Ceramic tile is an extremely good way to cover such an entryway, for it will hold up well under the high level of traffic the area receives.

Raising sections of a floor visually separates areas of a room. Covering the entire floor with tile joins areas. The combination, as shown here, has subtle architectural effects.

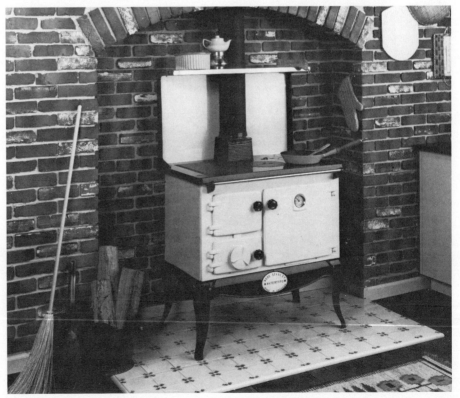

Protect the floor under a woodstove with ceramic tile. The color of this tile matches the stove; the delicacy of the design provides a contrasting touch to the rough brick wall.

Framework

Creating a raised area requires quite a bit of structural carpentry, so you may wish to have a contractor do this job for you. If you wish to attempt it yourself, build a wood frame of 2x4s or 2x6s as shown. Connect the framing with 16d nails, and use 8d nails to fasten any interconnecting 1x4 bridging. Once the frame is complete, cover it with ¾ particleboard or ¾ inch Exterior plywood. Then toe-nail the entire structure to the joists in the existing floor. (If you are working over a concrete floor, you should use epoxy to fasten down the frame.) To allow for the height of the floor and/or tiles, raise the lower edges of all doors by cutting off the bottoms with a sabre saw. If your doors are hollow-cored, you may have to replace them if they cannot be adjusted to the new height.

Tiling

Preparing the surface. Repair any mars and nicks in the plywood surface as discussed in Chapter 2. Then use a belt sander and coarse-grain sandpaper to smooth the surface; vacuum up all sanding dust before you apply the adhesive.

Laying the tile. Select a tile, adhesive and grout that will hold up under heavy foot traffic. Then lay out the working lines. Plan to cover the steps first, going up each riser and then over the tread. Begin at the bottom riser. Cut tile should fall at the top of the riser. In this way, the curl of quarter round, which will begin the covering of the tread, covers the cut edge of the top row on the riser.

Once the steps are finished, cover the floor of the entryway, laying the tile as you would for a conventional floor surface.

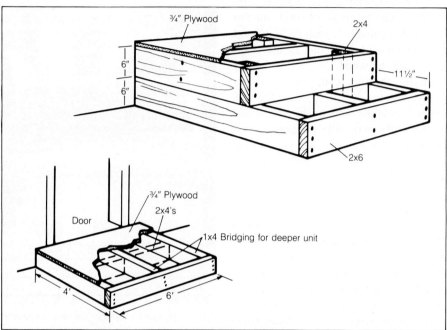

The framing for a raised entryway is made of 2x4s set on edge. If your design is wider than this one, insert 1x4 bridging between the 2x4s. Cover the framing with ¾ inch Exterior plywood.

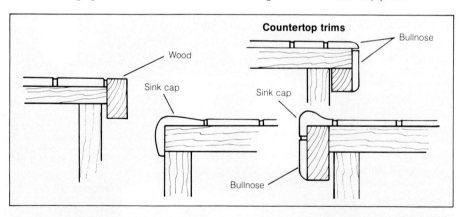

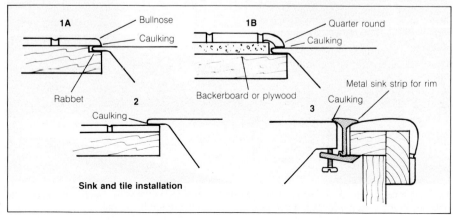

Sink and tile installation

KITCHENS

Ceramic tile countertops are quite popular, and with good reason. They are easy to clean and good-looking. More importantly, hot pans in a kitchen can be set on one without causing any damage: water can saturate a counter in a kitchen or a bathroom and the surface will never suffer. On an open shelf in any room, ceramic tile adds durability and elegance.

Installation Principles

In all of these installations, the tiling method is basically the same. Any one is a good project for the beginning tile setter. Ceramic tile can be laid over most of the materials usually found on a countertop, including old ceramic tile, plastic laminate and, of course, the plywood support found in a new countertop installation.

Special edge trims. Before you begin a counter installation, decide upon the type of trim you want along the edge of the countertop. In areas of meal preparation you may choose to have a smooth curved edge of bullnose trim so you can scrape chopped vegetables or batter mixtures from the work area into mixing bowls and can easily clean the counter area. However, in the sink area, take advantage of special edge trim that prevents water from dripping onto the floor.

Sink installation. Another option that you must consider is the method of installing a sink, if one is in the countertop. There are three common methods. In the first, the sink is installed before the tile. The sink rim is supported by the existing surface of the countertop. Then the tile is laid. Special trim tile covers the sink rim. In the second, the sink is installed after the tile is laid. Tiles are cut to fit around the opening for the sink. The sink itself then rests on top of the cut tiles, covering the cut edges. This finishing technique gives the installation a more professional appearance. Finally, the sink can be supported by a metal edge trim. In this installation, the sink rests upon the existing surface, the cut tile meets the surface opening, and the joint between the two is covered by the metal trim. This alternative has several advantages. The tile does not have to support the weight of the sink, which in some instances could cause the tile to crack. A metal sink rim is necessary if the sink rim itself is not made to support the sink. The biggest disadvantage of metal sink trim is that it creates two seams that are difficult to keep clean. Whatever method you choose, heavily caulk the joints between the sink and countertop and the sink and tile.

The most common choice for a countertop installation is glazed ceramic tile, either in single tiles or in sheets. Do not, however, use the pregrouted sheets. Before deciding upon a tile, verify its water-resistance with your tile dealer.

Installing Tile on a New Plywood Countertop

Underlayment. Because ceramic tile is heavy, and because many countertops are exposed to moisture, the underlayment should be made of ¾ inch Exterior plywood (minimum B-D). To support the top, install crossbraces of either 1x2s or 2x4s laid flat. Do not place the braces more than three feet apart. To hold an apron or other drip edge trim, nail a 2x2 furring strip to the front edge of the top. This will also be covered with tile.

In the installation pictured here, the right hand side of the countertop has been cut ½ inch shorter than the base cabinet upon which it sits. The tile will follow the cut edge of the plywood, creating a flush edge so that an appliance can be stored in the opening next to the counter. If that small space were not left, the trim tile would protrude and possibly scratch the appliance whenever it slid in or out of the

The tile used for this countertop and backsplash has the same color and texture as that of the floor tile, although the floor tile units are larger.

This new base is Exterior plywood cut with a ⅜ in. overhang at the front. It is ½ in. shorter at the end (the thickness of a tile) to permit flush installation of an appliance. A 2-inch-wide furring strip nails to the front edge of the plywood countertop — apron trim tile will be applied to this strip.

Trim tile usually must be cut to fit above the door of a dishwasher.

Dry lay the tiles first. Since this installation had the sink in the corner, the tile layout moved from the ends of the countertop toward the sink opening, as detailed below.

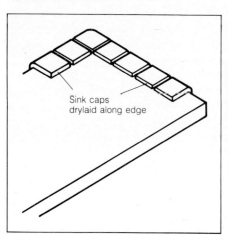

Sink caps drylaid along edge

opening. The other alternative, of course, is to extend the countertop over the appliance, after removing the surface on top. If a dishwasher, most portables are built with this option in mind. In this latter case, the trim tile must be adjusted to allow clearance of the dishwasher door.

Once you have installed the underlayment, check the surface. It should be sound. No nails or other obstructions should protrude. Fill any holes and defects

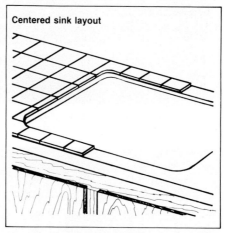

Centered sink layout

Tile layout here begins in front of sink and is filled in for half the counter. Tiles around edges are cut to create curved edge.

Corner sinks involve odd cuts of tile to fit the sink edge. In this arrangement, the sink rim overlaps and hides rough tile edges.

Countertop deck tiles begin at the corner and are laid working toward the corner sink.

with spackling compound and sand smooth.

Step one: dry layout. First do a dry layout so you can have the least number of cut tiles, especially very small cut tiles. Work from the front to the back of the countertop so that any cut tiles will fall at the back rather than the front of the countertop.

In the installation shown, cove tile was not added to finish the back. Instead, a single bullnose course of tile was used for the backsplash. Because of the spacing on this countertop, the backsplash tile was set in back of the countertop tile. This spacing was determined during the layout.

The starting point of your layout will depend upon whether or not you are working around a sink and, if you are, the sink's location.

Countertop without a sink. Measuring from end to end, find the center of the countertop. Draw a centerline. Lay out the tile along it, allowing for grout lines if your tile has no self-spacers. Use a carpenter's square to ensure that the courses are straight. Once you lay the tile up to the edges of the countertop you will be able to see the types of cuts you must make. If any tiles must be cut to less than half their width, go back and shift the original lines so that this situation will not occur. Take your time and shift the tiles around like a crossword puzzle until you get the result you desire.

Countertop with a sink set parallel to the wall. Rather than working with the centerline of the top, in this case you will work from the center of the sink toward the ends of the countertop. Again, dry set the tile and work for an arrangement that will require the fewest cut tiles. Of course, there is no way to avoid cutting tiles in order to allow for the sink opening.

Countertop with a corner sink. An L-shaped countertop with a corner sink must be handled differently than are the two earlier settings. Since there is no way to avoid very odd cuts of tile around the sink, the best method is to work from the ends of each leg of the top toward the sink opening.

Step two: trim tile installation. Once the dry layout is in place, the first step on a countertop is to install the edge trim along the front of the lip. Use the countertop tiles to maintain the spacing upon which you have decided. Apply a coat of adhesive to the edge surface. Then "butter" the backs of the edge tiles, and install them in line with the rows of tiles on the countertop. The sample installation uses apron tile along the edge. The bottom of the apron tile is fairly smooth. The first countertop row is bullnose tile. It creates a smooth joint with the apron tile.

Once the edge tiles are in place, you can move the countertop tiles without losing your layout design. With the edge complete, install any special trim tiles for sink openings, in corners, or in other special locations.

Step three: tile the countertop deck. Lift some of the dry-laid tiles and apply your adhesive. The typical adhesive for countertops is organic mastic, although some installers prefer epoxy. Don't spread more than you can cover readily before it starts to harden. Maintain careful spacing. Set each tile firmly in place, with a slight wiggling motion to ensure a good bond. Lay all the full tiles and leave spaces for the cut tile. Cut tiles to fill in, using a tile cutter or glass cutter.

All through the installation, lay your carpenter's square across the tops of the tiles to make sure that the rows are straight and square with each other. This will prevent wobbly grout lines. After placing the tiles, use a block of wood covered with carpet to set the tiles into the adhesive. Move the plywood block over the surface of the tile while tapping the block with a hammer. Do not hammer so hard that you break the tile or push it out of alignment as you slide the block across the surface.

Step four: the backsplash. The installation shown utilized only one course of bullnose tile for a backsplash. The unfinished edge of the bullnose was set directly on the countertop. In many installations, however, cove tiles bridge the space between the counter and the backsplash, and the backsplash extends to the underside of the overhanging cabinets. In my opinion, these arrangements provide for more continuity of design.

Apply a coat of adhesive to the area you will use as a backsplash. Then butter the backs of the tiles before you install them. You will have to cut tiles to fit around outlets, light switches and window sills. Do not neglect to break the circuit that feeds any light switch or fixture before you tile in the area around it. If necessary, finish off the backsplash top edge with a trim piece.

Step five: apply grout. Run a wide

strip of masking tape along the underside of the front apron tiles. This will keep the grout from dripping out from between the tiles before it has a chance to set up. You should also mask any surrounding wood surfaces to protect them from stains from

Cut pieces of tile are next installed on the front; bullnose tiles overlap the unfinished edges of the front tiles.

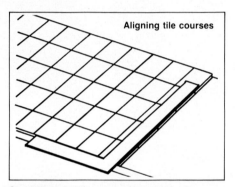
Check that the tile rows are square to tile countertop edge.

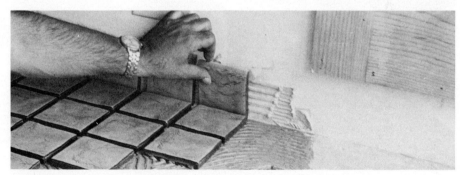
Position backsplash tiles to line up with the countertop tiles. In this instance, the one row of bullnose tile used for the backsplash was set down behind the counter tiles.

Apply masking tape to the bottom edge of the apron before grouting. This helps keep the grout from dripping out before it has set.

the grout. Then mix the grout and apply it with a rubber squeegee.

Once the grout has set, clean the surface with a damp sponge to remove excess grout. Then polish the tile with a soft cloth.

The rest of the tiles are added, spaced with spacing lugs or purchased spacers.

Spread adhesive on the backsplash wall and butter the backs of the tiles before applying.

Mix the grout and apply it on a diagonal, according to manufacturer's instructions, using a rubber-faced trowel or squeegee.

Installing Mosaic Sheets Over Plastic Laminate

Old plastic laminate can be an excellent surface on which to apply ceramic tile.

Removing the sink. Shut off the water supply or the shutoff valves, which will be either in the basement directly under the sink location or in the cabinet beneath the sink. Place a bucket under the sink trap. Use a pipe wrench or an adjustable wrench to loosen the water supply fittings. Use water pipe pliers to loosen the drain line. Loosen the sink holding clamps with a large screwdriver and carefully lift out the

sink. If the sink is porcelain, store it in a protected area, since porcelain will break easily.

Preparing the surface. Use a pry bar and hammer to remove the plastic laminate backsplash. Then roughen the laminate surface with coarse sandpaper.

Laying the sheets. As with single tiles, arrange a dry layout before you permanently bond any of the tile sheets. Once you have determined the arrangement, install the edge and corner trim tiles. Be sure to maintain straight joint lines.

After the countertop area is done, and before applying adhesive to the backsplash area, protect the newly laid tiles with spread newspapers. Apply cove molding to the corner of the wall; then lay the sheets. (Note the special corner cove piece for this particular installation.) With the tiling completed, gently but firmly tap in the sheets with the carpet-covered wood block and a hammer.

Wait for 24 hours before applying the grout. Remove any excess with a sponge; polish with a soft cloth.

In this example, ceramic tile was installed over an old plastic laminate countertop.

Remove the laminated backsplash, using a wide chisel and a hammer.

Ungrouted sheets of ceramic allow fast installation on countertop and backsplash. Add cove tile at the back and corners of wall.

Draw a line to indicate how far up the wall the tile will extend. Plan layout of the tile sheets, allowing for a cove base at back of the counter and bullnose trim on front. Sand the surface.

Begin at the front edge of the countertop to draw working lines. Spread the adhesive.

Start installation at the corner, using 2x2 in. bullnose trim at the front of the counter and 1x2 in. trim on the apron.

Lay the sheets, making sure you align joints and follow the working lines.

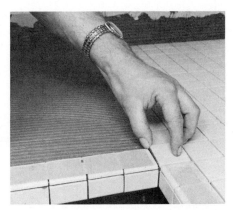

Install a special internal corner trim piece at the joint of the corners.

A 1x2 inch corner bullnose trim finishes the edge of the countertop corner.

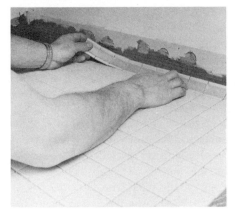

Apply cove base at back of countertop. This often is done before application of main sheet.

Tile sheets can be cut using a mechanical cutter; the equipment can be rented.

A thin tile strip is used at back of sink opening. The lip of the sink rests on this.

Internal cove tile trims a wall corner.

A special corner cove trim piece can be used.

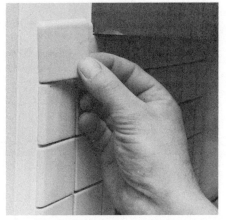

Cover exposed edges with bullnose tile.

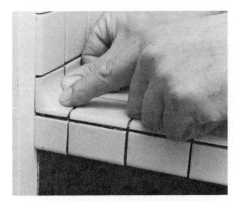

An internal cove corner piece fills in an awkwardly shaped area at the backsplash.

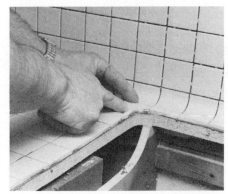

As the sink curves, tiles must be nipped to create a smooth, rounded line.

Let the tile set 24 hours; then apply the grout. Allow no air spaces in grout lines.

Range Hood Covering

One unusual use of ceramic tile is as a covering for the inside and outside of a range hood. Glazed ceramic tile can be particularly useful on a hood because it is easy to clean and impervious to the heat, grease and steam from cooking. The covered hood on page 20 has a built-in book holder so that you can scan your favorite recipe as you prepare a meal. This particular hood must be constructed of heavy-gauge sheet metal. The accompanying diagram sets out the dimensions. Unless you have extensive experience in sheet-metal work, however, you should have the hood constructed by a professional.

Not only this hood, but also any other, can be covered with a ceramic tile. Glazed ceramic tile is preferred. If your hood has a curved surface, sheets of ceramic mosaics are a good choice, for they can follow the curve of the surface. Use epoxy adhesive and grout, for they are the most heat-resistant and will ensure a long lasting bond.

Preparing the surface. Although it might seem easiest to work on a hood before it is hung in place, it is better to have the hood installed before beginning tiling (with the power off, of course). The ceramic tile will add a great deal of weight to the hood, and it may be difficult to install after the tiles are on. Once the hood is in place, clean the surface thoroughly and sand with either wet or dry 80 grit sandpaper on a belt sander.

Tiling the Hood

Establish working lines. The few cut tiles in the layout should fall near the high edges of the hood. First, find the vertical working line, which will run vertically through the center of the hood. The bottom edge of the hood will serve as the horizontal base line.

Layout pattern. Tile the hood as you would a jack-on-jack wall. The size of cut tiles on both sides of the hood should be equal. Always plan on a full-size row at the front edge of the hood, since that edge will be the most visible. Use groutlines that are at least ¼ inch thick, since epoxy grout is difficult to apply in lines that are any thinner.

Applying the adhesive. Mix the two elements — the epoxy resin and the catalyst — thoroughly in the proportions dictated by the manufacturer. Usually each can must be completely emptied. Apply with the prescribed trowel (often this is a square-notched one). Epoxy hardens due to a chemical reaction, not because of evaporation; do not apply more adhesive at one time than you can cover in 30 minutes. The area must be well-ventilated, and it should not be overly warm, since heat speeds up the setting time.

Laying the tile. Tile as much as the inside of the hood as you desire. Most often the amount of tiling there depends upon how much of the hood can be seen. Apply the tile to the inside before you cover the outside — in that way you will finish the hardest part first. Use trim tile with a quarter round finishing edge along the rim of the hood, and follow the vertical line established for the outside of the hood, so that the grout lines are consistent.

Apply the adhesive and set the tile from the hood edge up. Do not worry about holding the tile in place as you go — epoxy adhesive forms a strong bond almost immediately, so there is little danger of the tile sliding off. Work carefully to ensure that the grout lines are straight. When the entire hood has been tiled, let the adhesive set for at least 10 hours before beginning to grout the installation.

Applying the grout. Epoxy grout also comes in two cans. Mix the two together gently. If you do this too rapidly you either will add air bubbles that can ruin the installation or you will raise the temperature of the grout and, as a result, quicken the chemical reaction. Spread the grout diagonally to prevent the formation of air bubbles in the grout lines. (Some companies recommend special grout applicators for this process. The aid these give the grout process repays the cost of the applicator.) Wipe away the excess; spray the tiles with a light mist of water (or water and a non-detergent soap) to remove any remaining film.

Apply epoxy grout as quickly as you can. The reaction of the resin and the catalyst is quicker when the substance is in a large mass than when it is spread thinly over the tiles. You cannot depend upon a long pot life with this grout.

CERAMIC TILE AND THE BATHROOM

The water-resistant nature of ceramic tile makes it a natural choice for a bathroom. It is necessary for such areas as shower and tub surrounds. It can also cover other walls, floors and vanity tops. However, where ceramic tile really shines in these

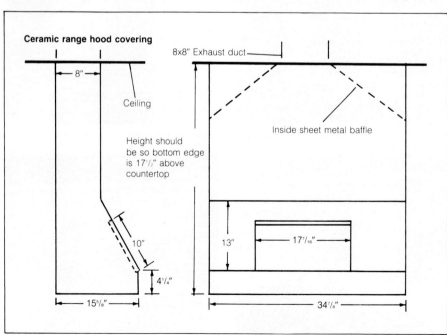

Ceramic range hood covering

8x8" Exhaust duct

8"

Ceiling

Height should be so bottom edge is 17½" above countertop

Inside sheet metal baffle

10"

13"   17⁷⁄₁₆"

4¼"

15⁵⁄₈"   34⁷⁄₈"

The basic dimensions for this range hood are given here, but they can be varied to suit your space. See page 20 for a color photograph of the finished unit.

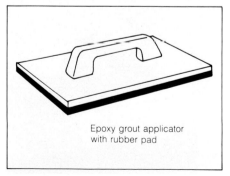

Epoxy grout applicator with rubber pad

For a smooth job, apply epoxy with a special, rubber based squeegee.

rooms is in glamorous sunken or raised tub creations. There are almost as many design ideas as there are people who build these unusual bathing areas. Indeed, many of today's bathrooms are in fact "bathing rooms," which feature his-and-her dressing areas and indoor-outdoor privacy areas for sunbathing and relaxing.

Because of the variety of projects that are appropriate for a bathroom, it is best to start with a discussion of the simplest and move to the most difficult. The range of difficulty runs from a simple shower enclosure using pregrouted sheets of ceramic tile to a completely hand-formed sunken tub of the owner's design.

Shower Surround

If you are retiling an existing shower area, you can use the old grout lines as guides, and the job is an easy one. For a newly added shower, there are two basic methods of tiling a shower enclosure. The first method incorporates a tiled shower floor. Because this installation requires the in-

staller to create his own shower pan out of mortar, the homeowner must have quite a bit of masonry skill. The second method, which is less work, involves use of a purchased shower floor pan. For both installations, check the flooring below the shower before you begin. The floor must be able to bear the additional weight of the pan and the tile. If it needs additional support, add 1x4 bridging between the floor joists.

Mortar-bed shower pan. The reason a homeowner usually chooses to create a pan rather than buy one is a purchased unit will not fit the exact space of the shower stall — a fairly common problem when people are remodeling an existing shower in an older home.

If you need a custom-made concrete shower pan, it is probably best to have one installed by a contractor. The pan must be watertight, and most amateurs have problems achieving the seal that is required. The shower pan is not formed with a standard wood form. Instead, it is hand-

shaped as the concrete is poured. This process is not a simple one, by any means, especially since the installer must create a slightly sloped surface that is level to within 1/8 inch. The slope guarantees that the water from the shower will drain off properly. The lip around the edge of the shower pan must also be built by hand. For all the above reasons, a professional contractor is our recommendation. The contractor will build a pan of reinforced concrete. Included in the pan will be steel reinforcing mesh and a plastic membrane for a water barrier. The completed pan will look like the drawing given here.

Purchased shower pan. Purchased shower pans are made of fiberglass. They are set in place over the drain pipe. Then the drain built into the pan is connected to the drain-and-trap, which comes out of the subfloor.

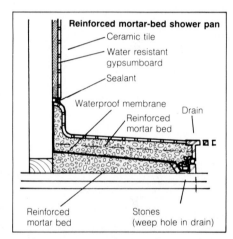

Creating a shower floor is a difficult task. This shows completed structure.

You need not confine yourself to a single pattern in your tile installation. Create an accent wall with an alternate tile design that complements your overall decor.

To connect up to the drain, this prefabricated shower pan requires an opening in the subfloor.

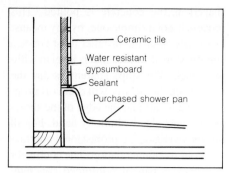

Cover the area surrounding the shower with special water-resistant gypsumboard or backer board. Seal the edges with the correct mastic.

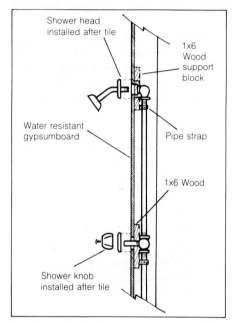

Install standardized plumbing fittings for the shower and faucets. Wood blocks between joists support the pipes. Special pipe strap adds support to the pipes.

Apply special fiberglass backer board.

The hole in the subfloor must be large enough to accommodate the drain attached to the pan — in most instances the drain will require a hole approximately 4½ inches in diameter. If you need to enlarge the old opening, or create a new one, use a sabre saw to cut the hole to size. Then set the pan on the shower subfloor or slab. Use a carpenter's level to check for level, and test the pan for a solid fit. In most instances you will not need to use any anchoring device. The weight of the tiles on the lip of the unit will hold it securely in place. The joint between the tile and the pan will allow for normal building settling, without damage to the tiles. Caulk and glue the drain. (Check specific requirements with your local building code.)

Installing the plumbing. The easiest way to be certain that the water knobs and showerhead are at the right level is to purchase prefitted pipes. Have a plumber install the pipes, or install them yourself. First connect the hot and cold faucets; then install the piping for the showerhead.

Once the pipes are in place between the wall studs, cut two 1x6 boards to fit between the studs. These boards support the pipes. Nail one board at the level of the showerhead; the other goes at the level of the water faucets. Fasten these boards with size 8 ringshank nails. Then take a piece of pipe strap — a soft, perforated metal strip. Nail one end of the strap to the showerhead support block. Cross in back of the showerhead to strap it in and nail the other end of the strap to the support block. Do the same with the faucet pipes.

Installing waterproof wall surface. Any area exposed to a great deal of wetness, such as a shower enclosure, needs a water-resistant backing. Choose either water-resistant gypsum board or special "backer board" made especially for this type of installation.

If the floor area of the shower is perfectly square, install the backer board before you insert the floor pan. Nail the backer board in place on all three sides; then slide the floor pan into position. The tiles will come down over the pan flange as shown. (The joint between the tiles and the pan is ¼ inch.) However, if the floor is out of square you will have to install the pan first. Then install the backer board down over the flange of the pan, inserting small blocks of wood (shims) between the board and the wall. Make sure all edges of the

shower pan are covered by the wallboard. Then cut the holes for the pipe fittings into the backer board. Do not install the projecting portions of the fittings until the tiling job has been completed.

Planning the layout. The back shower wall is the one that is most visible, so establish the working lines on that wall. In a shower where the shower walls project in on each side of the front opening, use the back corners of the shower stall as working lines. Check that the corners are vertical. If they are not, make a working vertical line at the center of the back wall, work outward from it, and cut tiles to fit at the corners. If the out-of-plumb condition is slight, use the grout lines in the corner to minimize the lack of an exact vertical.

Decide whether the tile will run all the way to the ceiling or will stop about six inches above the top of the showerhead and finish off the tile with a row of bull-nose. You also may tile the ceiling, but you will need to hold the tiles in place with pieces of plywood held by long wooden props until the adhesive sets up. Because of the difficulties — and the dangers from falling ceramic tiles — most manufacturers recommend that ceilings not be tiled.

Applying the adhesive. Apply a skim coat of adhesive to the wall area. Then pack all openings around plumbing fittings with ample amounts of adhesive. Protect the drain and floor pan with cardboard to keep them from being covered with adhesive and to avoid clogging the drain with debris while you set the tile.

Laying the tile. Install the tile just as you would on any other wall. Shape cut tiles with a pair of tile nippers. Trim the tiles carefully to fit them around the handle pipes. As you go along, install any ceramic tile fixtures, such as soap dishes.

Use a nipper for cutting tiles to fit around shower knobs and other fittings.

Grout the tile and install shower knob flanges and shower knobs.

Closing off the shower. The shower opening can be finished in several ways, such as a purchased door. This will come with a built-in frame, which screws to the wall; the bottom edge rests on top of the lip of the floor flange.

An alternative method is to build stub walls on either side of the shower opening. These walls must be added before you tile the shower. The stub walls are then covered with tile, along with the rest of the shower stall. In this situation, install a low threshold that joins the bottoms of the two walls. Fit a door between the stub walls,

or hang a shower curtain from a rod suspended between the two walls.

Tiling a Shower with Pregrouted Sheets

Probably the easiest way to tile a shower enclosure is with pregrouted sheets of ceramic tile. These come in 12x12 inch squares. Each sheet holds 9 tiles that are 4x4 inches in size. A silicone grout has already been injected between the tiles. Two edges of each sheet are preformed with finished bullnose edges so you need no finish trim for exposed edges or corners.

Use standard tile setting procedures to lay the tile sheets. Then grout the joints between the sheets, using a special silicone rubber grout that is applied with a caulking gun. The gun is relatively easy to use; however, some practice will increase your proficiency before you begin to grout the tiles. Follow exactly all instructions that come with the gun. The size of the opening that is cut in the nozzle of the silicone applicator varies for different caulking guns. If you do not follow the size requirements closely, the gun will not function properly and you can ruin your tile installation.

When the grouting is finished, remove any excess with alcohol. The result is an extremely waterproof tile job that will

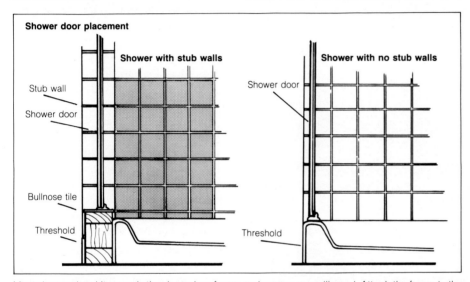

Most shower door kits supply the door, door frame and screws you will need. Attach the frame to the walls and to the pan flange or to a tile covered threshold.

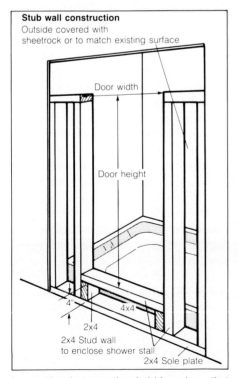

Insert shims between threshold boards so that the threshold's height corresponds to your tile size. Then you will need no cut tiles.

Pregrouted sheets make tiling a shower surround a quick and simple task. Lay the sheets as you would individual tiles. Then apply silicone grout between the sheets.

Traditional in a tub area, ceramic tile can be laid singly or in sets of pregrouted sheets. This design utilizes both a contrasting color and diagonal course and grout lines.

Pregrouted sheets come in kits for tiling a tub surround. All tools are included.

In the installation shown, plastic tiles have been removed from the tub surround.

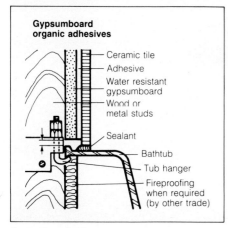

Gypsumboard organic adhesives

— Ceramic tile
— Adhesive
— Water resistant gypsumboard
— Wood or metal studs
— Sealant
— Bathtub
— Tub hanger
— Fireproofing when required (by other trade)

Secure a new tub with a metal hanger attached to the wall studs.

Trowel on a skim coating of adhesive and pack it into all openings around the plumbing.

hold up to the heavy moisture conditions of a shower.

Allow the tile to set for at least 24 hours. Then apply the grout suggested by your tile dealer. Once the grout has cured, install the finishing portion of the shower knobs as well as the shower head.

Conventional Tub Enclosures

A tub enclosure tiling job can be tackled by nearly anyone, especially if the installer uses pregrouted sheets of ceramic tile. These come with as many as 64 tiles to a square sheet. Kits designed to fit most standard size tub enclosures include the pregrouted sheets, matching internal cove corner strips and tile leg strips to finish the vertical edges of the tub. The corner trim pieces allow for variance in wall plumbness and provide a curved, easy-to-clean corner.

Pregrouted sheets are installed with dry-set mortar or with the recommended organic mastic. Dow Corning 784 white grout, applied with a caulking gun, is used for all grouting and caulking. You need do very little grouting — only between the large sheets, along the corner strips and joints between tiles and other surfaces. It usually takes less than one hour to install a tub surround with one of these kits. The tub can then be put to use within 6 hours.

The basic working methods for a tub surround installation are the same for pregrouted sheets and for individual tiles. Only the finishing and grouting methods vary. Incidentally, if you plan to tile all the walls of a bathroom, begin with the tub enclosure. Then do the remaining walls; finish with the floor.

Preparing the surface. The first step is to prepare the backing surface. If you are installing new tile over old, carefully re-adhere any loose tiles, and clean and prepare the surface as discussed in Chapter 2. If you remove the old tile in order to install backing, check for water damage before you install the new backing over the walls. If tiling a new surround, install new backing after the plumbing is in place, including the shower or tub fittings and the showerhead. Choose either water-resistant gypsum board or special backer board. Pack all holes around plumbing connections and accessory openings with adhesive. Apply a skim coat of adhesive to the wall surface; let the skim coat dry thoroughly.

Creating working lines. As with any

other tiling job, once you have prepared the surface, establish horizontal and vertical working lines. These ensure straight up-and-down, level courses and grout lines. Working lines are especially important in an old home whose walls or corners may be out of plumb.

Horizontal working lines. The placement of a horizontal working line depends upon the levelness of the tub. See Chapter 2 for instructions for establishing the horizontal working line above a tub.

Vertical working lines. You need to establish a vertical working line on each of the walls in the tub surround. The method for finding these differs from the standard method.

To establish the vertical working line on the center of the back wall of the tub surround, check with the layout stick, or layout a trial run along the edge of the tub, to determine the size of any cut tiles at the corners. If there will be less than half a tile at each end, move the centerline a distance equal to one half the width of one tile. Then use a chalkline and plumb bob or a level to mark the vertical working lines.

Because of the layout pattern involved, vertical lines on the end walls are established somewhat by trial and error. The layout requires that cut tiles fall at the back corners of the walls — the corners that meet the back tub wall. You want as few cut tiles as possible. To determine the best layout and the location of the line, lay a dry run of tiles (or use a layout stick) from the outer to the inner corner of the wall. Mark the vertical line at the middle of the layout. Placement of the vertical line will depend to a great extent on the width of the end wall as well as on the width of the tub. If the surround is designed to contain a newer tub, you probably will not have to use any cut tiles — unless the wall protrudes past the tub more than is usual. Tub sizes in recent years have been standardized to correspond to multiples of standard ceramic tile size.

Take your time in setting up working lines. If they are incorrectly established, the project will become difficult, since you will be forced to cut and fit tiny pieces of tile. Allow for the thickness of the tiles on the back wall when you lay out the end walls. If possible, plan so the tiles that must be cut at the corners will be the same sizes at both corners.

Laying the first course of tile. After you have marked working lines on all the walls, lay the lowest course on the back wall. Use a putty knife to smear adhesive lightly on the wall area where the first course will fall. Then "butter" the back of at least 60 to 70 percent of the back of each tile. (Don't apply too much, or the adhesive will ooze out and get on the fronts of the tiles.) Starting in the center of the back or center wall, work toward the ends, fitting each tile in place. Leave about ⅛ inch gap between the bottom row of tiles and the tub to allow for building expansion and contraction.

If the tub is fairly level and you started your horizontal working lines from the high point of the tub, the row will have only full-size tiles. Shim each tile with a toothpick to keep the tops of the tiles aligned with the working line. If you started with the low point on a tub that is not level, this first course is made up of cut tiles. Measure the distance between the tub and the horizontal working line for each tile. Cut each tile individually and fit it in place as you work.

Laying tile with a batten. If the lowest course is less than a full tile, you can tack a thin piece of wood just below the horizontal working line. Then install all the field tiles above this line before you lay the row of cut tiles. After the uncut tiles have set enough so they won't slide down, remove the wooden strip and cut the individual tiles for the bottom row. Use the "buttering" method given above. The choice of method is up to you. For some, the batten method ensures an easier and straighter starting course than does a course of individually cut bottom tiles.

Completing the back wall. Spread the adhesive on the wall, but do not apply so much that you cannot cover it before it dries. Fill in the wall with either the jack-on-jack or the running bond pattern in Chapter 2. After you completed the top row you can finish it with bullnose tiles. Use a bullnose corner to finish off the corner. If you are tiling all the way to the ceiling, cut and fit the last row of tiles one at a time for an even, straight upper course. Tap the ties into the adhesive.

Before quitting work on the back wall, step back and examine it carefully. Are all tiles straight and aligned properly? Are they all flush, with none protruding? If not, adjust as needed. Then, using a finishing nail or a toothpick, scrape away any excess adhesive that has squeezed out from between joints.

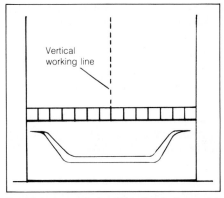

Establish the vertical working line in the center of the back wall and adjust it to avoid cutting small tiles where the walls meet.

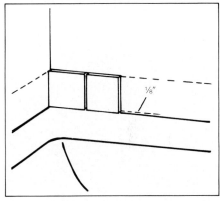

Leave a ⅛ inch space between the tub and the tile course directly above it.

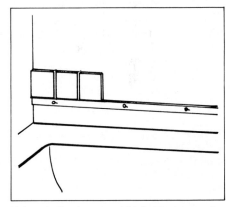

Using a batten to support the first course you lay will help you achieve straight rows.

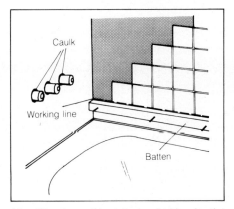

After filling the wall in stair-step fashion, lay the row of cut tiles.

Covering the end walls. Now tile the end walls. I find it best to do the wall with the fixtures first because it is the hardest and once it is done the rest of the job goes quickly. Since this wall will take a bit more time, do not spread too much adhesive.

Cover the end walls by starting at the vertical working line and laying tile back to the corner. After these walls are covered, install the tile around the front of the tub and down to the floor on the front of the end wall, cutting tiles to fit. Make absolutely certain the initial row of tiles in front of the tub is straight and level. Use the block of wood and hammer to set the tiles into the adhesive.

Quite often you will have an exposed edge on either of the end walls. Finish off this edge with bullnose tile. Use a bullnose corner tile at the corner top. Leave openings for the accessories; install them later as previously described. If there is a showerhead, run at least one or two courses above it. Grab bars should be mounted to the wall studs or with special fasteners. Allow the tiles to set before grouting.

Apply grout as discussed earlier. Clean grout from the tiles and caulk the seam between the bathtub and the bottom row of tiles. Use a good silicone-rubber bathtub caulk. Caulk also around all openings between the pipe and tiles. Install the fitting caps and accessories.

Raised Tub Enclosures

Tub enclosures can be as personal as your particular lifestyle and may incorporate any number of features. A raised platform brings the tub up off the floor. The platform around the edge of the tub results in a

This installer cut a diamond into the original tile and inserted a contrasting set.

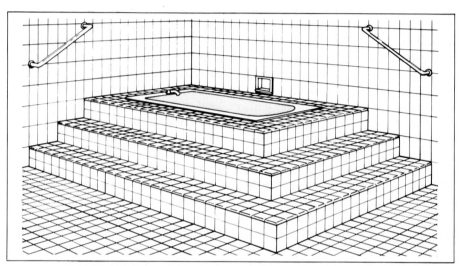

One way to acquire a "sunken" tub is to build a platform, into which you insert a purchased tub. Extend the tile over the platform and surrounding walls and floors.

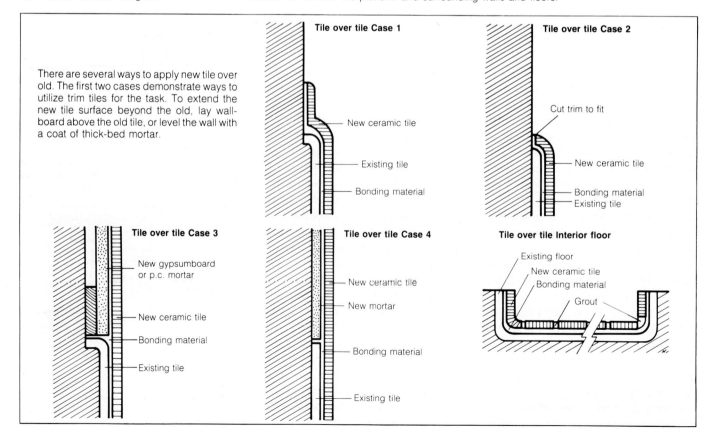

There are several ways to apply new tile over old. The first two cases demonstrate ways to utilize trim tiles for the task. To extend the new tile surface beyond the old, lay wallboard above the old tile, or level the wall with a coat of thick-bed mortar.

Tile over tile Case 1
New ceramic tile
Existing tile
Bonding material

Tile over tile Case 2
Cut trim to fit
New ceramic tile
Bonding material
Existing tile

Tile over tile Case 3
New gypsumboard or p.c. mortar
New ceramic tile
Bonding material
Existing tile

Tile over tile Case 4
New ceramic tile
New mortar
Bonding material
Existing tile

Tile over tile Interior floor
Existing floor
New ceramic tile
Bonding material
Grout

visually exciting room and provides space for toiletries, wash cloths, towels and other items you wish to keep near the tub.

Constructing the framework. Creating a sunken tub by building an enclosure for a purchased tub is fairly easy, but you must use sound construction methods so that the frame will support the weight of the tub and the tile. Use wood framing for the basic construction. Cover the surface with ¾ inch Exterior plywood. Use 16d nails to cover the surface with ¾ inch Exterior plywood. Then cover the structure with a coat of wood primer.

Inserting the tub. There are two methods for inserting a tub in a platform. The first calls for laying the tiles and then setting the tub in place over the tiles. The second sets the tub on the wood frame; then the tiles are laid up to the tub edge.

There are advantages and disadvantages to each. In the first method, the weight of the tub lip can crack the tiles, unless the edge where the tub is to sit is well supported. However, this method provides a much neater finished appearance because you do not have to worry too much about the cut edge of the tiles — the tub lip

covers them. In the second method, a row of quarter round surrounds the tub itself. Then tiles are cut to fit against the row of quarter round. This means that the cut edges are visible. To achieve a neat finished appearance, you must be patient and proficient as you cut the tiles, for the cut edges will not be covered by the tub lip.

In both cases, the tub lip should be well sealed with bathtub caulk to prevent water from running back under the lip and eventually rotting out the wooden platform.

Tiling procedures. The design of the platform holding a sunken tub can aid the tiling process. Once the tile has been chosen, design the size of the steps of the platform to correspond to the tile size so that no tiles need be cut. Do the same for the platform size.

Another way to simplify the tiling process is to think of the tub structure in terms of the large surfaces as wall or floor surfaces rather than seeing the structure as a continuous whole. Plan to tile one section at a time. Tile the steps first, then the tub area, then any wall space behind the tub. Finally cover the sides of the platform.

Steps. To get a watertight seal, work up the steps. Tread tiles should overhang those that come up the riser for a tight seal. Use a three-quarter round or other trim. Start at the bottom of the lowest riser and work up to the top of the platform. Find the horizontal and vertical working lines on the risers and the tread, just as for other tile installations. If you must cut tiles, cut the row at the top of the riser, the one that will be partially covered with the trim tile that curls around the edge of the step. If there are cut tiles at the sides of the riser, make sure that they are of equal size on both sides.

Tub enclosure. Once you have reached the top of the platform, snap working lines

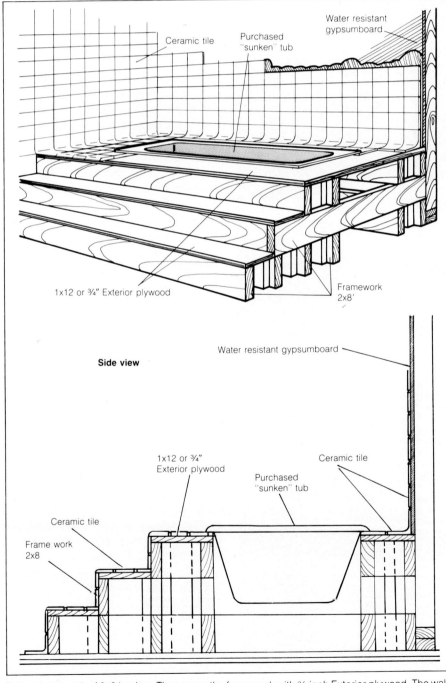

Side view

Build a framework of 2x8 lumber. Then cover the framework with ¾ inch Exterior plywood. The walls behind the tub need water-resistant backing.

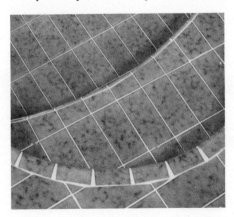

If the tub lip falls under the tiles, adjust grout lines to create a smooth edge.

that cross through the center of the tub. These will look like the crossed working lines of a typical floor installation. Plan for cut tiles so they fall around the tub rim; you will have to make odd-shaped cuts there no matter how well you plan.

Remaining areas. Once you have covered the tub platform and enclosure, cover the sides of the platform and any walls.

Sunken Roman Tub

Creating a Roman tub of your own design is an exciting project, and a great way to show off your tiling talents. It also is hard, back-breaking work that requires not a little skill in concrete work, plumbing and tiling. However, it can and has been tackled successfully by many do-it-yourselfers. If properly constructed, a sunken

Roman tub is a truly personalized architectural addition that not only will be admired by all your friends, but also will increase the value of your home.

As opposed to the wood frame tub enclosure discussed earlier, a sunken Roman tub is hand-constructed. Then it is covered with ceramic tile. There are two common construction methods for this type of tub. The first, and the one that has been used for years, is to construct a metal tank, which is covered with a thick bed of mortar. Once the bed is properly cured, the tile is set in thin-set adhesive. The procedure is a fairly complicated one and requires a great deal of skill in the construction of the metal tank and the application of the thick bed of mortar.

The second method, and the one used by me in my home, involves building a watertight tub of concrete — much like one would use to construct a swimming pool. This method is now being used by several builders, and tubs so constructed do not suffer from the leakage problems that occur in the metal tanks. The only structural requirement for a cast concrete tub is that the bottom of the tub be at ground level or just below it. You cannot suspend a concrete tub without a great deal of forming knowledge and special support construction.

If you do not feel you are capable of casting your own tub, have a concrete contractor construct one. Or, if you prefer, have the tub constructed of metal and installed by a contractor.

Since this tub rests on the ground, it can only be installed between the joists in a new room addition or a new home construction. It cannot be built in an existing bathroom over a basement.

Tub base preparation. Before you build a sunken Roman tub, prepare and compact the soil so it will accept the weight of the structure without later settlement, drainage, or heaving problems. Building an appropriate base involves several steps. You must dig a hole at least 6 inches larger than the tub on all sides, build forms to hold the concrete, add fill (if you need it), and finish with concrete.

The depth to which the base must extend depends upon your location. Areas with little freezing require less base than areas with a great deal of freezing. Layers of gravel and sand may be required as part of the base construction. To determine the best method for your particular environ-

A true sunken tub is based on either a metal or a concrete form. The tub itself can take any shape it pleases. Not only the surround but the tub itself is covered with tile.

The installation instructions given here for a sunken tub are those for my tub. The poured concrete tank is designed to simplify plumbing installation.

ment, check the standards of your local building code. They will tell you how deep to dig for an adequate foundation. Design your tub, complete with base specifications, plumbing schematics and wood formwork. Then have your community or county building inspector approve the plans before you begin work.

Digging the base. Once you know the necessary depth, mark out with wooden stakes an area (6 inches larger than the tub on all sides) on which the tub will rest. Dig out all the soil within the stakes to the depth required. Then tamp the soil surface firmly with a large roller or a mechancial tamper. (These usually can be rented.) The floor of the hole must be level. To check this, lay a 2x4 board across the tamped soil and place a carpenter's level on top of the board. Check the level in as many directions as possible, including diagonally. If the surface is not level, correct the situation by adding fill in those areas which are low. Tamp the added fill well. Otherwise you will have problems with moisture buildup below the base.

Formwork for the concrete footing. Dig trenches just outside the tub excavation area. They should be 2 inches wide and as deep as the hole dug previously. Place 2x12s on their edges in the trenches. The top edge of a 2x12 should extend above the level of the earth to the desired height of the finished slab — usually about 1-2 inches above ground level. Attach a stake to the outside of the board with special 16d nails called duplex or scaffolding nails. The "double heads" of these nails makes them easy to remove, so you can knock down the forms when the concrete has cured. Check that the form is square.

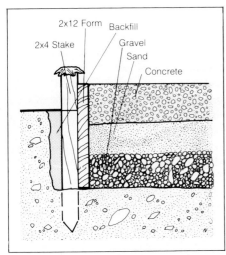

A gravel and sand footing prevent damage to the tub form due to freezing and heaving.

Repeat this operation for the other form boards on the other sides of the hole. Stake 2x4s every 16 inches around the entire perimeter of 2x12s. Cut all stakes off just below form height. Having staked the perimeter, you have set the exterior formwork. With the dirt that was removed during initial excavation, fill in around the outside of the boards. (This process is called "backfilling.") Tamp the dirt against the forms; this will prevent unwanted movement of the form boards. On the inside of the form, tamp the earth so it is just below the bottom of the form board; if necessary, compact or refill to relevel and regrade the entire area.

Estimating material quantities. The base courses are usually composed of gravel, sand and concrete. These materials are available in most areas, and they are relatively inexpensive. They are usually measured in terms of cubic yards. Since base materials are ordered by volume rather than by weight, it is important to make sure that the quantities you order are adequate. Sand and gravel compact to half their original depth. That means you must put in twice as much as the final depth requirement to have the correct amount once you finish tamping.

After excavating for the footing, and once you know the depth of a given base material, multiply the length times the width times the depth to figure the amount of base material you need. The dimensions of the tub here — 81x41 inches provide a good example of how to determine amounts.

Since the base is 6 inches larger on all sides of the tub, the base measurements are 93x53. If the information received from the local building inspector dictates a 4 inch layer of gravel, double the depth requirement to 8 inches to allow for compacting. By multiplying 93x53x8 (length times width times depth) you learn that you need 39,432 cubic inches of gravel. To convert cubic inches to cubic yards, divide 39,432 by 46,656 — the number of cubic inches in a cubic yard. The result tells you that you need less than one cubic yard of gravel. Use the same technique to determine the amounts of cement, gravel and sand you require for the batches of concrete you mix later.

Filling the base. You are now ready to prepare the base with the gravel and sand. Your reference point will be the top of the form board. Place the gravel over the en-

tire base floor. Lay it down in two layers of 4 inches each. Make sure that each layer is tamped thoroughly until firm. The gravel should be tamped down to at least two thirds of its original height. You are now ready to place the sand over the gravel course. To do this, place the sand uniformly over the entire area in a 2 inch layer. Tamp the sand down. If the gravel shows through, do not be alarmed. Add sand until the difference between the top of the sand and the top of the formboard will be approximately 4 inches. If the space is less, remove some sand.

Oiling the forms. You can now oil the interior part of the form. This helps later in the removal of the form. Use an inexpensive grade of motor oil or an oil spray.

Mixing the concrete. You can purchase premixed concrete, to which you need only add water, or you can mix your own. The basic formula for a concrete footing is as follows: mix 1 part cement, 3 parts sand, and 4 parts gravel. The maximum aggregate size should be 1½ inch. The amount of water required depends upon the sand. If you are mixing up one whole bag of cement (which would result in 5 cubic feet of concrete) the water amounts are as follows: dry sand requires 7 gallons, damp sand requires 6¼ gallons, wet sand requires 5½ gallons, and very wet sand requires 4¾ gallons.

The proportion of the four ingredients is important. Careful measurement makes the difference between a durable, longlasting job and one that may crack, flake or chip. There has to be plenty of larger aggregates to make an economical mix, yet enough small aggregates to fill in the holes around the larger ones, and enough cement to hold it all together. Hold to these proportions, even though you will not need this much concrete. One way to do so is to work in terms of "shovelsful." In this recipe, then, 1 shovel of cement would require 3 of sand and 4 of gravel. Adjust the water requirements to fit the amount of concrete you are creating.

A flat board is a good mixing site. Use a hoe to mix all the ingredients carefully and thoroughly together. Test the mix to see if it is correct by making the slump test. Place a small amount of concrete on a flat, level surface. The material should slump down to about two thirds of its original height if you have the correct amount of water and ingredients. Another test is to use a hoe to pull the concrete up in a series

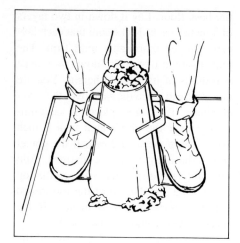

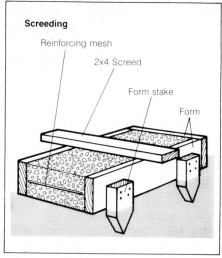

The slump cone is 12 in. high, with a base diameter of 8 in. and a top diameter of 4 in. Set cone on a firm surface and hold down by placing feet onto cone projections. Fill cone with 3 layers of concrete. Tamp each layer 25 times before adding the next layer.

Level off the concrete when cone is filled. Lift the cone and allow the concrete to settle. Stand the cone next to the concrete in order to measure. A large slump indicates a wet consistency; a slight slump is due to a stiff consistency.

Fill the form to the top. Watch out for air pockets in the corners. Slide a 2x4 screed across the top of the form, moving the screed from side to side as you work down.

of ridges. If the ridges slump back down and cannot be easily seen, there is too much water. If the ridges cannot be distinctly formed, there is not enough water. It is easy to add too much water, so mix in just a little at a time until you have the right mix.

Making the pour. Begin at one end of the form. Place the concrete mixture evenly from that end to the other. Spread the concrete with a short, square-end shovel as you go. Moving the concrete mix is difficult work, because the mix has a tendency to suck a shovel down, and the consistency of the mixture is such that you must turn the shovel sideways slightly and allow it to ''slide'' out rather than lift it straight up. In some operations, you will use the shovel to lift material and place it in odd areas — then you will find that not only is the concrete hard to handle, but it is very heavy.

Do not use a regular rake or hoe to shift the mixture about the form, because they cause the larger pieces of gravel or stone to separate from the cement paste of the mixture (this separation is called segregation). You can, however, purchase special concrete hoes, which do not cause such problems.

As you place the material, do not let it drop over 3 feet in height, because the drop from that height can also cause segregation. Use a shovel to ''spade'' the concrete — push the shovel vertically in and out at the corners of the form. Do not overdo this, however. If you do, the material could separate, causing the water to float to the surface.

Screeding. Screeding is the process of slicing off any excess concrete from the poured slab. It must be done immediately after you have poured the entire area. It is also a way to attain the desired level of the completed pour. First, find a helper. Select a very straight 2x4 or 2x6 board that is longer than the form is wide. This board is called the screed. Place the screed across the upper edges of the form boards. Beginning at that point, slide the screed back and forth as you move slowly down toward the other end of the form. Make sure that all high spots are leveled and that low spots are filled in. When filling in the low spots, go back and rescreed the area. Continue the operation until the entire slab has been leveled. This is the only finishing you need do for a foundation slab.

Curing the slab. Normal curing of concrete consists of allowing it to set for about 4 or 5 hours, then dampening it with a fine mist from a garden hose. Make sure the water pressure is not too high — if it is, it will wash out the finish. Alternative methods of curing concrete are to cover it with burlap or old newspapers soaked with water. Keep the covering well soaked. Continue the curing process for at least 3 days at the proper temperature. If the temperature goes below 50 degrees continue curing for another 3 days. Most contractors cure concrete for at least a week.

Pouring the tub. After the footing has cured, construct the inner and outer forms for the tub, as shown. Center the outer form on the foundation. To brace the outer form, cut 6 stakes of 2x4s to measure 24 inches long. Pound these in next to the

slab, one at each corner and one at the half-way point along either long side. These stakes will support 2x4 braces for the outside form. Fasten a 2x4 (on edge) with 8d nails so that one end supports the end wall of the form and the other end braces against the stake at that corner. The brace should form a right angle with the form wall and with the stake. Do this for all corners. The braces at the mid-points of the long walls push in against the walls. Finally cut 2 additional 2x4 braces that are 60 inches long. Nail one of these across the top of each short form wall for additional stability.

Once the outer form is secure, the inner form is suspended inside the outer form. The box-like opening in one short wall provides an open space through which the plumbing pipes are installed. This box rests on the footing. The rest of the inner form walls hang 3 inches above the footing. The open space thus created allows for the floor of the tub. Be sure to align the inner form so that the fixtures fall in the directions you desire.

Pouring the floor of the tub. If you do not use premixed concrete, use the following proportions to create the mixture for a watertight tank: for 1 part of cement, use 2¼ parts of sand and 3 parts of gravel whose maximum aggregate size is 1 inch. If you are using 1 bag of cement, use the following amounts of water for a given type of sand: dry sand requires 6 gallons, damp sand requires 5½ gallons, wet sand requires 5 gallons, and very wet sand requires 4¼ gallons. Again, hold to these proportions, even though you need less

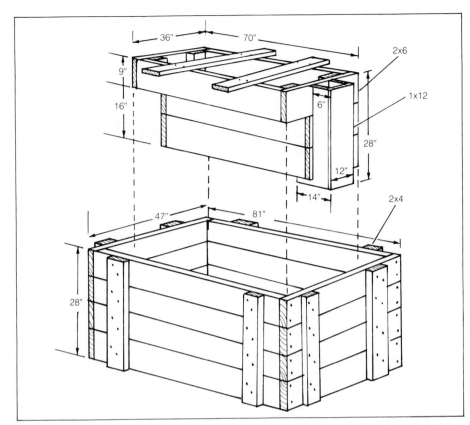

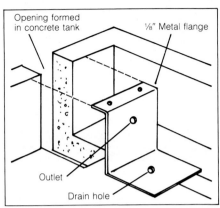

To house and protect the plumbing, install a large metal flange over one end of the tub.

Do not pour concrete into the 12x14 in. rectangular area at the end of this tub. Once the tub has cured, run the plumbing and drain pipes through this opening.

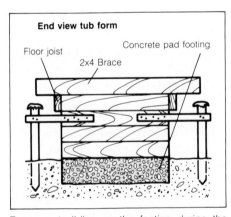

End view tub form

To prevent sliding on the footing during the pour, install braces along the form sides.

concrete than a full bag of cement will yield.

Before you begin the pour, insert reinforcing mesh. To support this, place 1-2 inch rocks along the bottom. The rocks should be 6 inches from each other and from the sides of the tub. On top of these set a layer of 6x6 and 10x10 metal reinforcing mesh; this is a mesh of welded 10 gauge wire with mesh squares of 6x6 inches. Reinforcing mesh is sold in rolls. Cut the mesh with metal snippers. Be sure when you lay the mesh that none of the edges touch the forms themselves — you do not want the metal to stick out of the form once the concrete has set.

Then begin the pour. Spread the concrete carefully to be sure that there are no gaps between the mixture and the corners. Since the inner form walls are shorter than the outer form walls, carefully spread the concrete in the area below the inner form wall. Continue the pour until the mixture is level with the lower edge of the inner form. If the mesh has sunk down during the pour, hook it with something like a coathanger and lift it back up.

Now you must screed the floor so that it is level. Since the forms are in place, the screeding is more of a hand job than the screeding of the footing. Cut a short board that will fit between the sides of the inner form. With the help of an assistant, pull the screed across the floor. Use a trowel to scoop out the excess concrete and level the section between the inner and outer walls. (Be alert, so you do not fall into the concrete!) Once the screeding is finished, trowel the tub floor as smooth and level as you can. Let the tub floor cure for seven days.

Pouring the walls. After the floor has set, pour the walls of the tub. These must be reinforced; use ⅜ inch reinforcing rods for the job. As you pour, insert vertical rods 6 inches apart all the way around the tub wall channel. Make sure that the rods

are located halfway between the inner and outer forms. Otherwise the rods might show through after the concrete has set. Every time you have gone 6 inches up the side, lay a horizontal row of rods. By the time the entire tub has been filled, you will have created within the pour a grid of reinforcing rods.

As the concrete is poured in the form, "jiggle" or tamp it in place to make sure that no air bubbles are trapped in the material. This is especially important next to the forms, since you will have to fill all air bubbles before you can install the tile. Keep the concrete damp and allow it to cure for at least seven days before removing the forms.

Installing the flange. Covering the end of the tub that contains the plumbing is a large, ⅛ inch thick piece of sheet metal, especially cut and formed to cover the entire surface of the tub front wall. Unless you have considerable metal-working experience, have a professional form this flange for you. Measure the depth and width of the completed, cured front wall and have the flange built to fit. Then fasten it in place by inserting masonry anchors into the tub itself and screwing the flange in place with masonry screws.

Preparing the surface. Remove all the form boards and supports. Use a hammer and chisel to break off any high spots or lumps created by the meeting of the form boards. Fill in any holes left by air bubbles that were not tamped out during the pouring. See Chapter 2 for repairing a concrete surface.

Levelling. Once the tub surface is repaired, cover it, including the metal flange area, with from two to four coats of portland mortar. These are intended to level out the surface. Apply each layer of mortar with a trowel to a thickness of ⅛ to ¼

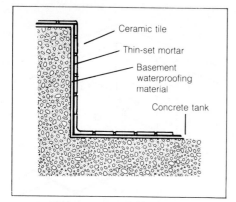

Layers of basement waterproofing material create a watertight concrete tank.

inch. Allow each coat to dry at least 24 hours before laying the next. As you apply the mortar, hold the trowel as flat against the surface as you can. If the angle is more than 45 degrees, there will be ridges in the surface. By the time you are finished, your tub should have a level, smooth surface.

Waterproofing. Once the mortar has dried completely, you are ready to waterproof the tub. The key to the success of this tub installation is this step. Cover the entire tub — especially the flange area — with basement waterproofing sealer. Apply the sealer with a brush or a roller. The

coat should be as thick as the manufacturer indicates. Let the waterproofing dry thoroughly. This will take about 4 to 6 hours, depending upon the humidity level in the air. Then sand the waterproofing smooth, using coarse sandpaper.

Repeat the entire process until you have applied four coats of waterproofing. Although this number might seem excessive, it is not. Because of the attention paid, my tub has never suffered from the leakage problems often encountered with sunken tubs — even those based upon metal tanks.

Plumbing. Now, in the opening provided in the forms and with the protection of the metal flange, run the plumbing connections into the tub. Vacuum away all debris and dust. Apply a prime coat of thin-set latex mortar adhesive. After the prime coat dries, you are ready to lay the tiles.

Laying the tile. First tile the interior walls of the tub. Then do the tub floor, and finish with the tub surface. Treat the walls and the floor as in any conventional installation. Lay along horizontal and vertical lines with care. If needed, cut tiles to allow for the plumbing fittings. When you do the upper edge of the tub, plan to have any cut tiles fall along the edges farthest from the tub. Always use the layout stick or a dry layout to arrange for as few cut tiles as possible.

Use portland-latex cement adhesive because of its water-resistant qualities. Apply a thin layer ($\frac{1}{8}$ to $\frac{1}{4}$ inch thick), lay the tile, and let the adhesive set for at least two days. Then install the chrome drain cap. Seal this well with the waterproofing sealer. Apply grout to all the surfaces and, when you have finished, clean off any excess. Finally, install the caps on the plumbing fixtures.

A second way to create a watertight tub is to install a water vapor barrier of 4 mil polyethylene. Fill about ½ of the form, insert the film, and finish the pour.

This installation of a sunken tub can be quite difficult. It is not uncommon to have professionals complete the construction work and plumbing. The homeowner then does the tiling. The variety of designs makes for a truly individualized project.

A band of ceramic mosaics renewed this endtable. To complete the installation, a wood strip was added and stained to match the table.

OUTDOOR CERAMIC TILE PROJECTS

Ceramic tile is an excellent material for outdoor use on patios, walks, entryways, and walls. It is, of course, popular as a material for edging swimming pools and also can be used for decorating ornate garden fountains. If you plan an outdoor project, however, check with the tile dealer to confirm that the tile you have chosen is suitable for exterior application. Some manufacturers do not recommend that their tile be used in localities in which the temperature falls below freezing for any period of time. Others have tiles that are designed for either indoor or outdoor use. In most cases, heavy-duty paver tiles are used for exterior application in areas of heavy traffic, while porcelain mosaic tiles are utilized for swimming pools, fountains or walls.

Steps for exterior tile application resemble those for indoor tile. Make sure to use appropriate adhesive and grout. If you do not, the effects of rain, snow, heat and cold will ruin your project in a very short period of time.

PATIOS

Patios may be covered with ceramic tile. Again, the most important rule is that the base be solid and smooth. Concrete is usually the best choice. If the concrete surface is an older existing surface, thoroughly clean and patch it before adding the tile.

If you are creating an entirely new patio or walkway, you will first have to construct the concrete base. The first step in construction of a tile-covered concrete patio or walkway is to "draw" the outline of the project with string and pegs. Then move pegs out by 6 to 12 inches. Excavate the entire area between the pegs down to at least 4 inches below the turf — or to the depth of excavation required by the

building codes for your area. These are based upon the soil type and frost line in your area. Always check your local building codes, as well as supply dealers, for the proper depth.

In areas not subject to severe winters or rainfall, a shallow excavation, without an edge stiffener, will be sufficient. In all other areas, however, an edge stiffener is desirable because it prevents erosion and frost heave.

Specifications

In our example we will assume a surface built directly on grade; that is, the surface is not raised above the ground more than 6 to 8 inches. The surface is usually located one or two feet below the interior floor level. If the patio is adjacent to the house, it is common to have steps or a small platform between the house and the exterior wearing surface. The small platform may be nothing more than a raised surface in a

similar material, or a wood platform extending over the patio itself. Since the patio is located on grade, you might want to raise it just enough (pour it thick enough) to eliminate the step or platform between the interior and exterior. The height limit would be about 18 inches above grade. Once over that size, should have intermediate steps or a platform. This is also much safer.

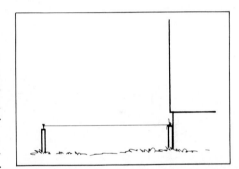

Lay out the patio with strings and pegs. Excavate the area inside the string and at least 6 more inches in each direction.

This walkway is made of rubble quarry tile — broken quarry whose coloring or surface texture is more irregular than standard quarry.

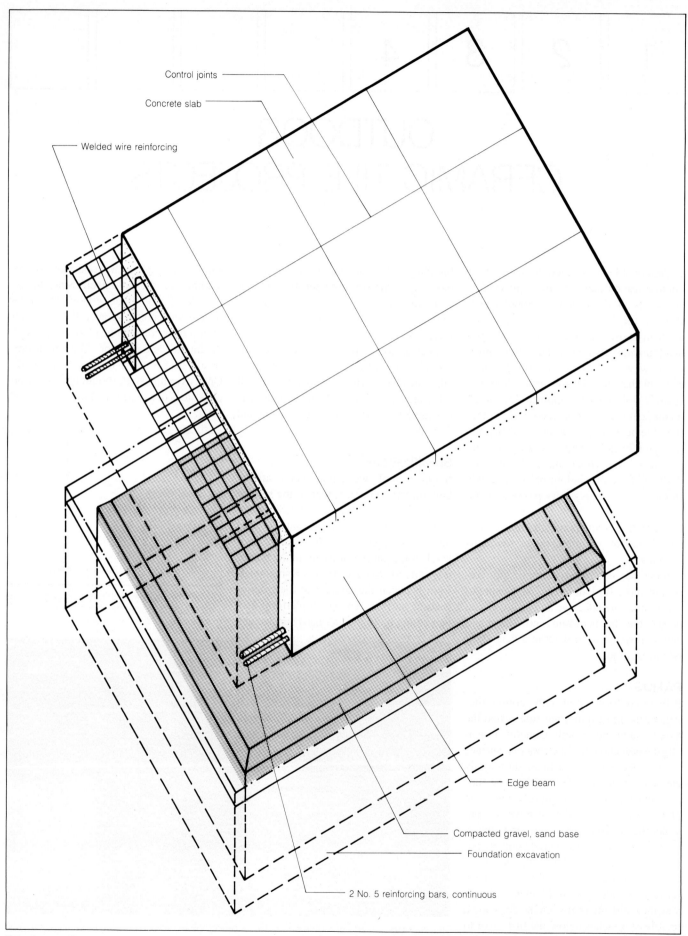

Control joints

Concrete slab

Welded wire reinforcing

Edge beam

Compacted gravel, sand base

Foundation excavation

2 No. 5 reinforcing bars, continuous

This diagram illustrates the construction of a patio slab with an edge stiffener. It encloses the base layers and prevents shifting and heaving.

If the patio is located adjacent to the foundation of your house or building, and you are in a climate where rain and/or snow are not prevalent, the patio surface should be gently pitched away from the foundation at a rate of ⅛ inch for every foot of distance. This figure is acceptable in climates where the annual rainfall is considered minimal. In a more northern climate, it is desirable to pitch the slope at ¼ inch per foot. This keeps the water away from the house interior and reduces the possibility of the patio surface being undermined. To check the accuracy of the grade, slide a 2x4 along the surface of the excavation. Place a carpenter's level on the edge of the board and measure the distance between the bottom of the 2x4 and the surface. As you move the board along, fill in any depressions in the surfaces below.

Patio Base Preparations

The base preparation of a patio is rarely seen. The purpose of the base is to prepare the soil so it will accept the surface material without later settlement, drainage, or heaving problems. The soil on which the patio will be placed must be prepared, compacted, and edged in order to keep the wearing surface in its correct position. Most materials placed under a patio surface are there to increase the density of the soil as well as to provide a leveling course (a course is a layer of material). Normally, the base courses are composed of gravel, sand or concrete. These materials are available in most regions. They are relatively inexpensive and their unit of measure is most often the cubic yard.

A slab on grade does not require a foundation; however, as mentioned earlier an edge stiffener is recommended as part of the design. This is simply an additional thickness of concrete added to the edge of the concrete slab to make sure that the edge keeps its position and shape.

Estimating Material Quantities

Since the base materials are ordered by volume rather than by weight, it is important to make sure that the quantities you order are adequate. To measure for base materials such as sand and gravel, you must know the size and depth of the areas using those materials.

ESTIMATING CUBIC YARDS OF CONCRETE FOR SLABS BEFORE ADDING IN EDGE STIFFENER

Thickness Inches	Area in square feet (width x length)					
	10	25	50	100	200	300
4	0.12	0.31	0.62	1.23	2.47	3.70
5	0.15	0.39	0.77	1.54	3.09	4.63
6	0.19	0.46	0.93	1.85	3.70	5.56

Remember that for a 6 inch slab, the lumber you would use is "dressed," which means it is surfaced to give smoothness and uniformity. This procedure reduces the size of the lumber. The 4 inch dimension of a 2x4 is actually between 3½ and 3⁹⁄₁₆ inches; the 6 inch dimension of a 2x6 will be between 5½ and 5⅝ inches. These differences are important when you purchase lumber for form construction.

Building Permits

Once you have completed your drawing and estimated your material quantities, but before placing your order, submit your plan for a building permit. Most communities will not permit you to proceed with your construction without a permit. In some cases, building inspectors have requested that work already completed be undone and corrected according to building code standards.

Site Preparation

Excavating. Remove all the topsoil and sod within the area you have designated as the patio area. Drive several stakes around the perimeter, allowing at least one foot (or more) beyond the actual edge of the proposed patio. Rake the ground, removing any large rocks, glass or debris in the excavation area. The depth of the excavation will depend on the thickness of your slab. For our example, the excavation will be 6 inches deep before grading for drainage. After you have levelled the site, and while you are excavating, you will have to grade the earth so that the corners of the patio furthest from the house will be lower than the point closest to it. Once this has been accomplished, smooth out the surface as much as possible by raking. In many cases you can grade just by moving the earth from low spots to the desired high areas.

Infilling. If your site slopes steeply away from or toward the house foundation, try to level and grade it as much as possible. To do this might require additional excavation below the layer of topsoil. It may be necessary to call in a landscape grader if the grade requires much earth fill.

If fill is required, determine the quantity by multiplying desired height by the area to be covered. This figure should then be doubled, as the fill will compact to almost one half of its original volume. To fill a site, put the greatest amount of soil where the greatest void exists, spread it around, and tamp. The tamping may be done by a large roller or by a mechanical tamper. Both can be rented. Continue to infill in 4 inch layers. Keep the soil moist but not wet. The soil will absorb the moisture and swell, which will be its natural state when covered by the concrete slab. To check for the desired level, lay a straight 2x4 down over the area. Place on it a 48 inch carpenter's level, on edge. You must have level ground before you can create a pitch. This will tell you which areas need more fill.

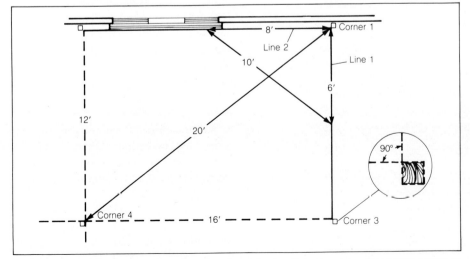

To check the square of a patio, stake and line the perimeter. Set extra stakes 3 feet from corner on line 1, and 4 feet from corner on line 2. The diagonal between stakes should be 5 feet. The dimensions of the triangle, as here, should always be multiples of the 3-4-5 triangle.

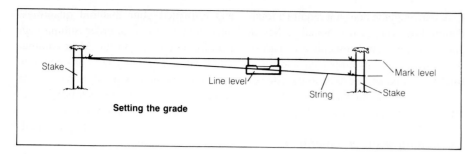

Setting the grade

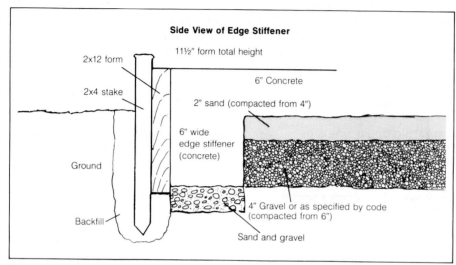

Side View of Edge Stiffener

Unlike the slab poured for a tub, in most areas a patio slab requires an edge stiffener made of concrete or some other substance. The edge stiffener prevents the slab from shifting.

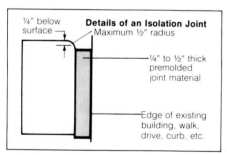

Details of an Isolation Joint

Isolation joints are designed to allow for the differing rates of expansion and contraction of unlike surfaces. Place the joint material between the patio and house and between concrete and brick or new and old concrete.

To give additional stability to the form for a large patio, supplement the 2x4 stakes. Add an extra 2x4 at every other stake. Set the extra 2x4 on an angle. Fasten with duplex nails.

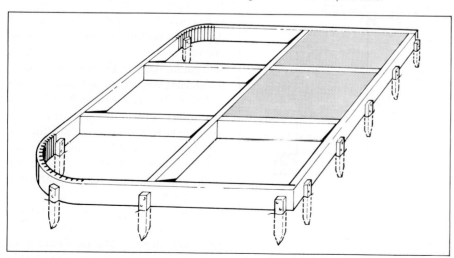

Set stakes closer together than usual at corners and curves to retain their shape during the pour. The interior forms of treated wood here stay in the patio as part of the basic design.

Formwork

Dig trenches just outside the patio excavation area. They should be as deep as the edging form (11¼ inches) and 2 inches wide. Place 2x12s in the trenches. At the corners farthest from the house the beam will be lower, in order to follow the pitch you graded. Place a stake outside the board and fasten the two together with 16d nails. Check that your square has not changed. Repeat this operation for the other form boards on the other sides of the patio. Stake 2x4s every 16 inches around the entire perimeter you have just laid out. The stake height should be just below the top of the 2x12. The stakes at the two farthest corners will be the same height relative to the foundation as those nearer the house, but will actually be longer due to the grade. Cut all stakes off just below form height. Having staked the perimeter, you have set the exterior formwork. Backfill the forms for stability. On the inside of the form, tamp the earth so it is level with the bottom of the form board. Then oil the forms.

Along the foundation wall of the house, install a preformed expansion material. This material comes in ½ inch by 4 inch strips. It is used to separate the concrete patio slab from the foundation of the house. To place it, lay it loosely along the foundation line. Once the concrete is poured it will remain in place.

Curved forms. Your patio design may call for curved forms. If so, use one-inch lumber rather than two-inch. You may also use ¼-to-½ inch thick plywood, sheet metal, or hardboard. Gentler, short-radius curves can use two-inch thick wood forms that have been saw-kerfed and then bent until the kerfs are held closed; or you can bend plywood, with the grain vertical. Wet lumber will be easier to bend than will dry lumber. For very tight curves, use ⅜ inch redwood or plywood bender boards. Sandwich together two or three boards against the stakes, and nail into position. Vertical curves can also be formed by saw kerfing. Another option is to bend the 2x4s during staking. When the slope changes sharply, shorter lengths of forming are best.

Lay out the curve with a string line that is tied to temporary stakes. Adjust the line up or down on the stakes to give a smooth curve. Short lengths of the forming are then set to the string line and are staked securely. To keep forms at proper curvature and grade, set the stakes closer on curves than on straight runs.

Forms for steps. There are several possibilites for the arrangement of the steps in relation to the patio. If you are building a patio which uses existing access to a back door, then you will already have steps in place and will simply have to set up the forms using the existing concrete steps as part of one side of the form. In this case, lay an isolation joint (expansion strip) where the bottom step will meet the patio.

If you are adding a patio and do not already have steps leading to it — for example, you have installed a sliding glass door to give access to a new patio area that is below the interior floor level — the procedure is a little more complicated. You

will need to form, place and partially cure the concrete steps before placing the concrete for your patio. This is because you will have to brace the step forms; you will want to remove the step bracing and forms before placing the concrete for the patio. You should place an isolation joint at the base of the top riser, and at the joint between the bottom step and the patio.

Footings. You will need footings underneath the steps. The footings should be at least 2 feet deep; in regions of hard frost, the footings should extend 6 inches below the frost line. Tie the steps to the foundation walls using anchor bolts or tie rods. One economical measure that will act as footings and prevent the steps from sinking is a grid of two or more 6-to-8-inch diameter postholes beneath the bottom tread. Fill these with concrete. The depth of these would be the same as a conventional footing. Tie the top step or landing form to the foundation using at least two metal anchors. Construct side braces of 2x4s to secure the form in place.

Pound stakes eighteen inches or so from the side form braces. Set 2x4s on their edges and prop them at an angle between the stakes and the form brace. Fasten at the back end with 16d nails.

The step forms will need a coat of oil to aid in their removal. Once the forms are built, put large rocks or broken concrete or bricks inside so you will not need to fill the whole volume with concrete. Keep this fill well away from the edges and the top so it will not be exposed. The concrete mix for steps uses gravel that is no larger than 1 inch in diameter.

If you are building a raised patio even with the interior floor, you will need steps leading down from the patio to your yard. These steps use the same forms as those leading from the house, but do not require footings. You would want to place expansion (isolation) strips at the base of the top riser and the base of the second-to-the-bottom riser.

Dimensions. Check your local building codes to find any minimum or maximum dimensions set. For flights of more than 5 feet (which is unlikely), a landing should be provided. A top landing should be no further than 7½ inches below the threshold. If the flight is less than 30 inches high, the minimum tread width is usually 11 inches and the maximum step rise 7½ inches. For higher step flights, the minimum tread width may be 12 inches and the step rise may become 6 inches. In some designs, steps with treads as wide as 19 inches and rises as low as 4 inches are sometimes built. One rule of thumb has it that the riser and tread should add to 17½ inches; however, patios and decks will often take more generous dimensions.

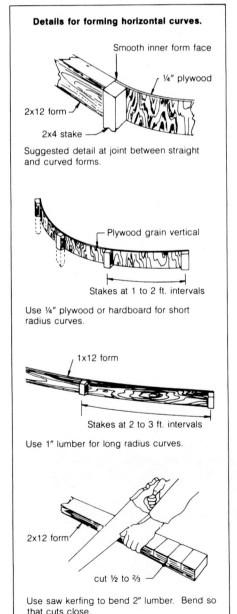

Details for forming horizontal curves.

Smooth inner form face

¼" plywood

2x12 form

2x4 stake

Suggested detail at joint between straight and curved forms.

Plywood grain vertical

Stakes at 1 to 2 ft. intervals

Use ¼" plywood or hardboard for short radius curves.

1x12 form

Stakes at 2 to 3 ft. intervals

Use 1" lumber for long radius curves.

2x12 form

cut ½ to ⅔

Use saw kerfing to bend 2" lumber. Bend so that cuts close.

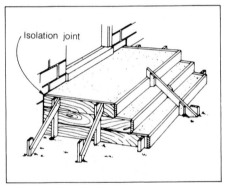

Isolation joint

Steps leading down from the house to your patio should be formed and poured before placement of the concrete for the patio. Bevel the bottom edge of the form boards for the risers so you can finish the treads under the forms.

Level risers from left to right and position them so the back of each tread is ¼ in. higher than the front. Begin placing the concrete in the bottom step and move up and toward the back.

Easier alternative. If you decide to buy precast steps and to bolt them to the house, place the steps in position before pouring the patio. You will need to dig posthole footings, place the steps and anchor them, and then put an isolation (expansion) joint between the steps and the patio.

Gravel and Sand

You are now ready to prepare the gravel and sand base. Your reference point will be the top of the form board. Place the gravel over the entire area. Lay it down in two layers of 3 inches each. Make sure that each layer is tamped thoroughly until firm. The 6-inch depth of the gravel should be tamped down to 4 inches. You are now ready to place the sand over the gravel course. To do this, place the sand uniformly over the entire area in a 2 inch layer. Tamp the sand down. If the gravel shows through, do not be alarmed. Place enough sand so that a difference between the top of the sand and the top of the form-board will be approximately 4 inches. If the space is less, remove some sand.

At this point the edge beam must be created. To do this, remove the earth from the inside perimeter of the formboard for a width of 6 inches; this 6 inch trough all around the perimeter should be about 6 inches deep after leaving about 2 inches each of gravel and sand on the bottom. It will be excavated to just below the bottom edge of the formboard, and then 2 inches each of the sand and gravel will be replaced. Moisten the area so the shape will hold. Having done this, check that the corners of the forms are braced and tightly connected, and that all alignments are still square and correct.

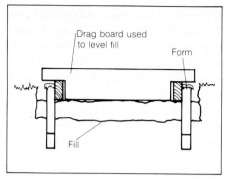

Cut a 1x10 as shown to match the depth of the concrete. Draw the board along the form and level the fill to the correct height.

Setting the Reinforcing Steel

Reinforcing comes in two forms. The first type used in the slab will come in rolls or sheets of 4x8 feet. This welded wire fabric is visually similar to wire mesh, but has a larger spacing and is welded at each intersection of the wire. It can be placed into the form in two ways: formed metal "chair rails" can be purchased to be placed in the sand on which the welded wire fabric sits. This ensures that the fabric will be in the middle of the concrete when it is poured. Another method is to place two-to-three inch stones inside the form; the fabric is placed on the stones. The chair rails allow for the fabric to be tied to them; the rocks are less stable. Either method will suffice. The main idea is to keep the fabric in the middle of the concrete, or 2 inches from the top of the slab. The second type of reinforcing is the #5 straight deformed rod, which comes in a variety of lengths. The rods are placed in the form in the perimeter trough you have created. To elevate them above the bottom of the trough, drive a wooden 2x4 into the bottom of the trough every three or four feet around the perimeter. This will keep the rod elevated. If the 2x4 is left unattached, it will float when the concrete is poured. Keep the steel as clean as you possibly can. Once the reinforcing steel has been placed in the forms, the concrete can be poured.

Pouring Concrete

Ready-mixed concrete is without a doubt the most desirable, since it is delivered mixed and ready for placement when you are at the right stage. Before pouring the concrete, prepare the ground area so that the truck can back in as closely as possible. This way the delivery can be directly into the form rather than having to barrow it in from some other location. It is strong-

ly recommended that you have a helper to assist you in this phase of the operation. A truck's capacity is usually 12 to 20 yards of concrete.

As you fill the forms, make sure that you place the material evenly over the entire area. Allow some overage, since you will want to work the concrete down into the forms by filling all the voids. Be careful not to let the material drop over 3 feet in height, or the mixture might separate. After adding each layer, compact by pushing the end of the shovel into the crevasses or corners. Start in a corner and continue laying each successive pour against the previous one until the entire form has been filled. When the form has been filled to overflowing, the truck will be ready to leave — your work, however, must continue. Spread the concrete with care, to prevent segregation. Work it uniformly, treating each square foot equally. If your reinforcing bends lift it with coat hangers when you work that particular area. Once the entire form has been worked over, you will be ready to finish the concrete.

Finishing the Slab

Place the concrete as quickly as you can, making sure it has been properly compacted in the forms. There is a tendency for the concrete to "bleed". This is the water rising to the surface due to the heavier materials settling on the bottom. The placing and screeding should be accomplished as quickly as possible to prevent this from occurring. If a large amount of water does rise to the surface, try to remove it by drawing a length of garden hose across the surface. "Bleeding" can cause future scaling or spalling of the surface. See Chapter 3 for screeding instructions.

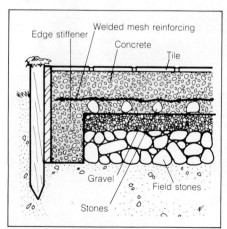

In a finished outdoor slab, a tamped layer of gravel and sand covers a layer of field stone. Then concrete is added.

Place small rocks inside the form. The rocks support reinforcing mesh during the pour.

Darbying. Once the surface has been screeded, the next step is to smooth the surface with a darby or a float. A float is a small, flat tool that one person can operate. It is fine for small sized projects. A darby is a large float. Often, it takes two people to operate. It has a long, wooden or steel handle, and can be rented or purchased from your local supplier. This is part of the process during which the final surface of the patio is set.

Edging. When all the bled water and surface water sheen have left the concrete, the concrete has begun to harden. You can now begin to perform the final finishing operations. Use an edger to round off the perimeter edges against the forms. This will prevent chipping or damage to the edge of the slab. Running the edger around the edge, form a uniform curve to the concrete corner. Work the material back and forth. If your first run does not work very well, try it again.

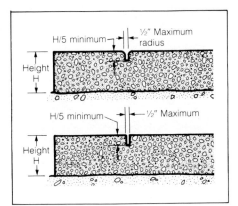

Once the concrete is set enough to hold a shape, make a 1 inch cut between the form and the concrete with a mason trowel or margin trowel. Then edge with an edging tool.

Jointing. Immediately after edging, put the joints into the slab. While a slab without any joints may look nice, a slab without joints will begin to crack. These joints allow the cracks to occur in the joint and not in the wearing surface. The depth of the joint should be one-fifth to one fourth of the thickness of the slab. Usually, all joints are put into the concrete at 10-foot intervals in each direction. In our sample slab, three joints will be required for the 16-foot direction and two joints will be required for the 12-foot direction. For putting in joints, it is good practice to use a straight board as a guide, and a tool with a ¾ inch bit. Exercise the same care in placing the joints as you did when edging. Set the board up on the spacing. Place the jointer into the concrete and pull towards you over the distance. You can use other boards to kneel on if you cannot reach across.

Finishing Air-Entrained Concrete

Because of the microscopic air bubbles, there is less water in the mixture. Since there is less water, there is less tendency to bleed. As a result, the floating and trowel-

ing can be done sooner, with less difficulty in arriving at a good surface. Better results are almost always achieved with air-entrained concrete. Air-entraining agents can be specified when the concrete is ordered.

Temperate Climates

In areas where rain and snow are uncommon, you can eliminate the edge stiffeners. In this case the forms can be built of 2x4s, as shown.

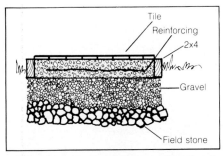

Areas which suffer from little ground heaving do not need an edge stiffener. Check local codes for area requirements.

Placing the Tile

After slab has cured properly, place a dry run of the paver or quarry tiles on the surface. Space them to suit. They can be spaced from ¼ inch to as wide as ¾ inch apart. After determining the spacing and layout of the tiles, make up a layout stick and use it to lay out the rest of the patio. Find the center of the patio in both directions just as for laying interior floor tile. Draw the working lines.

Trowel on the adhesive — either dry-set mortar or latex-portland-cement mortar. Both these adhesives have a fairly firm body. The consistency, coupled with the type of trowel they require, is such that the trowel does not have to be held as firmly against the surface as is the case with organic adhesives. You can do some slight leveling with cement mortar, although it cannot solve major problems. Follow directions specified by the tile and adhesive manufacturer. In most cases they will suggest the use of a skim coat applied with the flat, smooth edge of the steel trowel. Apply pressure as you spread the adhesive. Let set. Then apply a second coat over the skim coat, to the thickness recommended by the manufacturer. Turn the trowel around and use the notched side to spread the adhesive into the desired position.

Place the first tiles into position. Then tap them in lightly, using a carpeted wooden block and a hammer. This is a very

Control joints are essential to a large concrete slab. Temperature changes then cause cracks only near the joint rather than in the entire slab. Run the jointing tool along a chalkline.

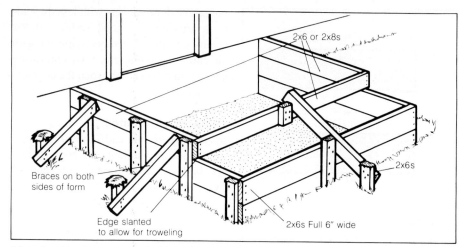

Braces on both sides of form

Edge slanted to allow for troweling

2x6 or 2x8s

2x6s

2x6s Full 6" wide

A form for steps is constructed of 2x6s. Double brace both of the sides to support the weight of the concrete pour and maintain straight sides. To ease the creation of the steps, pour them before you place the patio forms — you will need space to work as you finish the steps.

Edging along a riser form gives a smooth, gradual curve to the edge of the tread. A ¼- to ½-inch radius tool is usually used. Soon after you edge the step, begin the troweling.

Remove the forms in order to trowel the step risers. However, since you plan to tile, do not trowel the concrete more than once — tile does not adhere to a slick surface.

Porcelain ceramic tile sheets provide an easy method for tiling large concrete expanses. Here they cover a garden walkway.

important step because it forces out the water in the mortar, enabling the adhesive to contact more of the back surface of the tile.

Apply the appropriate grout. This can be either commercial portland-cement grout or sand portland-cement grout, dry-set grout or latex-portland-cement grout.

ENTRYWAY

A raised entry and steps covered with ceramic tile forms an excellent and elegant entrance — one that is easy to care for as well as beautiful. The tile used should be a good paver or quarry tile. Don't use a glazed wall tile for this purpose, since it not only is less sturdy, but the slick finish can be dangerous when damp. The tiles can be applied over a wood base if necessary; this type of application requires a complex construction in order to support the weight of the tiles. Most homeowners choose a concrete base with a thick mortar bed. The concrete base must be solid, with no surface defects, free of dirt, grease and other surface problems. Clean and prepare the surface as illustrated in Chapter 8, and install ceramic tile as in Chapter 2. Use trim tile to overhang tops of the treads.

Although the dimensions are larger, a raised entryway is constructed the same way as is a patio. Follow the same steps given for patios.

WALKS

Stake out the area for the walk, using pegs and a string — as for patios, above. Excavate at least 4 to 6 inches, depending upon climate and frost line. (Forming for a walk is done in much the same manner as for patios.)

Provide about 2 inches or so of field stone fill. You can use more if the walk excavation is deeper. Add about 2 inches of gravel fill on top of that. Level out the fill and place welded wire mesh down on top of the stones. Use larger stones (as for patios) to lift it up above the gravel surface to approximately the middle of the depth of the concrete pour. Now pour the concrete; screed the surface; finish it with a trowel. The level of the surface should not vary more than ⅛ inch in 10 feet for proper adhesion of the tiles. The surface should be even, but it should not be troweled to a slick finish as would be the case for most normal concrete finishing jobs. The slick finish would not bond well with the tile adhesive. Then use a fine broom to finish off the slab. Place the control joints every 10 to 12 feet.

In all cases of installing ceramic tile on walkways, patios and entryways, a dry-set mortar or latex-portland-cement mortar bond or skim coat should first be applied before the actual adhesive coat used to set the tiles.

GARDEN FENCE

A fence covered with ceramic tile usually has a base of poured concrete. The surface must be clean, sound and dimensionally stable with no cracks or defects. It must be free of coatings, oil, wax. All concrete surfaces should be rough; older walls may need sandblasting.

Use a dry-set or latex-portland cement mortar. First apply a thin bond coat of about ⅛ inch thickness, followed by the adhesive coat of from ⅛ to ¼ inch. Any grout except silicone may be applied.

Installation of the tiles to the fence follows basically the same procedures as for interior walls. However, choose an out-

When staking out a walk or other area, tack the string to the stakes or wrap it around so the string will not slip or become loose. Wraparounds should all be at the same height.

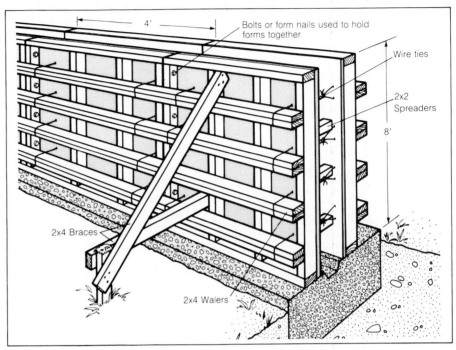

Use 4x8 prefabricated forms of ¾ in. plywood sheathing nailed to 2x4 frames. Set forms on their long or short sides; fasten together if needed. Hold forms in place with 2x4 walers connected with wire ties. Pass wire ends through forms and twist together inside. To ensure wall thickness, add 2x2 blocks inside forms. Brace the structure with 2x4 bracing and stakes.

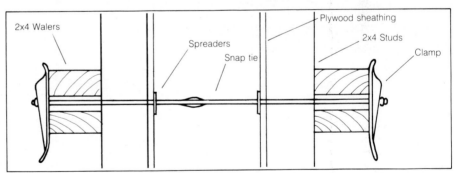

Instead of using wire loops, you can use manufactured units called snap ties. The ties not only hold the forms together but space them properly for the wall width as well. When the forms are removed, the ties merely snap off, leaving portions of the ties inside the wall.

Use 2x4s for stakes to support the form boards Otherwise they will sag or fall during the pour. Align the string with the inside edge of the top of the form board.

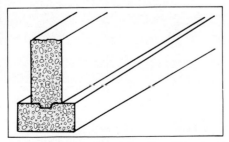

Add stability with a foundation "key." Bevel and oil the edges of a 2x4. About ½ hour after pouring the foundation, press the 2x4 into the concrete; let sit until mix has set.

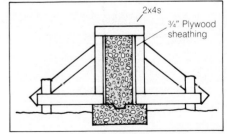

Small walls (less than 3 feet high) can be formed with sections of ¾ inch plywood. Support the sides with 2x4 braces. Secure the top opening with 2x4 strips every 2 ft.

door tile, since it is not water-permeable. Check with your local tile dealer for suggestions regarding suitable types of tile.

GARDEN POOL AND FOUNTAIN

You can tile the entire pool or fountain or use the tile as a decorative accent to the pool. Probably the easiest way to build a pool is to build a simple saucer-shaped

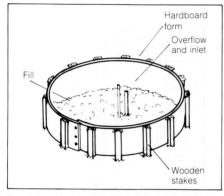

Create fountain form with hardboard sheets — this installation called for 2. Hold sheets together with 3 carriage bolts; stake securely.

pool, as shown. It can be raised above the surface of the patio or just below the edge. The pool may be fitted with a recirculating pump and fountain jet to add the sound and beauty of moving water.

Pool Construction Steps

Decide upon the dimensions of the pool. The example given here is 54 inches in diameter, standing 6 inches above the level of the proposed patio. The bowl of the pool is 42 inches in diameter and 9 inches deep. Obviously, the pool you build need not hold to these dimensions.

Step one: plumbing. Once you know the pool's dimensions, dig the hole for the footing and base, following local code requirements for depth. Then install the plumbing. Run in two lines of ½ inch plastic piping, one for the drain outlet and one for the water inlet. Measure from the bend in the outlet pipe to 2 inches above the proposed level of the base of bowl, then to the proposed water level. Create

the vertical length of the outlet with two pieces of pipe that fit the two measurements (remember to account for the coupling). In that way the upper section of pipe can be unscrewed so the pool can be drained in the fall.

If you wish, provide the pool with a jet spray head and a recirculating pump. This permits a fountain in addition to the reflecting pool. The hole you dig to house the pump must be sunk deep enough to accommodate the pump and to maintain level pipes.

Step two: the base. Once the piping is in, you must place, tamp and level the gravel and sand base of the footing, as discussed in the section on tubs in Chapter 3.

Step three: the forms. Once you know the pool's dimensions, construct a form for the pool from ¼ inch hardboard. The form must be deep enough to run from the level of the gravel footing beneath the concrete bed up to 6 inches above the patio level. Therefore, if the concrete pour for the patio will be about 6 inches deep, the pour for the pool must be 12 inches high in order to achieve the pool elevation. Now multiply the diameter of the pool by 3.2 to find the circumference. This will be the length of hardboard needed for the form. In this example, the hardboard must be 170 inches long. Fasten ends of the hardboard together with small ¼x1 inch carriage bolts. Insert the form in the hole. Place stakes every 12 to 18 inches to hold the form securely.

Step four: placing the concrete. Once the form is staked, pour a watertight concrete mix. Hand-place the concrete, following the basic shape of the bowl of the pool. Be sure that the concrete is spaded, to get rid of air pockets, especially around the plastic pipes. Then tamp and level.

Step five: screeding the concrete. Now create a specially shaped screed as shown. Take a piece of 1x12 that is 1 foot longer than the width of the pool. This will be used as the screed. Find the center of the screed; then measure out toward both ends to determine where the rim of the bowl will fall. Since this bowl is 42 inches across, the rim will fall 21 inches on either side of the center. Draw in the shape of the bowl, and cut the board to that shape, using a sabre saw. When you reach the end of the rim line, saw straight over to the end of the screed. The resulting screed should resemble the one shown here.

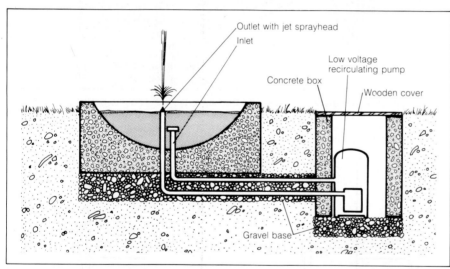

To add a fountain to the pool, install a low voltage recirculating pump. The outlet pipe creates the fountain; the inlet pipe draws the water back to the pump; the water is then recirculated through the fountain. Some pumps are built for installation in the bottom of the pool.

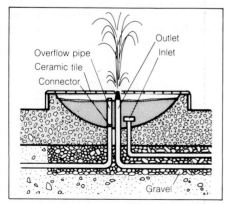

A third pipe completes the plumbing for the pool. The overflow pipe will drain off extra water — for example, from rainfalls.

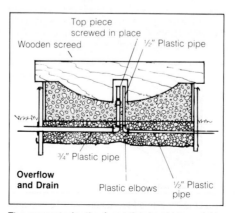

The concrete for the fountain should be a fairly stiff mix — do not add too much water. Then use a shaped screed to form the bowl.

Sit the screed on the form, next to the plastic pipes. (Center the bowl in the form.) Sketch in an allowance for the pipes and an opening for the pipes. Again place the screed into the form. Now, with a helper, move the screed in a circular motion to rough-shape the bottom of the pool. Remove excess concrete with a trowel. Fill in any low spots as you go. Continue the movement around the form until the surface is smooth.

Step six: finishing the pool. Wait until the concrete has set up enough to take a thumb print (this will take approximately 1 to 3 hours). Then use a small masonry trowel to smooth and round the bowl of the pool. Pay particular attention to the areas around the drain and inlet.

Tiling the Pool

Let the concrete cure for at least 7 days. Apply a bond coat of latex-portland-cement mortar. Let this dry thoroughly; then plot your working lines. These should cross in the center of the bowl. If you must cut some tiles, let them fall at the rim of the bowl and at the outer edge of the lip. (Of course, you will have to cut tiles to fit around the pipes.)

Once the bond coat has dried, apply the adhesive coat of latex-portland-cement mortar and lay the tile according to your design. Allow the adhesive to set for the time required by the manufacturer. Grout with a mixture of 1 part portland cement plus 1 part sand, by volume. You also can lay the tile in a thick bed of mortar. This is especially valuable if the bowl surface is not level. For instructions on this technique, see the following section on swimming pool construction.

Variation: Square Garden Pool

Another pool design produces a rectangular or box-shaped pool. It is formed of 2x6s and 1x8s. The result is a beautiful garden pool that provides space for growing aquatic plants. The bottom of the pool can be painted, or tiled in a dark color to make the pool appear deeper and to help disguise the soil buckets holding the plants. The upper rim can be tiled in any color you desire.

SWIMMING POOLS
Building a Pool

Ceramic tile is a traditional material for covering swimming pools, but installing them on a pool requires a high degree of skill. Once the pool is constructed and has cured, the appropriate drain and inlet pipes are installed and a commercially prepared waterproofing material is applied to the concrete. The construction of such a large project is beyond the scope of this book — and of most do-it-yourselfers. The best course is to have a professional install the pool itself. This should be proven to be watertight before the tile is installed. Fill the pool with water — the water level should not fall at all over a period of a day. Then empty the pool, let it dry thoroughly and clean any oil or grease from the concrete surface.

Tiling a Pool

Most people tile only the coping of the pool, since the entire job is so extensive. However, if you plan to tile the whole pool, cover the coping first, then the sides and finally the walls. Work on one section at a time.

Apply a scratch coat and then a thick bed of mortar. Usually, the mixture of both is as follows: 1 part portland cement, 1/2 part lime, and 4 parts of dry sand (5 parts damp sand). Mix with water according to the directions on the mortar package. As always, check the instructions on your particular product; manufacturers' instructions vary. Let the mixture set for at least fifteen minutes so it homogenizes completely.

Then lay the scratch coat of the mortar to seal off the concrete. Using a mortar trowel, lay rough coat, about 1/4 to 1/2 inch thick. Once this scratch coat has set, trowel on a bed of mortar that is at least 1 1/2 inches thick. The purpose of this bed is to level the concrete surface, fill in any depressions, seams or other variations in the surface of the concrete tank. Hold the

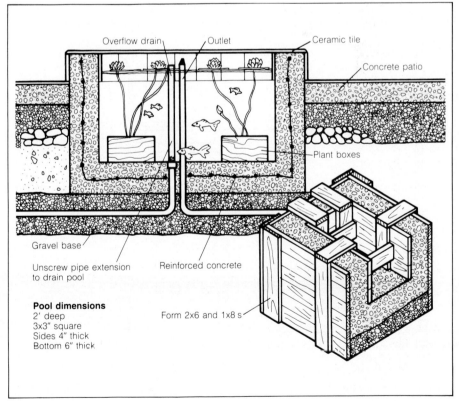

Overflow drain   Outlet   Ceramic tile
Concrete patio
Plant boxes
Gravel base
Unscrew pipe extension to drain pool
Reinforced concrete
Form 2x6 and 1x8 s

Pool dimensions
2' deep
3x3" square
Sides 4" thick
Bottom 6" thick

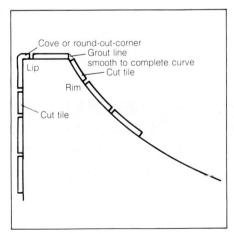

Cove or round-out-corner
Grout line
smooth to complete curve
Lip
Cut tile
Rim
Cut tile

Once the pool has cured, apply tile with a cement based adhesive. Use cove or round out-corner trim for the lip; smooth out the grout line to create the curve at the bowl rim.

Square pool: Once the plumbing is installed, build the forms of 2x6s fastened together with 1x8s. To keep walls spaced correctly, install 1x8 braces across the top of the forms and between the inside walls. Pour the pool base — leave no air spaces under the inside form walls. Then complete the pour. Tile the entire pool or only the edges above the water.

trowel as flat as possible to achieve a flat surface and to prevent what is called the "washboard effect" — ridges in the surface of the mortar. Troweling mortar is a

difficult skill to learn. The job itself will take some time to complete.

Once the mortar is laid, install the tiles into the mortar bed before the bed has set. (At this stage, the mortar is said to be "plastic.") Soak the tiles for approximately one half hour before you place the tiles in the mortar. Otherwise, they will draw water from the mortar, which weakens the bond. Plan horizontal and vertical working lines as you would for any other project. Cut tiles should fall along the wall edges and near the top of the pool rim. Place the tiles on the mortar; their weight will settle them into the mortar surface. Once you have covered the entire pool, the installation is grouted.

The second method for setting the tile is to allow the mortar bed to damp cure for seven days. At that time, apply a bond coat of portland cement or dry-set adhesive. This installation does not require that the tiles be soaked before they are laid.

SMALL PROJECTS

Ceramic tile makes an excellent material for small projects around the backyard and exterior of your home. Set the tile into the front steps or in "alcove" portions of a

brick or stone house front for a bit of color. Use broken pieces of tile or mosaics to cover patio tables in the same manner as for wood tiles (see Chapter 6).

Planter

The tile-covered planter on page 22 calls for a poured concrete form. You can create a planter of any size you wish by following the basic framework given here. Cover the planter with porcelain ceramic sheets — they will conform to the curve of the planter.

Creating the forms. The outside form is made of a sheet of ⅛ inch tempered hardboard. Use a sheet that is three times longer than the desired width of the planter, and as wide as the planter is high. Curve the sheet into a circle and secure it with at least two lengths of 14 or 16 gauge wire. Then center the outside form on a piece of plywood that is at least 6 inches wider than the form, on a patio or lawn. You cannot set the form directly on a patio because there is no way to secure it during the pour. The form might slide or the concrete ooze out from beneath the bottom of the form. (If you want the planter to sit directly on the ground, it must have a footing.) Oil the form. Do not work very far from the planter's ultimate position, since the planter will be very heavy and you will not want to move it very far.

The inside form will remain in place after the concrete has cured. Use a metal or plastic can that is no more than three quarters the width of the outside form. A 24-inch-wide planter, therefore, would have a center opening that was no larger

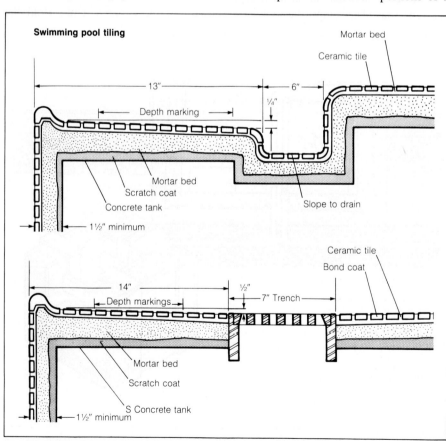

Swimming pools are watertight concrete tanks. Once the tank itself has cured properly, the pool is covered with a rough, "scratch" coat of mortar. Let this dry thoroughly.

Once the scratch coat has cured, apply a thick bed of mortar. The mortar bed is a levelling bed, creating gradual curves and slopes required for proper tile application and proper drainage. The bed's thickness will vary but it must be between 1 and 1½ inch thick.

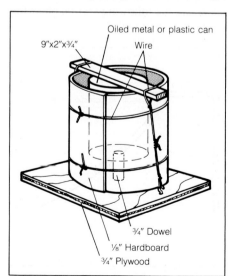

A garden planter has two forms: a hardboard outer form and an inner form made of a metal or plastic can. Do not remove the inner form.

than 18 inches. Cut a length of ¾ inch dowel to equal the distance between the bottom of the can and the plywood base. This will prop the can in place. Cut a piece of 2x2 that is at least as long as the plywood base. Place it across the top of the form to keep the inner form from rising up as the concrete is poured. Screw two eyebolts to the base, directly aligned on either side of the outside form. Loop a length of wire through one bolt and up and around the 2x2 brace. Twist the wire ends together securely. Place the dowel and the metal can inside the hardwood form. Fasten down the other end of the brace with a wire loop through the other eyebolt.

Pouring the concrete. Mix a concrete mix for a watertight container (use the same proportions as given for the sunken tub discussion in Chapter 3). Pour the concrete with care and tamp often so that there are no air pockets (or as few as possible) beneath the inner form and along its sides.

Once the sides are filled, screed the surface. Damp cure the concrete for seven days before you remove the outside form.

Positioning the planter. Then with a helper's assistance, move the planter to the spot you have selected for it. The planter will be very heavy, so you will have to push and roll it into positon.

Preparing the surface. Once the planter is positioned, smooth the outside, the lip and the portion of the inside of the planter that you plan to tile. (There is no need to tile the entire inside area.) Pay particular attention to the ridge formed by the overlap of the outer form. To smooth, chisel off any excess. Sand the area smooth with a carborundum stone or a grinder wheel and electric drill. Patch all holes with plaster patching material.

Laying the tile. Use either epoxy or portland cement adhesives for this installation. Spread a bond coat of the material recommended by the tile manufacturer. Let this dry thoroughly. Plot the working lines so that the tiles fall in true horizontal and vertical lines. Cut tiles should fall at the base of the planter. Utilize edge trim tiles to create a smooth corner between the top and the side of the planter.

Barbecue cart. Make 1½x1½ inch notches in back corners of the bottom. Attach furring strips to top, and shelf sides to bottom. Slide back legs through notches; nail to corners. Drill holes through back legs and furring strips to fasten handles. Insert front legs. Prepare plywood underlayment top. Tile furring strips and top; use trim tiles as needed, or form corners with grout lines. Plot working lines so cut tiles fall at edges. Apply sealer after grout dries.

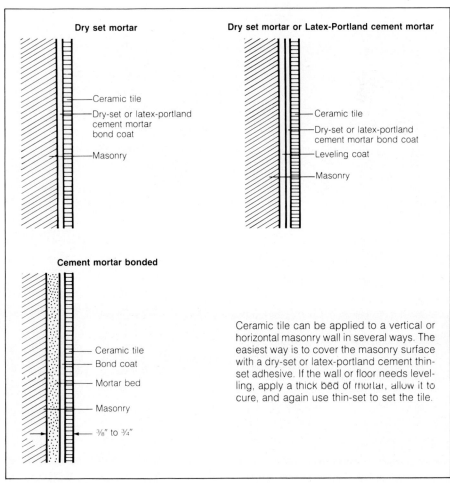

Materials list:

2 pc. ⅜x30x48 (top and bottom)
2 pc. ⅜x6x48¾ (shelve sides)
2 pc. ⅜x6x30 (shelve sides)
2 pc. 2x2x26 (front legs)
2 pc. 2x2x36 (back legs)
2x2x36 (lower shelf brace)
2 pc. 1x2x48¾ furring strip (top)
2 pc. 1x2x30 furring strip (top)
2 preformed handles
2 10 in. bicycle wheels, axle, fasteners
6d nails
2 3 in. bolts

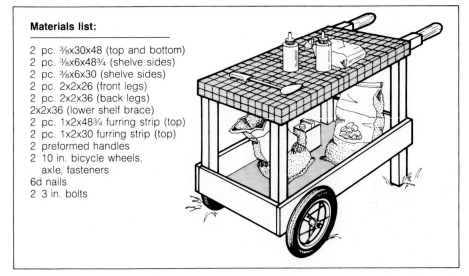

Dry set mortar

— Ceramic tile
— Dry-set or latex-portland cement mortar bond coat
— Masonry

Dry set mortar or Latex-Portland cement mortar

— Ceramic tile
— Dry-set or latex-portland cement mortar bond coat
— Leveling coat
— Masonry

Cement mortar bonded

— Ceramic tile
— Bond coat
— Mortar bed
— Masonry
— ⅜" to ¾"

Ceramic tile can be applied to a vertical or horizontal masonry wall in several ways. The easiest way is to cover the masonry surface with a dry-set or latex-portland cement thinset adhesive. If the wall or floor needs levelling, apply a thick bed of mortar, allow it to cure, and again use thin-set to set the tile.

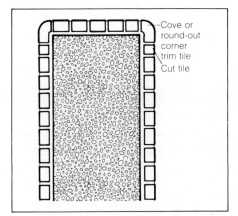

— Cove or round-out corner trim tile
— Cut tile

Choose porcelain ceramic mosaic tiles for this project, since the sheets follow a curved form. Use cove or round out-corner trim tiles; place cut tiles at the top or bottom of planter.

RESILIENT TILE

The resilient tile of today is appropriate in any setting. It requires adhesive or, as here, has a self-stick backing. The new no-wax finishes cut floor-care time to a minimum.

Resilient tile can resemble other materials — ceramic tile, wood parquet, marble or stone.

Resilient tile, one of the easiest materials to install, is available in a wide variety of styles and colors, and is low in cost and easy to clean. A do-it-yourselfer can tile the floor of an average 10x15 foot room in a few hours at a cost of about $150.00.

The installation of resilient tile requires few special tools. You need the following: a chalkline; a utility knife or heavy-duty scissors to cut the tiles; a notched steel trowel to spread the adhesive; a prybar; a yardstick or steel tape; a hammer; a rolling pin to secure the bond between the tiles, the adhesive and the subfloor; and clean rags. The only special tools you may need are a floor sander to smooth and clean the subfloor and a 150-pound, 3-section roller to roll the tile. These last two can be either rented or borrowed from a flooring contractor. Also available is a special home installation kit which can be rented or borrowed from flooring, building materials or hardware stores.

TILING FLOORS

Resilient tile is most commonly used on floors. The primary benefits, especially of the new vinyl tile, include resilience and longevity. However, unless the tile is set according to specified guidelines, the completed installation will be less than satisfactory. Choose a tile and adhesive that are compatible. Clean all grease and dirt from the existing floor. Carefully plot working lines to ensure an even, over-all pattern in the finished floor. Follow all manufacturer's instructions. The result of such care will be a long-lasting and attractive floor.

Estimating Materials

Measure the lengths of two adjoining walls, and multiply the two lengths. The result is the square footage of floor space to be covered. If the room is not square, but includes an additional area such as an entryway, divide the room into separate squares. Measure each square and add the square footage figures together to find the total area. If you are using 12x12 inch tile, the square footage will equal the number of tile pieces necessary.

If you select 9x9 inch tiles, convert each wall dimension from feet to inches; then multiply the two dimensions. Divide the square inches by 81 (the number of square inches in a 9x9 inch tile). The result equals the number of tiles required. To the total number of tiles add 5 percent to allow for cut tiles and trimming errors.

Store the tile and the adhesive required for your installation at 70°F. for about 48 hours before installation.

Preparing the Floor

Resilient tile can be laid above grade or below, over concrete, wood, terrazzo, or tightly bonded, smooth-surfaced asphalt or vinyl asbestos tile. Use the pry bar to remove the cove or quarter round molding but do not remove the baseboard unless you plan to replace it. If the room has no cove molding, consider adding it after the installation. Cove molding creates an attractive and smooth joint between the floor and the walls.

Because resilient tile conforms to the subfloor on which it is laid, the finished job will reflect any imperfections or unevenness in the subfloor. It is therefore very important to begin the installation with a carefully and properly prepared subfloor.

Preparing a concrete floor. The floor must be sound, dry and above all, smooth. Use a heavy-duty detergent to clean grease or oil from the floor. Fill all depressions, cracks, and score marks with the material recommended by the tile manufacturer. Usually this will be either spackling compound or plaster patching material. See Chapter 2 for repair instructions. If the floor is covered with paint, wax, or a high-sheen coating, clean and roughen it with a floor sander. Vacuum up all sanding dust.

Preparing a wood floor. A wood subfloor should be at least 18 inches above ground level and well ventilated. Make certain the subfloor has a double construction — a lower layer of rough wood (any type) flooring covered by a top layer of strip wood flooring. If the floor is of sin-

gle-wood construction, install an underlayment of ⅜ inch Exterior plywood or tempered particleboard or ¼ inch hardboard. (Hardboard and particleboard are recommended because they provide a harder surface than plywood.) There are other circumstances that also require an underlayment. The boards of your double construction wood floor may be so rough, loose, broken or warped that they cannot be made to provide a smooth and firm surface. Any floor having boards that are over 3 inches wide also needs an underlayment. To add the underlayment, place the plywood sheets so they butt against each other but are staggered from row to row. To do so, offset corner joints 6 inches or more. Nail the plywood securely in place

Usually an underlayment is ⅜ in. Exterior plywood or ¼ in. particle board or hardboard.

with 1½ inch ringshank nails. Space the nails 6 inches apart along the seams, ½ inch from the edges. Fill the joints with the patching material specified by the tile manufacturer — this usually will be the adhesive you will later use to lay the tiles.

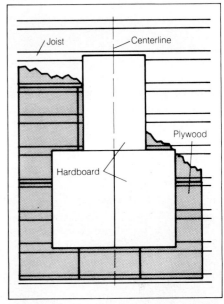

Sheets of new underlayment must fasten to joists, but the joints should not fall over those in the old floor. Staggered placement increases the new floor's structural strength.

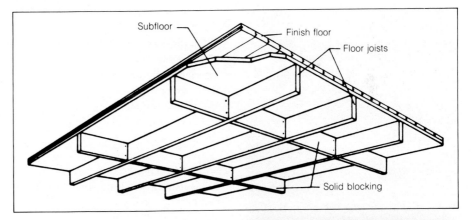

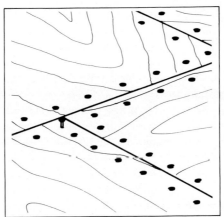

For added strength, stagger the top and bottom joints of the underlayment sheets. Then place nails 6 inches apart along the seams.

Patch cracks or defects in the existing floor with the appropriate patching material. See Chapter 2 for recommendations.

To ensure straight courses, snap 2 chalklines that cross in the center of the floor.

Dry-lay tiles from the center to both walls. Measure the distance left over.

If the space is less than half a tile, move the chalkline a half-width, and resnap.

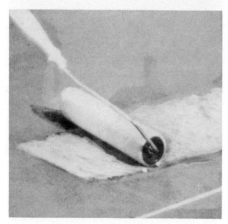

To apply adhesive, use a brush, a trowel or a roller. Do not apply too much adhesive.

Then sand the underlayment smooth, vacuum up the sanding dust, and coat the entire surface with a light coat of shellac or other wood sealer to keep the wood from absorbing the adhesive.

If the present subfloor needs no underlayment, nail down any loose and springy boards. Clean off any grease and oil with a detergent, and sand lightly to remove any wax or paint. Some manufacturers require that a felt underlayment be placed over a hardwood subfloor. Check your tile instructions for installation procedures.

Preparing old tile floors. You can install new resilient tile over an old asphalt or vinyl asbestos tile floor if the floor is firmly bonded. If it is not, the old flooring may crack and peel up and, in the process, loosen and crack the new tiles.

Cement down any loose tiles in the old floor and roll them with a heavy roller. Single loose tiles can usually be removed with a wide chisel or scraper. If you must remove the entire floor, use a floor scraper, a tool that is similar to a sidewalk ice scraper. This task is not an easy one. In some cases, heating the tiles with an old iron will help soften and loosen them, but be careful not to start a fire or melt the tiles. Place a protective cloth over the tiles while ironing.

If the tiles are too stubborn to come up, do not attempt to sand them off with a floor sander. Some tiles contain asbestos fibers, which can easily damage your lungs if you inhale them. Instead, add an underlayment of ⅜ inch Exterior plywood.

Laying the Tile

Establishing working lines. Find the center of the room by snapping two chalklines. These will run through the center of the floor, between facing walls. The two lines will form right angles at the center of the room. Check that the lines are at right angles by laying a tile (or a carpenter's square) in one of the corners created by the crossed lines.

Now dry-lay a row of tiles along one chalkline. Measure the distance between the wall and the last full tile. If this space is less than half a tile wide, move the chalkline over a distance equal to half a tile and snap a new line. Do the same with the other chalkline. Recheck for square.

Applying the adhesive. Always choose the correct type of adhesive for your particular situation. There are specific adhe-

sives for use on floors of concrete, wood or any other surface. The flooring dealer can help you select the correct adhesive. Then read all instructions very carefully — not all adhesives require the same application methods, and drying times often differ. In all cases, you will achieve the best results if the room temperature is no lower than 70°.

The trowel usually required for resilient tile application has notches that are about ¹/₃₂ deep and ³/₃₂ inch between centers. Do not apply too much adhesive. Press the trowel firmly enough against the floor so that adhesive only passes through the notched openings. Let no adhesive remain in the areas over which the trowel's teeth pass. Hold the trowel at a 45° angle for the best results. Too much adhesive will "bleed" through between the tiles. It will also form a soft coating under the tile, permitting heavy objects to dent the tile. On the other hand, too little adhesive will result in loose tiles and possible cracking.

Vinyl asbestos installation. Start spreading the adhesive near the wall in one of the quarters marked by the chalkline. Work out towards the crossed lines. Spread the adhesive close to the chalklines, but do not cover them. Make sure the coating of adhesive is uniform. Then allow the adhesive to set. In most instances this takes from 15 to 25 minutes, depending on temperature and humidity conditions. The adhesive should become tacky; none should transfer to your finger if you touch the adhesive. The open time of most adhesives for vinyl asbestos tile is quite long. Check your particular brand for specifics. You then will know how much working time you have before the adhesive becomes too hardened to hold the tiles.

Vinyl tile installation. Most adhesives for vinyl tile have a short open time. Unless your brand states otherwise, begin at the crossed working lines and apply no more than five or six square feet of adhesive at a time. Lay the tiles immediately.

Layout patterns. There are several layout patterns for floor installation of resilient tile. Your choice depends in part on the design of the tile and the amount of time required for the adhesive to dry. (This is called the "open time" of the adhesive.) Often, layout instructions for a chosen tile come with the tile. Some tile designs, particularly smooth-surface patterns, look best when the direction of the pattern is alternated in adjacent tiles. Others, such as those with embossed patterns, look better when they are laid in the same direction. Some tiles even come with arrows printed on the back, indicating the direction in which they are to be placed. No matter which arrangement you choose, do not slide the tiles into place, since this only causes the adhesive to ooze up between the tiles. Press the tiles into place, butting each tile tightly and neatly against the adjoining tile.

One-quarter layout. The pattern given below is probably the most common method utilized. For this method, start laying the tile in the first quarter section. Place the first tile into the corner created by the crossed working lines. Place the second tile next to it and a third tile above it. Then fill in the rest of the quarter in a stair-step pattern until you have laid all possible full-size tiles in that quarter. Repeat the process for the remaining three quarters.

One-half layout. If the room is fairly small — or if your adhesive has a long open time — you can fill in one-half of the floor space at a time. Again, begin by placing one tile in a corner created by the crossed working lines. (From now on this tile will be referred to as Tile 1.) Place a second tile (Tile 2) in the corner adjacent to Tile 1, next to it. Tile 3 then goes on the other side of Tile 1. You now have three tiles in a row. Place Tile 4 directly above Tile 1. This creates a pyramid shape. Continue the layout by filling in the pyramid sides, using a stair-step pattern.

Diagonal layout. An interesting variation of the layout pattern is to work diagonally. This is particularly effective when you use tiles of two contrasting colors. To establish the diagonal working lines, first create the same working lines as described before. Then on both lines, measure 3 feet from the center intersection and place

marks there. Use a carpenter's level to draw in lines at marks, crossing the working lines at right angles. Do the same for the other two working lines, creating

small boxes in each quarter. Using a long steel ruler or tape, connect the diagonal corners of the boxes. Carry these lines to the walls of the rooms. (If the room is

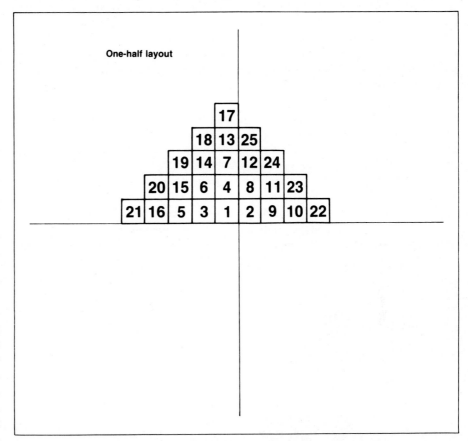

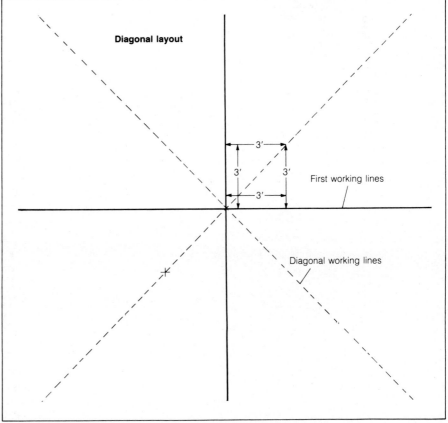

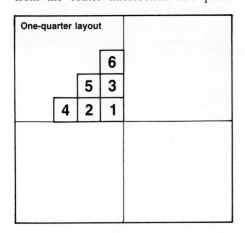

rectangular rather than square, these diagonal lines will not run to the corners of the room.)

The diagonal lines you have just drawn are the new working lines. Ignore the originals. Place Tile 1 in a corner created by the crossed diagonal lines. Tile 2 and 3 will be of the contrasting color of tile. Lay Tile 2 beside Tile 1 and Tile 3 above Tile 2. The layout will run according to a quarter-room plan. Alternate colors for every other row.

Feature strips and designs. As with ceramic installations, resilient tile floors can incorporate designs and patterns. Such designs require careful planning. (See Chapter 2 for instructions on planning a design.) One way to build a pattern into the installation is to utilize feature strips. These strips come in multiples of the tile size. They are laid in place according to the design created prior to beginning the layout. If you do include feature strips, keep two things in mind. First, fill in all the tiles that will border the strip. Do not lay the strip so that part of it extends beyond the rows of tile you have laid. This assures that the strip will be straight and that there will be no narrow spaces between a row of tiles laid later and the strip placed earlier. Put the strip down exactly as if it were a tile — do not slide it into position, but place it firmly against the tiles already laid and then lower it into the adhesive.

Removing excess adhesive. Whenever you finish the portion of the room on which you are working, whether a quarter or a half, go over the tiles and remove any adhesive on their surfaces before it hardens. In most cases, use a damp cloth or very fine steel wool. Check the method specified by the tile manufacturer.

Cutting resilient tile. Once all the full-size tiles are in place, cut the tiles that fall between the finished floor and the wall. Determine cutting lines according to the instructions in Chapter 2. Then heat the tile slightly with a lamp and cut it with a pair of utility scissors or a sharp knife. Be careful that you don't scorch or burn the tiles. They should be warm enough to be flexible, but they should not be so hot that you cannot handle them.

If the tiles must fit around door jambs, pipes or other obstructions, first make a pattern from a piece of heavy paper. Use

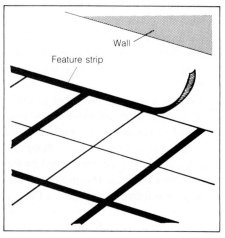

Install feature strips in the same way as tiles. Place the edge of the strip firmly against the laid tile; lower into the adhesive.

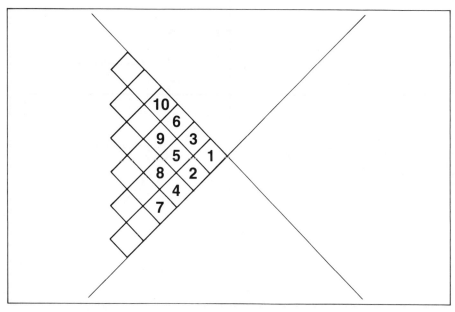

Here feature strips combine with vinyl composition tile to create a design in the tile expanse. The large blocks contain 4 tiles each.

Make a paper pattern to fit around pipes and obstructions. Trace onto the tile.

A contour gauge provides an accurate copy of the profile of a molding or other structure.

The rods in the gauge adjust to the shape being copied. Draw the outline onto a tile.

Setting tiles with a rolling pin requires much effort. You can rent a special roller.

this to trace the outline onto the tile and then cut the opening. If a tile must be slipped over a pipe or other object, use a single-blade razor (the kind that comes in a holder) to cut a slit in from one edge of the tile. A razor cut is the least easy to see. Then cut to fit the opening.

Fitting tile around door jambs need not be difficult, if you take your time. The simplest method is to use a special — and inexpensive — device called a contour gauge. Approximately five inches long, this device consists of two sturdy metal plates, one on top of the other. Clamped between the plates are more than a hundred metal rods, each of which is no more than $1/32$ inch in diameter. The rods slide between the plates. As a result, when pressed against a door molding, the rods take on the outline of the molding. To use, press the gauge against the molding; then place the gauge on a tile, trace the outline and cut the tile. Do not handle the gauge carelessly, however, because the rods can slip free of the plates, and they are difficult to reinsert.

You also can use a pair of compasses. One leg follows the outline of the door

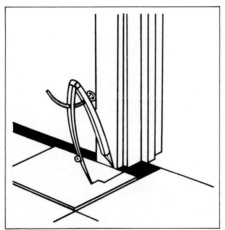

Run one leg of the compasses along the molding; the other draws the outline on a tile.

Finish off a new resilient floor with vinyl wall base, available in a number of colors.

jamb; the other draws in the outline on the tile.

The method that creates the neatest joint between tile and molding involves cutting a recess in the molding rather than cutting the tile. The door jamb is not a structural support. Use a carpenter's saw to remove about $1/8$ inch of the base of the frame at the floor level. Slide your border tile snugly against the wall. This eliminates the need to cut the tile around the door frame and hides ragged edges.

Rolling the tile. Depending on the type of tile and the manufacturer's directions, you may have to roll the floor to assure a tight bond and a smooth floor. Do this after you have laid all the tiles. The easiest method of rolling is with a 150-pound floor roller that can be rented or borrowed from the flooring dealer. Because of its size, the roller requires two people to operate it. (You can roll the floor using an ordinary household roller and plenty of pressure.) Be careful that as you use the roller you don't push the tiles or cause them to slide out of position. Before you begin, clean all adhesive from all tiles. Otherwise you will merely spread adhesive over more of the tile faces. Clean the tiles again once you have finished.

Once the floor has been rolled, reinstall the baseboard or shoe molding. However, you may decide to replace it with vinyl wall base molding to match the floor tiles.

Vinyl wall base. This molding completely seals the joint where the floor meets the wall. The base eliminates dirt accumulation in the joint and provides a smooth, tough surface that never needs paint, cannot chip and cleans quite easily. Both straight strips and preformed inside and outside corners are available.

To use vinyl wall base, remove all old molding at the base of the walls at the time you prepare your underfloor for the tile installation. The wall surface must be dry and free from oil, grease, loose paint, or other foreign matter. The wall surface must also be continuous all the way down to the floor. If warping has caused gaps in the floor joint, do not use the wall base to correct the problem. Do not install vinyl molding on outside walls that might be in contact with the earth (such as basement walls). The moisture present there will loosen the adhesive and the molding will come off. Do not install over vinyl covered walls or over paint less than two weeks old.

The first step in application is to apply the proper adhesive to the ribbed back of the wall base, using the same notched trowel as for the floor adhesive. Leave

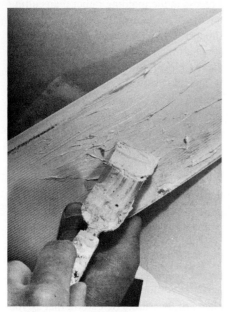

To install wall base, apply the adhesive to its ribbed back with a notched trowel.

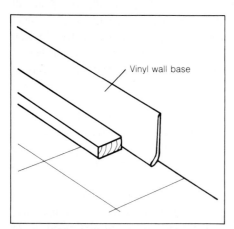

After installing, roll the base with a steel hand roller or glass jar. Then press toe of the base firmly against the wall with a 1x2.

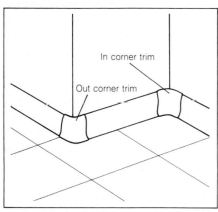

To provide a smooth and continuous base line around the room, install preformed inside and outside corners to finish off the job.

about ¼ inch bare along the top edge of the base so that the adhesive will not ooze above the base. Immediately press the wall base firmly against the wall. The toe must fit tightly against the floor and the wall.

Roll the entire surface of the base with a steel hand roller. You may instead use any smooth, even, cylindrical object. Exert pressure so that the wall base will adhere

Because this basement was not part of the "living" area of the home, it collected things that families don't know where to store.

to the wall at all points. After rolling, press the toe of the base firmly against the wall using a straight piece of wood.

WALL APPLICATION

It is possible to apply resilient tile to a wall. Usually this is done to visually increase the size of a room — the tile is laid across the floor and up the wall. This installation then is finished off with a chair

New walls, folding doors and ceiling enclosed work and storage areas. Vinyl asbestos tile was laid with contrasting feature strips.

Some manufacturers, such as Azrock, recommend installing resilient tile on floors and other surfaces as well. Here the tile becomes a major decorating factor in a living room area.

rail to create a "wainscotting" look. Instructions appear below. However, most manufacturers do not recommend placing resilient on a wall. The material does not respond to heating and cooling as will the wall surface. As a result, the tiles may break away from the adhesive and pop off the wall. On the other hand, some homeowners have installed resilient tile on walls, and they have had no complaints or problems with the tile. So, whether or not you attempt this depends upon how much you want the installation. There are no guarantees.

Preparing the Surface

Wall tile installation calls for correct preparation of the wall surface. Preparation basically is the same as for floors. First, remove any wall molding, such as base or chair rail. Do not lift off the molding around windows or doors. Remove all receptacle or light switch covers. If the wall is a new wall covered with gypsumboard, it must first be primed with the primer recommended by the tile manufacturer. A wallpapered surface should also be primed — if all the old wallpaper is securely fastened to the wall and has no loose or sagging areas. If there are loose spots, steam the paper from the wall before priming the surface and applying the tiles. Tile can be installed over panelling, once the surface is lightly sanded to remove the finish and provide a gripping surface to which the adhesive can adhere. Apply a light priming coat first, so the wood will not soak up the adhesive moisture too quickly. Patch and fill all holes or irregularities with the correct filling material, as suggested by the tile or adhesive manufacturers.

Layout

Working lines. To create right-angle centered (or diagonal) working lines, use a level to find the lowest spot on the floor. At this point, place a mark about ¼ inch below the top edge of the area from which the wall base molding has been removed. Then again using the level, draw in a level line at this point. Taking this line as a starting point, measure up the height of four or five tiles and draw in the horizontal working line. Now snap a chalkline at the working line. Measure from corner to corner on this line and find the center point for a vertical line. Drop a plumb bob from the ceiling until it crosses the center point marked on the horizontal line; then snap

Quite often the same resilient tile that is installed on a floor can also be used on the walls. In this room, tile was placed above wood shelves to create the unusual wall decor.

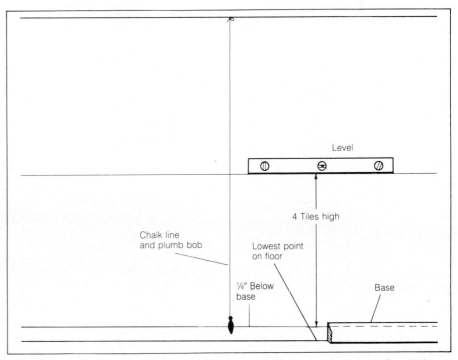

Locate the center of the wall and snap a chalkline to create the vertical working line. Find the lowest point of the floor and measure 4 tiles up from there. Use a carpenter's square to be sure the working lines cross at right angles.

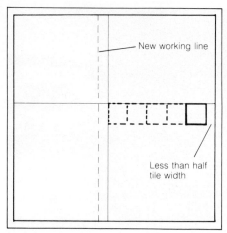

Shift the vertical working line the width of half a tile to avoid cutting very narrow tiles. Have even widths at each corner.

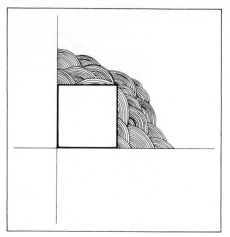

Adhesive for wall installation has a very short open time, so apply very little at a time. Do not slide the tiles into place.

the vertical chalkline. An alternative method utilizes a carpenter's square instead of a plumb bob. Place a tile at the intersection (or, a carpenter's square) to ensure that lines are at right angles to each other.

Avoid having narrow tiles at both corners of the room. To discover how the tiles will end up, use a tile to measure from the centerline to one corner. If the last tile width comes out less than half a tile, then move the center working line over by the width of half a tile.

Installation of the tiles follows the same steps as for floor installation, but you should use only the adhesive specified by the manufacturer for wall installation. Again, start in one corner of a quarter section of the wall marked by the working lines. Spread only a little adhesive at a time and press the tiles firmly in place. Follow directions for set-up time required for the adhesive before placing the tiles. If installed too soon, the weight of the tiles can cause them to sag. The result will be an uneven appearance.

USING SELF-STICK TILES
Some resilient tiles come with an adhesive already on their backs. A protective paper covers the adhesive. Most self-sticking tiles can be installed on sound, clean subfloors of concrete, above or below grade, or over wood, terrazzo or existing floors of tightly bonded, smooth surface linoleum or resilient tile. Do not apply self-sticking tiles to wall surfaces. Instead, use ordinary dry-backed tiles.

Although these tiles are self-sticking and quick to install, do not omit the preliminary steps. Prepare the floor surface very carefully, just as for dry-backed tiles. Straight and plumb working lines guarantee a good-looking, neat installation. Once the lines are drawn, peel off the paper back on each tile and press the tile in place. Start at the center point of the room and make sure that the first tiles are absolutely flush with the chalklines. Do not slide the tile into position. Butt each tile square to the adjoining tile. The corners should meet exactly before you press the tile into position. The strong adhesive backing makes the tile extremely difficult to remove once pressure has been applied. Work on only one small portion of the room at a time. Cut and fit the border and cut tiles before removing the backing. Allow the floor to set for at least 24 hours before washing or waxing.

Lay self-stick tile in a quarter of the room at a time. Position; press into place.

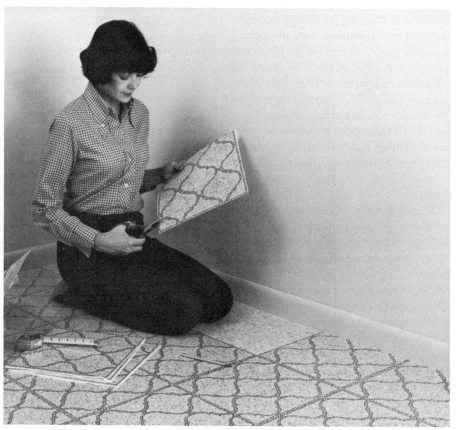

The border tiles for the perimeter of the room are easily cut to size with a pair of ordinary household shears. Do not remove the paper backing before you cut the tiles.

INSTALLING RESILIENT TILE OUTDOORS

Some resilient tile may be utilized outdoors on concrete slabs for patios. Check with your local floor tile dealer as to which tiles should be selected for use in outdoor situations. Plan the layout as you would for a conventional tile floor installation, carefully setting up the working lines.

The concrete slab must be firm and even. Fill and smooth all expansion joints and cracks with an appropriate patching material. (See Chapter 2 for subfloor repair.) The concrete must be free of paint, oil, grease or dirt.

In most cases the adhesive recommended for outdoor installation is an epoxy, spread with a finely notched trowel. This type of adhesive creates a very strong bond. The chemical reaction that takes place in epoxy is accelerated by high temperatures and retarded by low temperatures. Thus, it is extremely important that the installation be done when the temperature is between 70 and 80 degrees. If the concrete is exposed to direct sunlight at the time of the installation, the sunlight can establish a temperature in excess of 175 degrees. Shade all sunny areas until the installation is completed. The heat of the direct sun will not be detrimental once the tile is in place and has been well rolled.

When spreading the adhesive, bear down hard on the trowel so that only the adhesive flowing through the notches remains on the surface rather than covering the entire back. Do not place tiles in adhesive too soon. Allow 30 minutes time for the adhesive to partially set before laying the tile. This prevents the tile from slipping and the adhesive from oozing through the joints. Cover fresh adhesive with tile within 1½ hours. Each tile should be laid snugly against the adjacent tile or be cut to fit a vertical surface. Be sure to roll thoroughly or press each tile firmly in place — the rolling flattens out the adhesive and assures a good bond between the tile and the slab.

Cut border tiles as the job progresses to prevent tile movement after the early tiles have been set. If at all possible, stay off the newly laid tile for at least 12 to 14 hours so the adhesive will set and hold the tile firmly. If the tiled area must be walked on, place plywood or boards on the surface to distribute the weight. The finished installation may be washed 48 hours after the installation has been completed.

Be certain your tile is appropriate for an outdoor installation. Prepare the surface; then use a finely notched trowel to spread a special epoxy adhesive.

Some home plans include "bathing relaxation centers." Such a room often features a sunken or raised tub and sliding doors leading to a fenced patio. To unify bathing area and patio, the same flooring material covers both. Resilient tile is one option for covering these surfaces.

WOOD TILE

Before the creation of wood tile, parquet floors were laid piece by piece. Now you can purchase tiles in which simple or intricate designs are already arranged. The tiles are fastened in place by one of three methods: they are nailed down, glued with adhesive or held in place by a self-stick backing. The edges are formed in two ways, either flat or tongue-in-groove. The flat-edged tiles butt together; tongue-and-groove tiles fit together. However, despite these differences, the major consideration when you install a wood tile floor is the design of the tiles themselves. The other considerations are minor.

Stone

Haddon Hall

Fountainebleau

Jeffersonian

Canterbury

Finger Block

Herringbone

Parallel Finger Block

Louisville

Wood parquet tiles come in a range of styles, from formal to very informal. The designs are created by bonding pieces of wood together.

FLOOR INSTALLATION

Wood tile is most commonly used to create parquet floors. A professional-looking, long-lasting floor depends upon several general principles. Do not use solid wood products below grade, or in damp, humid locations. The humidity will warp the tiles, and they will ultimately pop off the floor. Laminated wood tiles, however, do not respond in the same way as solid tiles and are suitable coverings in damp settings.

Read all manufacturer's instructions. Follow the recommendations for adhesive

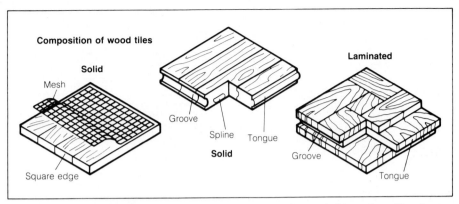

Solid wood tiles are made of blocks of one thickness of wood that are held together with splines or glue. Laminated tiles consist of several layers of hardwood glued together.

Simple wood tiles enhance the renovation of this old Victorian home. They blend with the other textures but do not detract from the overall decor.

A complex pattern such as this one is simple to install with preformed wood tiles. Directions for installing the pattern are on page 110.

and trowel type, for both squares and planks. Nail all solid wood planks that are ¾ inch wide. When gluing planks that are less than ¾ inch thick, use the proper adhesive and roll the planks within three hours after installation. Finally, dry lay the tiles before you fasten them down, in order to be sure that the appearance of the finished floor is to your satisfaction. Often, in the case of more complex tiles, the manufacturer will have layout suggestions — follow these carefully.

Tools

You need these tools for laying wood parquet tile: tape measure, broom, chalkline and chalk, hammer, coping or sabre saw, handsaw, brush and the proper adhesive trowel.

Surface Preparation

As with all other tiles, the first step in a wood tile installation is to prepare the surface. Check with your tile dealer as to which types of tile should be used on your room's existing floor surface. Most wood tile can be installed over subfloors of concrete, dressed and matched wood, or plywood. Under certain conditions, subfloors of resilient tile are suitable. Before you prepare the floor, remove base and shoe molding and doorway thresholds.

Concrete subfloor. A concrete subfloor should be sound, level, dry, smooth and clean. Remove grease or oil stains with a garage floor cleaner. Level high spots with a carborundum stone or a terrazzo grinder (a special drill head for an electric drill). Fill low areas to the general subfloor level with a good-quality latex concrete patching mix prepared according to the directions on the container.

Damp-proofing. In some cases, a concrete floor may require a membrane of 4 or 6 mil polyethylene to create a water vapor barrier. This barrier prevents moisture from seeping upward through the concrete and ruining the wood tile. (Such seepage is called capillary moisture.) One would be necessary if the concrete is in contact with the ground, especially if any moisture seepage is suspected. A membrane is also required before installing tile over "green concrete" — concrete that has had insufficient time to dry — or over an old concrete floor that probably did not have the barrier installed during construction. A vapor barrier is not required if you are laying tile over wood or plywood sub-

Renovation in this home created a balcony library above a general sitting room. A parquet floor blends as well in this modern room as in the Victorian setting pictured earlier.

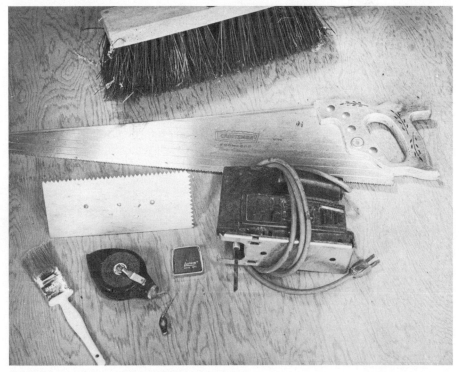

You will need these tools to install a wood tile floor: tape measure, broom, chalkline and chalk, hammer, coping or sabre saw, handsaw, brush and adhesive trowel.

floors, or over a concrete subfloor above ground level.

To install the vapor barrier, first sweep the subfloor. Then mop or squeegee a primer over the floor. The tile manufacturer will probably suggest an organic adhesive. Allow 30 minutes for the primer to dry thoroughly; then use the flat side of the tiling trowel to apply a skim coating of adhesive. Allow the skim coat to become tacky, as required by the manufacturer's directions.

Starting at the entrance to the room, roll a 3- or 4-foot wide polyethylene film to the opposite wall. Cut the strip off at the wall edge, and lay another alongside the first. The sheets should overlap by 4 inches. Cover the entire floor in this manner. You need apply only one layer of the film, and occasional blisters or bubbles will not impair the film's effectiveness. The tiles will be installed directly over the film.

Radiant-heated subfloor. Wood tile can be installed over a radiant-heated subfloor with adhesive, if the subfloor surface temperature does not exceed 85 degrees F. Turn the system off and allow the slab to cool before installing the floor. The system can be turned on immediately after installation.

Wood or plywood. On an existing floor of ⅝ inch tongue-and-groove or ¾ inch plywood, nail the edges and centers of each board with annular-grooved underlayment nails spaced 6 inches apart. Renail old wood subfloors or old surface flooring where necessary. Fasten down loose or squeaky boards with rosin-coated box nails. Rough sand to level any raised areas and board edges.

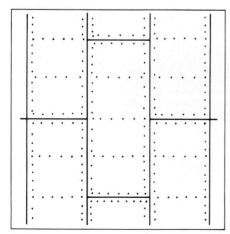

Before applying tile to an existing wooden subfloor, the surface must be solid and sound. If necessary, install a new plywood underlayment. Stagger the sheet joints.

The underlayment or the subfloor under a glued installation of parquet wood tiles must be ¾ inch thick. A ¾ inch plank floor can be nailed over a floor only if the plywood is at least ½ inch thick. The floor under a ⅜ inch plank installation must be at least ¾ inch thick — and the planks must be nailed, rather than glued.

Resilient tile. Some parquet tiles can be installed directly over old asphalt or vinyl asbestos tile, if the old tiles have not crumbled, come loose or otherwise lapsed into poor condition. The tiles must be firmly bonded. If not, remove all tile down to the subfloor level and scrape the subfloor to remove all traces of old adhesive. If the old resilient tiles are well-bonded, remove old wax by cleaning them with water and a good quality household scouring powder. Allow ample drying time afterward.

Border Designs

Because of the various designs and grains in wood tiles, and the availability of squares and plank styles, a wood tile installation can have built-in borders and design patterns. Investigate the variety of styles available before you begin. Plan ahead carefully. If you include planks in a border section, complete the section of small blocks before you lay the plank. In that way the edge of the plank will be correctly aligned.

Installation Techniques

Butt-edged wood blocks. In many cases, these blocks are made up of several thin wood strips that are edge-glued and laminated together. Because they will expand and contract, this type of block should never be laid with all strips lined up in the same direction from one wall to the other. This layout could cause buckling. Instead turn adjoining blocks at right angles to each other, creating a "checkerboard" look with the grain of wood. Other than that one limitation, the tiles can be laid in almost any pattern, including a diagonal one.

Tongue-and-groove wood blocks. These tiles are fitted together as they are laid. Lay one tile; then slide the groove of the next tile over the tongue in the first. The fit is usually fairly tight, so you may have to hammer the second one in place. In order to protect the tongue edge of the block you are placing, use a special piece of wood between the tile and the hammer.

Hardwood block flooring in various finishes usually comes tongue-and-grooved. Tongue-and-grooved tiles create a floor that is structurally stronger than a floor of flat-edged tiles.

To match the grain or create patterns, first lay the tiles without adhesive, in a pyramid pattern. Mark each as you take it up, for later reference. Then you can relay the design quickly.

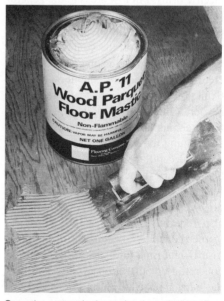

Once the pattern is determined, apply the adhesive with a notched trowel of the correct size.

Align the tongue in the groove and lower the tile into the adhesive.

Tap stubborn tiles into position for a tongue-and-groove lock. Then press tiles into the adhesive. Remove any excess adhesive that oozes out between the tiles as you go along.

The back of a set tile should be thoroughly covered with mastic in order for it to adhere properly.

Cut a special groove in the wood piece to allow for the tongue you want to protect. At this time you also will need to determine where cut tiles (if any) will fall.

Spreading adhesive. Using a notched trowel, spread the adhesive as recommended by the manufacturer. Apply the adhesive in the one quarter of the room that is created by the working lines. Do not cover the lines themselves.

You will have the best results when the adhesive is above 70 degrees F. If it is less than 70 degrees, warm the adhesive before applying, by storing it in a heated room. Trowel on the adhesive to the recommended thickness. Too little adhesive will result in a poor bond. Too much will result in bleeding between the parquet units. Remove a tile occasionally to be sure the adhesive completely covers the back of the tile.

Spread only the amount of adhesive that you can cover with tiles within 3 hours. After spreading the adhesive, let it sit for one hour in order to become tacky before you install the tiles.

Laying the blocks. Begin laying the tiles in a corner created by the crossed working lines. When positioning the tiles, put them lightly into place without sliding. Sliding will cause the adhesive to pile up

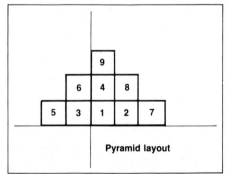

Lay the wood tiles in the standard pyramid style used for all floor tile installations.

Use a sabre or coping saw to cut tiles to fit between the wall and installed squares.

on the leading edge, creating poor-fitting joints. Place them so the tiles merely touch together — do not force them together.

As the installation proceeds, lay plywood or boards over the installed units to prevent foot traffic from sliding the blocks out of place.

Layout patterns. Wood tile is installed in a pyramid fashion, as are other tiles. See Chapters 2 and 5 for quarter room and half room methods; you can also choose a diagonal layout as discussed in Chapter 5.

Cutting tiles. Use a fine-toothed or metal-cutting blade in a sabre saw to trim solid squares at walls and other vertical obstructions. Allow ½ inch or more for expansion at these locations. Use base and shoe moldings to cover these voids. Nail moldings into the wall, not the floor. At door moldings, trim the tile or cut away the bottom of the molding. Trimming the tiles to fit irregular shapes requires either a paper pattern or a contour gauge. See Chapter 5 for a discussion of these methods.

Finishing the installation. When the floor has been completed, step on every joint line to ensure uniform seating into the adhesive. You may prefer instead to roll the floor with a 100 or 150 lb. roller, which can be rented. If there is any appreciable difference in elevation between the new floor and floors in adjoining rooms, install a special "reducing" nose strip at the juncture. Finally, clean all adhesive off the tools and flooring with mineral spirits.

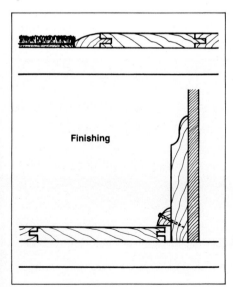

Cut tiles to allow ½ in. expansion. Install base molding to hide the open space. Nail the molding to the wall, not the tiles. Add a reducer strip to smooth the joint between the tiles and adjoining flooring.

Laying Octagonal Block

Most octagonal blocks are made of a square block to which pointed end pieces (called "pickets") are attached. The tiles are butted together, and the layout follows the standard half-room layout of resilient tiles. Placement of the first tile, however, is especially important in this installation.

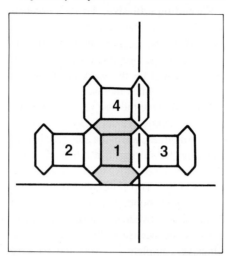

Begin in a corner created by the two crossed working lines, Line A and Line B. Place the tile so that the outside edge of one picket follows Line A, and the points of both pickets touch Line B. The side of a picket in Tile 2 fits up against one side of the square block of Tile 1. Tile 3 is similarly placed on the other side of Tile 1. Now position the side of the square block of Tile 4 against the top picket of Tile 1. This completes the pyramid base of the layout. Continue placing the blocks, fitting pickets and square sides together, until the floor has been filled in.

Installing Laminated Tiles

Laminated tile does not expand and contract as solid wood tile does. Consequently, a laminated wood tile floor does not require the ½ inch expansion space between the last course and the wall. Instead, trim the tiles so that they fit snugly and will not slip. If you wish, insert small shingle wedges between the tile and the wall. Another method that prevents the tiles from slipping is to nail them down. Use small finishing nails. Pound them in through the top of the tile; then lightly countersink the nails with a nailset. Fill the depressions with a putty stick.

Installing Self-stick Wood Parquet Tiles

Self-sticking wood parquet tiles are manufactured with an adhesive backing applied at the factory. No other adhesive is necessary. These tiles butt together for a quick and easy installation.

Surface preparation. Self-stick tile can be installed over any subfloor of concrete, dressed and matched wood, or plywood, and over old subfloors of well-bonded resilient tile. Self-stick tile should not be installed on below grade or radiant-heated concrete subfloors. The subfloor surface must be warmer than 60° F. The surface must be absolutely dust-free — mop and vacuum the surface thoroughly.

Laying the tiles. Establish working lines as before; then lay tiles, first peeling the protective paper off the back of the parquet to expose the sticky-foam surface. Place the tile in position at the corner of the crossed working lines. Do not apply pressure until the block is positioned properly.

Then press down in the center of each tile with your hand. Once a block is in place, it cannot be pulled up and used

To install self-stick wood tiles, peel away the paper that protects the adhesive backing.

Fit the edges together so they meet exactly; then lower the tile and press to secure.

again. If it has to be removed for any reason, such as poor alignment, the block should be discarded.

Then lay the corresponding blocks to make up the pyramid. To ensure a good fit with block No. 6 (page 109), align the bottom edge with the top edge of unit No. 3. Keeping the edges flush, ease the block down into position. Examine it carefully to make sure you have the starting blocks of the pyramid correctly in place. This is very important. At the edge of the floor, trim the squares to allow for ½ inch clearance at the wall joint and vertical obstructions.

Installing Wooden Planks with Adhesives

Wood planks, which come in various lengths and widths, usually are laid so that their lengths are parallel to the long walls in a room. In a square room the choice is optional. They are placed in the same way as are square blocks, but planks require only one working line. To ensure a straight installation, you must first find out if the floor is square.

Determining if the floor is square. Lay a carpenter's square in the corners of the room to find the most square of the four. Using a metal straight edge, extend a straight line from top of the leg which lies along the long wall. The line goes all the way across the room to the opposite wall. At each corner, measure the distance between the line and the wall. If the dimensions are equal, the room is square, and you will measure out from the wall to locate the working line. If the distances are not the same, you must measure out from the straight line to find the working line.

Laying the planks. Now determine the width of three course of wood planks, and snap a chalkline. Here, the total width is 15¾ inches. Spread adhesive from the working line to the closest parallel wall. Lay the three courses; then cut and fit planks as required to finish off the installation. As you work, fit the tongue-and-grooves of the planks together — both those on the sides and the ends. When this section is finished, roll the rows with a 150 lb. roller. Then apply the adhesive on the remainder of the room, lay and roll the planks.

Installing Wooden Planks with Nails

Establishing working lines. Snap a line along side the starting wall, at a dis-

tance of one plank plus ½ inch to allow for expansion. Secure the first row in place by face-nailing down through the top of the flooring. Then set nail heads lightly with a nail set. You can later fill in these holes, using a putty stick. Install the second row by sliding the grooves of the tiles in the second row over the tongue of the tiles in the first row. In most cases you will have to use a scrap of plank with the groove in it to tap the plank securely in place.

Blind-nailed installation. The tradi-

tional method for installation of wooden planks — especially those that are ⅜ inch thick or more — is to blind-nail them in place through the tongue. This can be done with a hammer, or a rented power-nailer especially designed for this purpose. The blind-nailing is done at a 45 degree angle through the tongue of the planks, back through the body of the tile into the floor. Place one at each end of the tongue and one at the center. When the groove of the next plank is slipped into

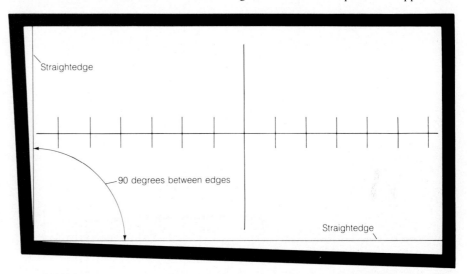

If a room is not square, your installation will appear uneven and unattractive. To remedy the situation, find the corner that is most square; draw a level working line from that corner to the adjacent corners. Continue around the room. Use a carpenter's square to create square corners. Then measure from the drawn lines to establish working lines.

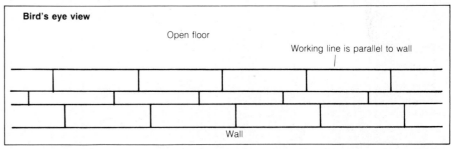

To install plank floors, draw in a working line that is three courses out from a long wall in the room. Then spread adhesive between the wall and the line.

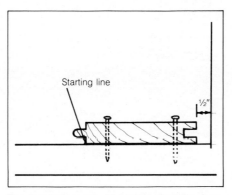

The beginning row of planks must be face-nailed. Set the nails below the plank surface with a nail set; later, fill the holes with wood putty and smooth.

To blind-nail solid wooden planks, use a rented power nailing machine. Or hammer nails part-way in and complete the process with a nail set to protect the tongue of the plank.

place, the nail will be completely hidden. If you use a powernailer, position it over the planks and strike the special driving head with a heavy hammer. This drives in a special fastener.

Finishing the floor. The last two strips must be face-nailed in place. Then add a reducer strip to make the new floor height fit that of the existing flooring in adjoining rooms. For exterior doors, remove the door and threshold and run the flooring under the threshold. Then cut off the door to suit. Reinstall the molding, nailing it into the wall, not the flooring.

Random placement. As you place the planks, do not have the joints in one course fall directly above those in the course below. Instead deliberately stagger the joints for an authentic-appearing hardwood floor installation.

WOOD TILE ON A WALL

Wood parquet tile also can be installed on a wall for an unusual and exciting room accent. Use butt-edged ⅜ inch parquet or planks. Install them with the adhesive suggested by the manufacturer, and apply them only to a solid, sound, clean and smooth surface, as suggested for other types of tiles. Incidentally, if you lay a pattern of plank tile diagonally rather than horizontally on a wall, the results are attractive and unusual.

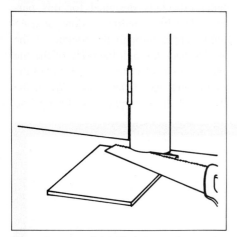

To create a smooth joint between a door casing and wood tile, shorten the door casing. Lay a tile or plank against the door casing, mark the height, and saw just above the mark.

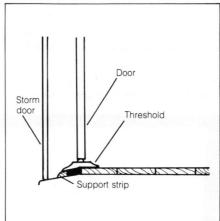

Remove an exterior door and its threshold. Lay flooring where the threshold originally was, and reinstall the threshold above the tile. Cut the door to fit and rehang.

To create a rustic setting in a den, cover a floor and wall with tile or plank. Set the design horizontally, vertically, or diagonally.

SMALL PROJECTS

One attractive and useful way to use wood parquet tiles is as coverings for tables or buffets. This is especially practical as a means of using up tiles left over from a flooring job. Although almost any style or pattern can be chosen, the prefinished smaller squares look best.

Small Table

Build a table according to the plans given here. (Alter the measurements of the top and the apron pieces as necessary so they are compatible with the size of the tile blocks you are using.) Then glue the tile in place on the top with the same adhesive that you used for the flooring installation. You also can refurbish an old tabletop by

applying wood tiles to the top. For a smooth finished edge, apply metal or wood facing strips around the top and the tile edges; fasten with small finishing nails.

Cube Table

For an unusual furniture piece, construct a cube table. The size of the cube will depend upon your wood tiles, so have the tiles on hand before you begin. (This particular cube is designed to handle tiles that are 13¼ inches square and ⅜ inch thick.) Nail the plywood box together with 10d nails. Then use the same adhesive as for floor installation to glue the wooden parquet blocks to the boxes. To hold the tiles in place while the adhesive dries, use

small brads. To finish the edge, apply brass or wooden molding strips, or stain the raw edges.

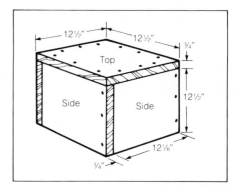

To cover a cube table, place the tiles in the adhesive and hold with brads until the adhesive dries. Remove any mesh backing before you begin, or it will show at the corners.

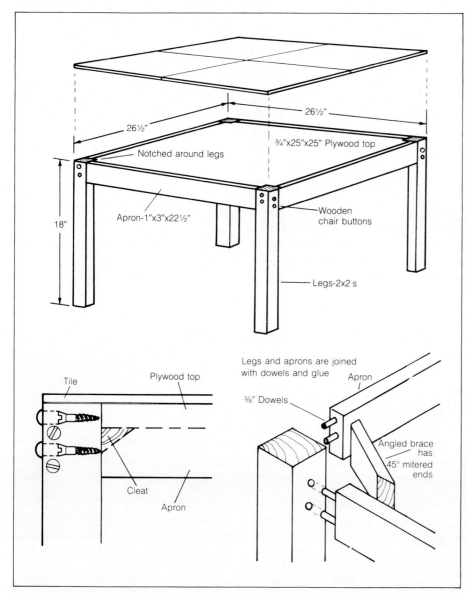

Cut apron and legs to length; sand. Cut top from ¾ in. plywood; notch each corner to fit 1½x1½ in. legs. Top fits flush inside aprons. To support top, install triangular wood cleats ¾ in. below upper inside edges of aprons. Join aprons and legs by one of the methods shown. See Chap. 7 for doweled joints. The screwed joint requires drilled holes that extend through the leg into the apron. Cover screw holes by gluing on chair buttons.

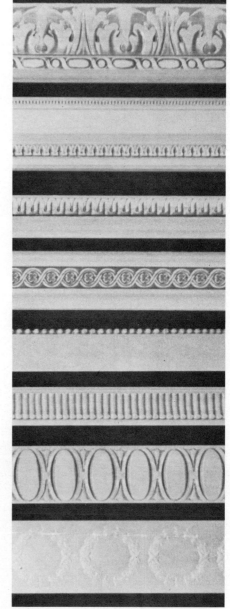

Wood molding at the wainscot level can attractively finish off a wood tile wall.

DESIGNER TILES

CARPET TILE

Carpet tile is easy to use, even for the beginner. It can be installed by any one of three methods. The first calls for double-faced tape around the edges of the tile.

The second method uses carpet adhesives, which are spread in place with a trowel. The third and easiest type of installation takes advantage of self-stick backing on the tiles.

Installation

Step one: room layout. For all three cases, the first step is to create working lines on the floor, just as for ceramic or resilient tile; divide the room into quar-

Because of its bulk, roll carpeting is difficult to install. Instead, use carpet tile for a quick, easy, wall-to-wall installation.

ters. Check that the working lines are at right angles (90°) to each other. Dry-lay carpet tiles along a line to determine how they come out at the walls. If there is less than half a tile width left between the last full tile and the wall, move the line over by half the width of a carpet tile and resnap. Then repeat the trial layout on the other working line. If necessary, adjust it in same manner.

Step two: tile at the doorway. Position a carpet tile against the doorway, and determine if the bottoms of the doors need to be raised. If so, mark the new level; then remove the door. You need not remove the molding base. However, if using carpet adhesive you may wish to remove the shoe molding. You can tack this back down over the carpet once the job has been completed. This gives a neater, more professional-appearing job.

Step three: placement with double-faced tape. Begin at a corner created by the crossed working lines. Lay a strip of double-faced tape all the way over to the wall; center tape on the working line. Lay the entire row of carpet tiles. Press the tiles in place so their top edges butt against

the working line. Do the same along the other working line, which crosses the first, so that you have outlined the quarter of the room you will fill first. Then work in the stair-step floor pattern discussed in Chapter 2. Place a square of tape in each corner of the individual tiles and press the tiles into place, one by one.

Step three: variation—using carpet adhesive. This gives a more secure surface than double-faced tape. Select the correct adhesive as suggested by your dealer and manufacturer. Spread adhesive over a section of one quarter of the room. Use a trowel, but do not attempt to spread more adhesive than you can comfortably cover before it sets up. Do not cover your working lines with the adhesive. Follow manufacturer's directions carefully.

Starting at one of the corners in the center of the room, position a row of carpet squares along one working line, making sure the edges of the tiles follow the working lines carefully. Then lay another row up against the other working line of the quarter and begin filling in the rest of the tiles. Position the tiles exactly and press them down firmly. Do not slide them

around on the adhesive or up against each other, or you will end up with adhesive on the tiles. This can become a real mess to clean up.

Position one end of each tile next to the previously laid tile, then hold the positioned end securely and let the rest of the tile fall into the adhesive. Press each tile securely in place.

Step four: cutting tiles to fit. Cut and fit tiles around the border of the room as you work, using heavy shears or a sharp knife and a wooden block as a cutting board. To cut the tiles to fit around obstacles, first make a paper pattern or use a contour gauge to determine the cutting line. Often, you can slit the tile and cut it to fit around a pipe. When the tile is adhered in place, the slit will not show. To finish off all edges at doorways, fasten down metal or vinyl door trim designed for carpet installations.

Variation: applying self-stick tiles. This carpet tile installation method utilizes self-sticking, foam-backed tiles. Peel the protective backing paper from the back of the tile and position the tile in place. Firmly press the entire surface of the tile with

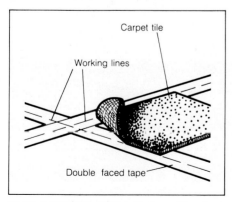

To find clearance needed for a door, measure from the floor by the height of one tile. Use a plane or a saw to shorten the door.

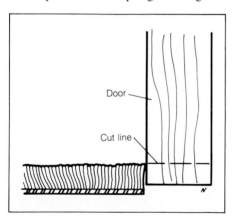

Install double-faced tape along working lines. Lay edges of the tile at the center of the tape. Then fill in the room quarter.

Once in position, self-stick tiles are difficult to remove.

One good use for carpet tile is to customize a van. Fasten ¼ in. plywood sheets to the metal wall struts and ½ in. plywood to the floor. Then install cabinets and other items.

The finished interior has bench seating that doubles as sleeping facilities. A plexiglass skylight supplements lighting. Some vans feature carpeted walls as well as floors.

the heel of your hand to seat the tiles securely. Align the tile exactly before placing it, since the tile will be very difficult to remove once it has adhered.

Projects

Carpeting a van. One unusual application of carpet tile, as shown here, is decoration of a van. The "van culture" is a growing American phenomenon and automotive boutiques exist to support customizing and outfitting of personalized vans. It is cheaper to do it yourself, however. You can dress up a van using self-stick carpet squares of thickly tufted pile. The self-sticking back eliminates use of messy adhesive. There also is little waste. Regardless of width and length of floor surface, surrounding walls or cut-outs, you buy only what you need. Using the roll materials would involve much more waste and expense.

The van shown here is the product of an industrious young fellow in Pennsylvania. The finished result is a cabin-on-wheels showplace fully equipped for weekend camping. His van not only has ample standard sleeping facilities, but the floor, which is padded with carpet squares, can provide extra space for sleeping bags, if necessary.

Laying the tile. Working lines for the van are plotted just as for any standard floor. Cut tiles should fall along the edges of the floor. You will have to trim the tiles to fit along moldings and other obstructions, such as the pedestal for the table shown here.

Lay working lines for the floor so that any cut tiles will fall opposite the side door opening and under tables or shelves. You may pad areas such as this map holder in the door.

Cat castles. A cat castle is simple to construct and the homemade model has several advantages. It provides a place for your pet to play or sleep and, because of the carpeted surface, it also serves as a scratching post, saving your furniture in the process.

Cutting the pieces. The first step is to cut all the pieces to size for the two boxes, which are of ½ inch plywood. Then using a sabre saw, cut the 6-inch diameter holes in the box sides. The bottom box has circular cutouts in three sides and in the top.

It also must have a 3½x3½ inch square hole through which the 4x4 support post extends. The top box has the same cutouts, but it also requires an additional one in the bottom, as well as an opening for the support post. After cutting the holes, smooth all cut edges with 80 grit sandpaper.

Assembly. Use 1-inch No. 6 ring shank nails and glue to assemble the boxes. After the glue on the boxes has dried, insert the post in the bottom box. Fasten it to the bottom of the bottom box with nails and

glue. Place the top box down over the post and fasten the two together, again with nails and glue. Cover the boxes and the post with carpet tile cut to fit. Set the tiles in the adhesive recommended by the carpet manufacturer. Do not use self-stick tile for this project — it will not hold up to the weight or strength of most cats.

Editor's note: the dimensions in the materials lists included here always refer to finished sizes.

Materials List

4 pcs., ½x17x17 inches ½ inch plywood
    (box tops and bottoms)
2 pcs., ½x17x17 inches ½ inch plywood
    (bottom box sides)
2 pcs., ½x17x18 inches ½ inch plywood
    (bottom box sides)
2 pcs., ½x12x18 inches ½ inch plywood
    (top box sides)
2 pcs., ½x12x17 inches (top box sides)
1 pc. 4x4x47 inches lumber (support post)
Carpet tiles, as needed to cover

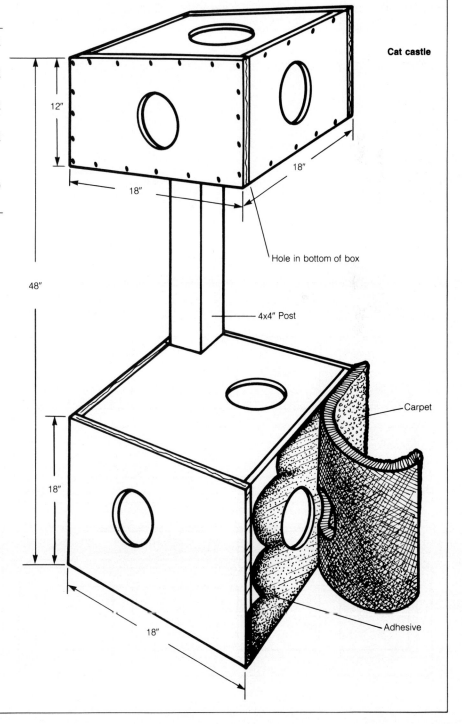

Cat castle

12″
18″
18″
Hole in bottom of box
4x4″ Post
48″
18″
18″
Carpet
Adhesive

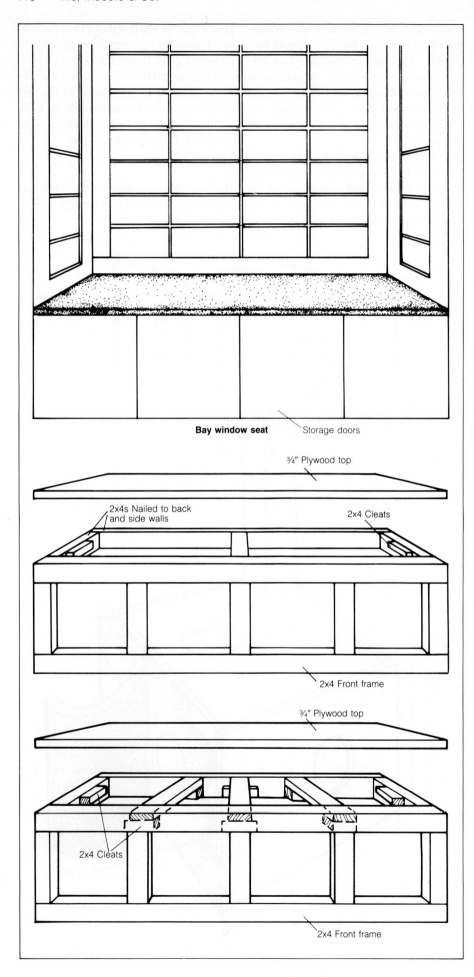

Bay window seat   Storage doors

¾" Plywood top

2x4s Nailed to back and side walls   2x4 Cleats

2x4 Front frame

¾" Plywood top

2x4 Cleats

2x4 Front frame

Bay window seat. Carpet tile, scraps of 2x4, and plywood can turn an open bay window space into an attractive and useful seating area. Use No. 8 ringshank nails throughout, since they will not work their way out over a period of time.

Structure. The first step is to make a frame of 2x4s to reach across the front of the bay area, as shown. The top edge of the frame should come up to 1 or 2 inches below the window sill. Nail a 2x4 across the back of the area, below the windows. This should be the same height as the front frame and should be nailed to the wall studs.

Now cut 2x4x4 cleats. These will support the cross braces and the seat platform. First, on each of the side walls install one cleat, 6 inches from the corners and flush with the top of the frame. Then nail three on the back strip and three to the front, directly across from each other. Because the cleats support cross braces for the top, the cleats should lie 1½ inches below the top edges of the back board and of the top of the frame. Then attach 2x4 braces laid flat to reach from front to back.

Cut the seat from a piece of ¾ inch plywood. The dimensions must be such that the piece fits in place over the framework and cleats, with the front projecting 1 to 1½ inches beyond the front of the frame. Fasten the seat in place.

The seat: storage variation. Although the easiest treatment for the front of the seat is to nail ½ inch plywood sheets across from wall to wall and then paint the front to match the room's existing decor (or cover it with carpet to match the carpeted seat), you can take advantage of the space below the seat by creating flush doors of ¾ inch plywood for access to the interior. Hinge the doors to the front with hidden hinges and touch latches to keep the doors nearly unnoticeable.

Covering with carpet tile. Consider the front edge of the top as your horizontal working line. The vertical working line is centered, running from the front to the back of the top. Over the top, the front edge and the 1 inch overhang, spread the adhesive recommended by the carpet manufacturer. Begin placement of the first tile underneath the top; roll it around the front and up onto the top. Fill in the tiles straight to the back; then work in a stairstep pattern across to the wall until half of the seat is covered. Fill in the other half.

If you wish, you can also cover the front of the seat with tiles. If you have doors, tile each one separately, following the method for a wall, using the floor as a horizontal working line. If you have not included doors, treat the entire front similar to a wall.

MIRROR TILE
Installation

Tools. You will need a straightedge, carpenter's square, plumb line, level, measuring tape, glass cutter, and double-faced mounting tape.

Estimating quantities needed. Before starting your tile job, draw up a diagram of the wall area to be covered, measuring the length and the width of the wall. Multiply the two numbers and divide the total by 144 to find how many 12x12 inch tiles you need. If there is a window or door space, deduct that square footage from the total. Add in about 10 percent of the square footage figure to allow for waste and breakage.

Preparing the wall surface. The wall should be clean, dry and smooth before you apply mirror tile. Remove any loose paint, old wax or dirt. Wallpapered surfaces must be firmly adhered to the wall and free of grease, blisters and flocking. Before placing mirror tiles on the wall, check the walls for plumb and square; walls often are not perfectly straight. Hang a plumb line from the ceiling to the floor in the center of the wall area to be covered. Draw a vertical line from the bottom to the top, or chalk the plumb line with builder's chalk and snap a chalkline for a working line. Then draw a horizontal line across the middle of the work area to be covered.

Use a carpenter's level to check level. Measure so your installation requires as few cut tiles as possible. If necessary, adjust the placement of the vertical working line to avoid cut tiles. Now you are ready to install your first tile. It is important that the first row be level, or the job will not look right.

Applying tile. Mirror tile traditionally is mounted in place with squares of double-faced tape, which comes in the box right along with the tiles. You can also purchase supplemental rolls. A special adhesive for mirror tile becomes available this spring; see the manufacturer's directions.

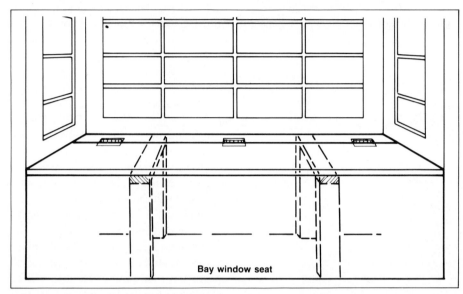

Bay window seat

An alternative design for the bench provides storage area access with a lift-top seat. The back top piece should be 6 to 8 in. wide; the forward piece finishes the top. Under both pieces, fasten braces that butt snugly for maximum support when the top is closed.

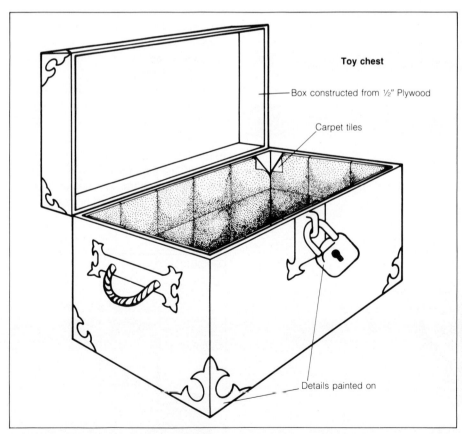

Toy chest

Box constructed from ½" Plywood

Carpet tiles

Details painted on

Indoor-outdoor carpet tile muffles noise and protects surfaces in a toybox. Using ½ in. plywood, 6d nails and glue, build a rectangular box. (Use the construction methods given for the cube table in Chapter 6.) When the glue dries, set a table saw for the desired height of the top; run the box through. Attach the top and bottom sections with outside hinges. Paint the outside a bright color; outline gold enamel details with black. Install the tile.

Place the tile face down on a smooth surface; affix double-faced tape in the corners.

Unpack the tiles and place them face down on a smooth surface. Peel off one face of the protective wax paper on the mounting tape. Apply the small cut squares of the mounting tape to each of the four corners; the side of the tape that still has the wax paper should be facing you. Peel off the second piece of wax paper on each of the pieces of tape to mount the tiles on the wall.

In one of the corners made by the intersection of the lines on the wall, place the first tile in position. Check that the tile is level and straight. Press the tile in firmly at each of the four corners to set the tile permanently in place. Working your way out from the center of the wall area, completely fill the first row.

Begin the second row directly beneath the first, placing tiles carefully next to each other and keeping them level. Proceed in this fashion until half of the wall has been filled in. Follow the same procedure for the other half of the wall.

Cutting mirror tile. The mirror tiles are cut with an ordinary glass cutter. The glass cutter must be kept sharp and the small cutting wheel should roll freely. Store the cutter in a jar of light oil between uses, if you own your own wheel. Always cut glass on a hard surface, with the painted side of tile facing down. Wear a pair of leather gloves for protection and goggles for eye protection. Snap the two pieces apart.

Installing mirror tile in problem areas. Often you will end up with a tile that must be placed where an obstacle, such as a light switch, is directly in the middle of a tile. Since you cannot cut a hole in the tile, you must cut it into four squares and fit them around the switch opening.

First, draw in a light outline of the place in which the full tile would fit if the switch opening were not there. The tile will be cut into four squares. As shown, Square A fits between the last full-size mirror tile and the opening for the switch. Measure the distance and mark it on a loose tile. Score a line the full length of a tile and snap the tile. Squares B and C fall above and below the switch opening. Measure the width of the opening, mark it on the loose tile, and score and snap. From this cut squares B and C. To cut Square B, measure the distance between the top of the switch opening and the top outline. Mark the height on the strip you just snapped and cut Square B. To cut Square C, measure from the switch opening to the lower outline. Mark and cut this from the same strip. Score and snap. The remaining long strip is Square D.

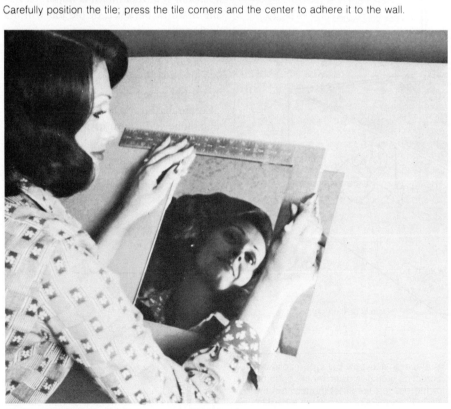

Carefully position the tile; press the tile corners and the center to adhere it to the wall.

When scoring, guide the glass cutter with a carpenter's square to ensure straight lines.

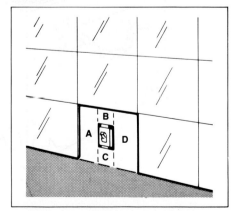

Cut three tile strips. Two fall on either side of the switch. One is cut into two pieces to fit above and below the opening.

When installing the switch plate covering, choose either a mirror plate or one that will not look out of place on the mirror wall — such as a brass or brushed silver cover. Wall receptacle cover plates also are available in these finishes.

To trim around doorways, particularly in areas where the tile would end up in a L-shape, you will have to cut the tile in two pieces for it to fit properly.

Projects

Use mirror tile on furniture surfaces and accessories. Another common use may be as a back-wall covering behind a portable bar or a china cabinet. The tile also can be adhered to sealed plywood boxes to create planters or decorator plant stands. Use beveled edge tiles to avoid the possibility of cuts.

Designs. One popular finishing touch

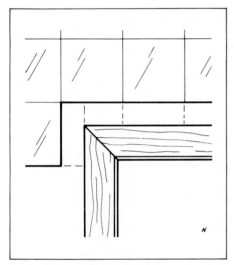

To fit tile around the upper corner of a door frame, cut it in three pieces. The first fits between the wall and the frame; the second fits above the frame; discard the third.

is to add small diamond-shaped decorative mirror pieces over each corner of the tiles. Other design arrangements include strips of tile alternated with cork or wood tiles, or with wood strips.

Mirror tile coffee table. A long, low coffee table with a mirror tile top adds sparkle to a living room. This table stands 12 inches high. The top measures 6x2 feet. No tiles need to be cut, since the table top is constructed in multiples of the size of the tile. Here, a protective acrylic sheet lies over the tiles. The sheet may not be necessary, since the tiles will not break under normal circumstances. However, the tabletop will be easier to clean with the acrylic sheet on it, especially if liquids spill on the top.

This array of planters displays several types of tile — mirror, metal, cork, and wood. Use only one type, or integrate two or three to create an unusual addition to your decor.

Materials List
6 pcs. lumber, 1½x1½x12 inches (legs)
2 pcs. lumber, ¾x1½x69 inches (long aprons)
3 pcs. lumber, ¾x1½x21 inches (short aprons and brace)
1 pc. plywood, ¾x26x74 inches (underlayment)
16 pcs. ⅜ inch dowel in 2-inch lengths
Brass edging or wood facing strips, 2½ inches x17 feet
12 mirror tiles (12x12 inches)
Acrylic sheet
White glue

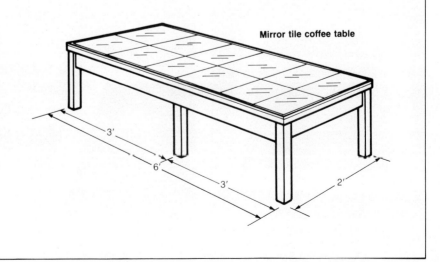

Mirror tile coffee table

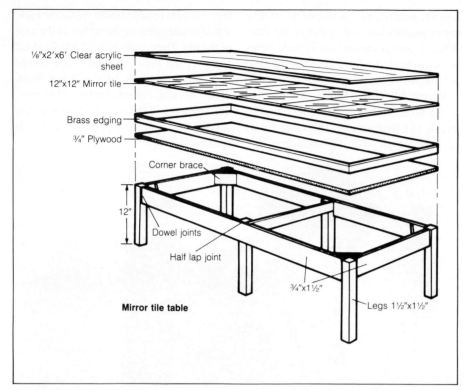

- ⅛"x2'x6' Clear acrylic sheet
- 12"x12" Mirror tile
- Brass edging
- ¾" Plywood
- Corner brace
- 12"
- Dowel joints
- Half lap joint
- ¾"x1½"
- Legs 1½"x1½"

Mirror tile table

Construction. Cut the legs to length from 1½x1½ inch turning blocks, and cut the aprons to the width of the table. Centered in each long apron, cut a half-lap joint to fit each of the 1½ inch legs. Then connect the end legs and the aprons using dowel joints made of 2-inch wooden dowel. Bore the holes, with a doweling jig, to the correct depth. Use white glue to coat

This exploded view shows the construction order for the mirror-tiled table. Note the location of the half-lap joints and corner braces. The top acrylic sheet is optional.

Before joining with glue and dowels, lay the pieces out in relation to one another.

Mark the ends of each adjoining piece, one half inch in from the edges of the lumber.

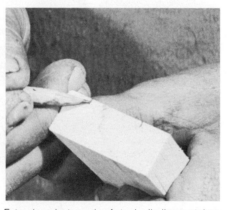

Extend marks to ends of stock. Jig line matches the marks to center the holes.

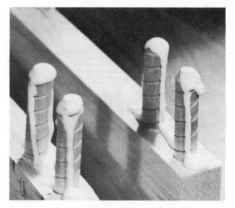

Gently rotate the dowels into one end of each board. Dribble glue onto the dowels.

Fit mating pieces loosely together. Do not hammer or force them together; if you do, the pieces are likely to end up out of square.

Join the pieces with a bar clamp, which may be purchased or rented. Apply pressure evenly and gradually to maintain square corners.

To make a bar clamp, nail 2 wood blocks to a 2x4 cut 12 in. longer than the frame. Fit wedges at the sides; tap alternately.

the insides of the holes as well as the leg and apron surfaces that will meet. All outside edges must be flush. Strengthen the joints with corner braces glued and screwed in place, as shown.

Because of the length of the table, center legs must be included. These are held in place with half-lap joints. Then fasten a crossbrace between the two center legs.

Assemble the table on a flat, smooth surface, and clamp the assembly so it is square. Check with a carpenter's square. Be sure that all the legs sit evenly on the surface and that the top is level. Let the table sit overnight.

While the glue dries, cut the ¾ inch plywood top piece and sand all its edges smooth. After the leg frame has set up and is secure, fasten the top in place. Place the top so it overhangs the framework one inch on all sides. Nail down with flathead wood screws. Countersink with a nailset;

fill with wood putty and sand level.

Finishing and tiling. Stain and finish the legs and frame to suit. Then adhere the mirror tiles to the plywood top, using the new, special mirror mastic as the tile adhesive. Add the acrylic sheet. To finish off the edges, tack on a thin brass band. If you prefer, use glue and finishing nails to attach a thin wooden molding instead of the brass band. Clamp the molding until the glue sets. The band or facing must be high enough above the table surface to hold the acrylic sheet in position.

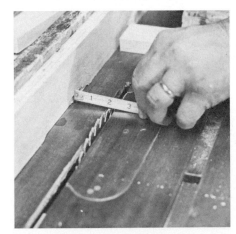

For a half-lap joint, first set the saw to the width of the cut to be made.

Set saw for overlap. With the board on end, run it through the blade with a push board.

Lay the legs side by side. The distance from the saw to the ends equals the overlap.

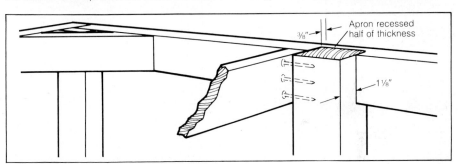

Fit the leg into the recess in the apron so that the outsides of the frame and the leg are flush. If the tops are not level, sand or plane the overlap.

Set the cut to equal half of the thickness of the board. Be sure that the cuts in the mating apron boards are of equal depth.

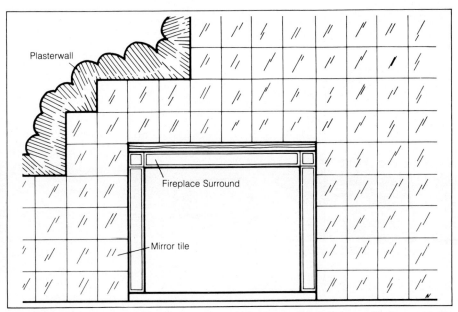

When installing tile and mounting tape for a mirror tile fireplace wall, begin the application next to the fireplace surround. Before placing tiles, seal any rough surface, such as brick, with plaster. Or, add a plywood underlayment, but follow code clearance requirements.

WALLPAPER TILE
Wall Preparation

Wallpaper tile can be installed on any smooth and sound surface. Soiled walls should be washed thoroughly with household detergent, preferably one with ammonia. Protruding nails should be set; fill holes with spackle and prime the wall once it is dry. Freshly painted walls should be permitted to dry at least 72 hours before the paper is applied. Surfaces with stains or paints that may bleed through should be sealed with shellac. Never apply squares to coarse or textured surfaces.

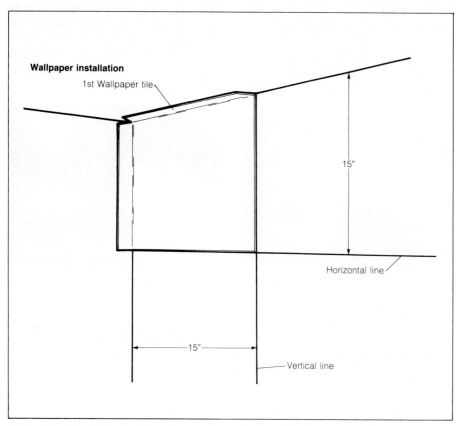

Measure from the ceiling and the wall corner for working lines. The distance should be 1 in. less than a tile's width. The wall lap will be covered; the ceiling lap will be trimmed.

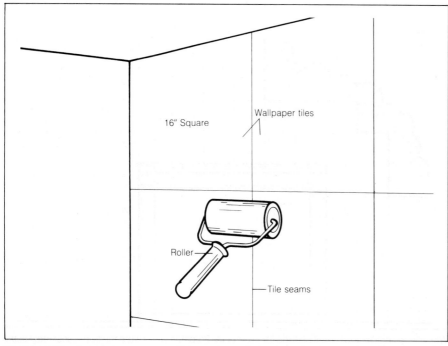

The edges of wallpaper squares sometimes curl, usually because the edges became too dry before the tiles were placed. Place squares quickly; roll seams with a small roller.

Consult the list below for your wall surface, and proceed accordingly.

Flat painted. Just prepare the wall as above and the wall will be ready.

Glossy paint. If a wall has a glossy covering — such as semi-gloss or gloss paint, shellac, or varnish — the walls should be sanded or dulled with a commercial dulling agent (available at paint stores). The roughened surface is necessary before the adhesive can bond.

Raw walls. For plasterboard, cured plaster, plywood, or wallboard walls, cover with a vinyl-latex primer, sealer or self-priming vinyl-latex paint. Allow at least 72 hours of drying time before applying the squares.

Old wallpaper. Wallpaper can be any one of many materials, from burlap to vinyl, and can come in different coatings and textures. As a result, it is advisable to remove all old wallpaper in order to achieve satisfactory adhesion. After the paper has been removed, thoroughly wash off all old paste. Then treat this surface the same as a raw wall.

Hard-surfaced panelboard. Either seal the wall with shellac, or check with your paint dealer for the primer sealer that will be the most effective.

Sizing. The above information covers the majority of wall surfaces. However, in some instances some of these surfaces also require sizing before installation. We recommend that you apply one wallpaper tile as a test. If the test wallpaper square remains securely in place after 24 hours, you may proceed as above without sizing.

Application Requirements

Tools. You will need these tools: a sponge (a nice flat one); a large, 17½x17½ inch load water pan, sink or tub (squares can be rolled loosely as long as all surfaces are soaked); plumb line; single-edged razor blades; a drop cloth or newspapers.

Working lines. A wallpaper tile installation requires two working lines. The vertical line is placed near a corner — preferably near the corner that is the least conspicuous in the room. Measure out from the corner a distance that is 1 inch less than the width of your tile pieces; snap a chalkline. A 16-inch tile will require a chalkline 15 inches from the corner. Be sure that the line is plumb. Then measure the distance between the line and the corner at several points to determine the plumbness of the corner. If there are positions that are more than 15 inches away, move the line over and snap again at 15 inches from the farthest point.

Place the horizontal line a distance from the ceiling equal to 1 inch less than the height of the wallpaper tile. Using a long metal straightedge and a carpenter's level, draw a level line across the wall. Measure this at several points, as you did the vertical line, and adjust as necessary to achieve a level line.

Patterns. The patterns on some wallpaper tiles have a definite horizontal or vertical direction to the design. Before you begin to lay the tiles, determine if your tile has this type of pattern. On striped tiles, the direction will be obvious. More complex designs, such as those with floral patterns, will be more difficult to evaluate. Select one element, such as a particular flower, and be certain that it always falls in the same position within the tile.

Before you begin, you must also discover whether your particular tiles are to be set side by side or staggered. If you are uncertain, dry lay some of the tiles on the floor. If the squares will have to be offset by one quarter or one half, the design requires a staggered layout.

Installation

Soaking the squares. Soak each square in room-temperature water for 45 to 60 seconds. Do not leave it in the water longer than one minute. Soaking the square for at least 45 seconds activates all of the adhesive and assures uniform expansion of each square. Remove the squares from the water and let the excess water drip off.

Placing the squares. The tiles are placed one vertical column at a time. Apply the first square in the box created by the crossed working lines, the wall and the ceiling. Fill in the space between the working line and the wall. The outside edge of the tile should overlap the corner by 1 inch. Align the square in its exact position and check for plumb and square with the carpenter's level before pressing it down. Smooth the wallpaper gently with the flat surface of the sponge in order to remove air bubbles. Place the next square as closely into position as possible, then slip it into exact alignment. The edges of the squares do not overlap, but should butt against each other.

Sponging and trimming. After positioning each square, hold it in place with the palm of one hand and gently sponge the square with the other hand. Sponge toward the previously applied squares to remove air bubbles and surface water. Do not stretch the paper; check that all vertical edges align.

To adjust for any irregularities of wall or ceiling joints, use a ruler to crease the paper at the joint line. Let the squares dry 15 to 20 minutes, and then trim them carefully with a razor.

Outlets and switches. When covering walls with light switches and outlets, turn off the electricity and remove the cover plate. Place a dry square over the outlet and cut a small hole over the opening. Then soak the square and apply, as above. Let the square dry 15 to 20 minutes. Trim with the razor until the cutout is slightly smaller than the cover plate. Replace the cover plate; it should just hide the edges of the cut.

Removing wallpaper tile. These tile are "strippable." Just peel off one corner of the square and pull. If adhered to a properly prepared wall, the squares will strip right off.

BEVELED GLASS TILE

Small beveled glass tiles fall more into the category of stained glass than of tile. The glass tiles cannot be adhered to a wall, because they are opaque and one can see through them to the adhesive-covered surface below. However, the beveled units can be leaded together, or they can be held in a wood frame to produce a formal, traditional door or room partition, or incorporated into a tabletop. The Whittemore-Durgin Company, for example, has beveled glass tiles in sizes from 2x2 to 6x9 and a number of shapes, so you can create either complex or simple designs. Before you proceed to complex projects, begin with a small project until you become familiar with the methods of handling the tiles.

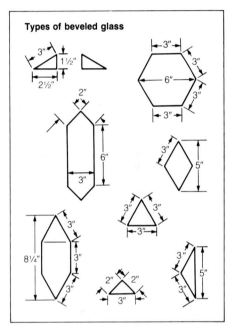

Types of beveled glass

The small tiles also come as triangles, diamonds, and hexagons. Consider using these unusual shapes in your layout plan.

Beveled glass tile usually comes in very large sheets that must be installed by a professional. However, small tiles are available in sizes from 2x2 to 6x9 inches.

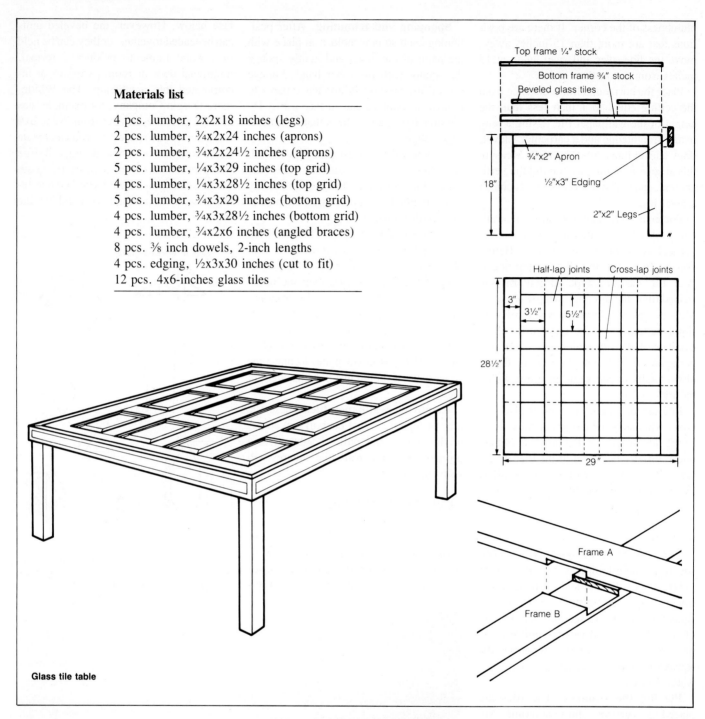

Materials list

4 pcs. lumber, 2x2x18 inches (legs)
2 pcs. lumber, ¾x2x24 inches (aprons)
2 pcs. lumber, ¾x2x24½ inches (aprons)
5 pcs. lumber, ¼x3x29 inches (top grid)
4 pcs. lumber, ¼x3x28½ inches (top grid)
5 pcs. lumber, ¾x3x29 inches (bottom grid)
4 pcs. lumber, ¾x3x28½ inches (bottom grid)
4 pcs. lumber, ¾x2x6 inches (angled braces)
8 pcs. ⅜ inch dowels, 2-inch lengths
4 pcs. edging, ½x3x30 inches (cut to fit)
12 pcs. 4x6-inches glass tiles

Top frame ¼" stock
Bottom frame ¾" stock
Beveled glass tiles
¾"x2" Apron
½"x3" Edging
18"
2"x2" Legs

Half-lap joints   Cross-lap joints
3"
3½"   5½"
28½"
29"

Frame A
Frame B

Glass tile table

Projects

Beveled glass decorator table. This unusual and elegant table utilizes beveled glass tiles as the focal point of its design. Two wood grids — one above and one below — support the tiles. Choose nearly any type of wood; however, a hardwood such as oak, ash or walnut would be the best choice. You also may create the frames from hardwood plywood, which comes in ¼ and ¾ inch thicknesses, and has a layer of oak on one or both sides of a plywood core. The only difficulty with using a plywood frame is attractively finishing the edges that will enclose the tiles. A hardwood frame would look better.

Cutting and assembling the table frame. Cut the four legs to size and sand all surfaces smooth. Then cut the side aprons and sand them as well. Make sure their ends are cut perfectly square so the table will sit firmly on the ground. Then glue and dowel the four aprons to the four legs. Use a doweling jig to bore the dowel holes. Clamp the pieces squarely together, using a carpenter's square to check for accuracy. Allow the glue to set up. Fasten the corner braces in each corner, using 1-inch No. 8 wood screws, again making sure the table frame is square.

Assembling the grids. Cut the bottom frame pieces to size and length and mark the locations of all cross- and half lap joints. Cut with a dado head in a radial arm saw, table saw or router. Glue the bottom pieces together, making sure all joints are square. Allow the glue to dry thoroughly; sand all the surfaces.

Fasten the bottom frame onto the top of the leg and apron, using glue and small 1-inch No. 8 flathead wood screws. Countersink the screws with a nailset, and fill with wood putty. When the putty dries, sand flush with the top surface of the frame.

First, draw the outlines of the rabbet joint onto the ends of the stock.

Set the saw to the depth required. Measure the distance from the blade to the fence.

Make the cut. Repeat the process for the second cut in order to complete the rabbet.

The lower grid supports the tiles on ½-inch-wide ledges. The upper grid secures the tiles with rabbet edges cut ⅛ inch high and ¼ inch deep. Cut the rabbets with a radial saw, table saw or router. The outside frame of the upper grid will be rabbeted only on its inner, lower edge. The interior gridwork pieces will be rabbeted on both lower edges, where they meet the beveled glass tiles.

After cutting the rabbet joints for the top grid, cut the cross-lap and half-lap joints. Dry fit the grid and set it over the bottom frame with the glass tiles in place to be sure the fit is correct. Draw in the position of each glass tile. Adjust as necessary; then fasten together the pieces of the grid, in the same manner as for the bottom.

Placing the tiles. Once the glue used in the grid has dried, center each of the glass tiles over the lower grid squares, following the marked outlines. Cover the inner face of the top frame with glue; position it over the tiles. Clamp the frame in place with C-clamps and gently set weights on the center to hold the frame in place until the glue has dried.

Adding the edging. Cover the edges of the table with a ½x3 inch edging that has 45 degree miter joints at all four corners. Hold the facing in place with glue; tap in 1 inch No. 8 flathead wood screws from the back of the frame aprons. Let dry.

"Stained glass" table top. To take full advantage of the variety of designs possible with beveled glass tiles, you can choose this alternative table construction and use one of the designs shown here.

Cut a sheet of acrylic to serve as an underlayment for the glass. Drill holes in the acrylic and fasten to the legs with screws and washers. Arrange the glass tiles in one of the patterns shown here, or your own design. Keep the tiles in place on the acrylic sheets by adding another acrylic sheet on top, or inserting very thin strips of wood molding, or adhering with special glass mastic. You can emphasize the wood joints as much or as little as you please. Finish by staining the table to suit.

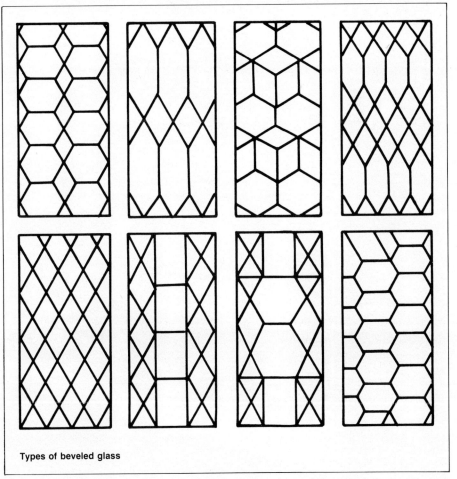

Types of beveled glass

Here are several optional designs that include beveled tiles of several sizes. Laid on an acrylic sheet and separated with thin wood molding, the tiles create an attractive table top.

METAL TILE

Metal tile is most often used on kitchen backsplashes, especially in the wall section behind the stove. The tiles are installed either with double-faced tape or adhesive. There is no need for finishing pieces because all four edges of the tiles are beveled. The tiles can be bent with a rented metal tile bender available from your tile dealer.

Mark the cutting line for a metal tile just as for ceramic. Cut it with a tin snips. To hide the cut edge, butt it against the wall.

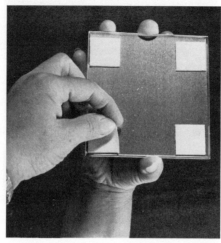

In most areas, tabs of double-faced tape hold metal tile securely in place. However, in very high heat areas, use adhesive instead.

Installation

The placement of metal tile with adhesive follows the same layout patterns and steps as for ceramic tile. The wall surface must be clean, firm, dry and flat. Working lines are required, as always. If you must cut the tiles, do so with a tin snips. Since you will create a sharp edge when you cut the tile, for safety's sake butt the cut edge up against a corner wall or other surface.

Double-faced tape method. To apply the tiles with double-faced tape, remove the backing on the tabs. Place the tabs in the corners of the tiles; press tiles onto any clean, flat, dry, firm surface. Cut the tiles with tin snips. To bend the tiles, use a metal tile bender to bend the tile and to fit it around corner.

Projects

Metal tile can fit in anywhere in your home. Since it comes in a variety of colors and finishes, you should take ad-

Metal tile is a useful covering for the area around a stove and oven. It is heat- and stain-resistant. These tiles are stainless steel.

vantage of that when you plan your installation. These tiles can be used to surface cubes, planter stands, work surfaces, as well as many of the other projects in the book offered for mirror, wood, or other types of tiles.

TIN TILE

Tin tile is made of stamped metal sheets. The three-dimensional design creates an uneven surface; in fact, the depth of the design can be as great as 2⅛ inches in some tiles. As a result, the tiles cannot be set in adhesive. This means that the existing surface requires no surface preparation other than cleaning, followed by installation of furring strips.

Installation

Tin tiles are nailed to furring strips that have been nailed to the wall studs. Thus, the surface beneath the tiles need not be repaired or sanded. The larger panels will look best on a ceiling or on a wall. The smaller tiles probably will work best if installed on a wall. Complementary moldings are available to finish off a wall at the ceiling or at the wainscot level.

The required thickness of the furring strips will vary according to the depth of the design stamped into your particular tile. Some come with a depth as great as 2⅛ inches. The furring strips usually are set 12 inches on center. Always check the furring strips for level as you install them, and shim as necessary. Once the furring strips are in place, nail up the tin tiles using 1-inch common nails spaced 6 inches apart. Use metal shears to cut tiles as needed. When the installation is completed, paint the surface with an oil-based paint or leave the tiles plain.

Projects

Tin tile fireplace front. Because they are fire-resistant, tin tiles can make an excellent fireplace front. If you combine the tiles with decorative wooden molding you can create a Victorian look of elegance and charm.

The tiles attach to wooden furring strips, which are anchored to the masonry fireplace face with masonry fasteners. Use wood that has been treated so that it is flame retardant, and keep the furring strips at least 12 inches away from the fireplace opening.

Mark the positions of the furring strips on the masonry. Then, using a ⅜ inch variable speed drill and a carbide-tipped masonry bit, bore holes for the masonry anchors. Install the plugs, bore holes in the furring strips and anchor the furring strips in place.

Then fasten the tin tiles in place with small flathead nails. Do not dent the tiles as you fasten them in place. Glue down decorative wooden molding over the edges of the tiles, to cover the nail heads. Then paint the surfaces.

MARBLE TILE

Marble tile comes in many sizes and colors. It is usually installed in the same manner as ceramic tile. Always use the adhesive suggested by the tile manufacturer.

One of marble tile's major disadvantages is that it is hard to cut. The job requires that you use a carbide grit blade in a hacksaw or tile nippers. The easiest method calls for power equipment and a cut-off masonry blade.

For project suggestions, see Chapters 3 and 4. Marble tile will substitute for many of the projects found there.

INTERIOR AND EXTERIOR SUGGESTED TILE USE

Type of Tile	Use
Carpet	Interior: walls, floors, dressing up vans, autos Exterior: patios, walkways, entryways and steps.
Wallpaper	Interior walls.
Cork	Interior walls.
Mirror	Walls, small projects. Use only in dry areas with tape installation.
Metal	Walls, Interior.
Tin	Interior walls, ceilings, furniture projects.

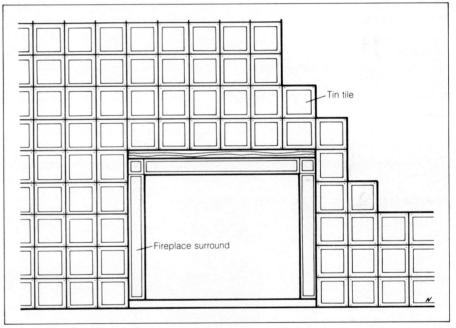

When tiling around a fireplace, be sure to leave a 12 in. space between the first row and the firebox opening, as codes require. This space is occupied by the fireplace surround.

TILE MAINTENANCE AND REPAIR

CERAMIC TILE

Ceramic tile's popularity with home-owners is partially due to its easy maintenance. In fact, Roman tiled floors over 1000 years old are still found in good condition, even after being buried underground or exposed to the elements.

Cleaning

Day-to-day cleaning of ceramic tile requires only water and a soft cloth. For stubborn stains, use a detergent. Do not use steel wool pads on ceramic tile because they may cause rust stains. Nor should you use harsh abrasives on ceramic tile. Naval jelly can be used to remove rust stains; organic stains such as coffee, mustard, or ink can be removed with chlorine bleach. Hardwater spots, such as in showers or tub enclosures can be cleaned away with a solution of half vinegar and half water.

Household bleach scrubbed in with a toothbrush helps keep grout clean and free of mildew. However, if your surface has colored grout, test first to make sure the bleach will not affect the coloring of the grout. A non-abrasive powdered cleanser or bathroom cleaning solution often is necessary for removing mildew, grease or other materials from grout lines. If this does not do the job, use a special liquid cleanser especially made for ceramic tile (this is available at tile centers).

STAIN REMOVAL GUIDE
For Cement Mortar And Silicone Rubber Grouts.

Type Of Stain	Stain Removal Agent
Grease and fats	Sal soda and water
Colored dyes	Household bleaches
Iodine	Ammonia
Mercurochrome	Liquid household bleach
Blood	Hydrogen peroxide or household bleach
Coffee, tea, food, fruit juices and lipstick.	Popular household cleaner in hot water followed by hydrogen peroxide or household bleach.

Caution: Ammonia and household bleaches should not be combined.

The application of special sealers to ceramic tile floors and walls adds extra protection. Contact your local tile dealer for sealers to use for your specific tile. Waxing and buffing tile floors will also help protect the floors and add even more beauty. Use only tile waxes suggested by your dealer; do not apply them in wet areas or they will create water stains.

Buffing

The simplest way to buff a ceramic tile floor — and any other tile floor, for that matter — is to rub it by hand or with a soft buffing pad on an ordinary floor mop. The latter is what is called a "weighted cloth," since you must bear down on the mop head to achieve a good shine. A method that is easier (and, some people believe, less satisfactory) is to use a rented floor buffer. In most cases, the buffer uses a soft lamb's wool polishing head, for the best results. Tile dealers carry several buffing compounds. Select the one that best suits the condition of your floor.

If grout lines become mildewed or especially grimy in areas that stay damp, such as tub enclosures, use a toothbrush dipped in household bleach to scrub the problem area.

Instructions come with the machine. The main thing to remember is to keep the buffer moving as you polish the floor to prevent any damage to the surface.

Loose Tiles

Loose wall tiles can be caused by several things, including the wrong adhesive or incorrect preparation of the wall surface before installation of the tile. The problem may also occur if standard rather than water-resistant gypsumboard was used in a bathroom. As a result, moisture may build up and break down the adhesive. Excessive vibration, such as that caused by the frequent slamming of doors, is another possible source of trouble. The first step is to correct the problem; otherwise, the tiles will loosen again after you replace them.

Only a few problem tiles. If only one or two tiles have become loose, the job is fairly simple. After locating the source of the trouble and correcting it, use a sharp knife, ice pick or other pointed object to dig out the grout around the tile. Lift out the tile. Carefully scrape the dried adhesive from both the wall and the back of the tile.

If you have some of the same adhesive originally used to set the tile, smear some of the adhesive over the void on the wall as well as on the back of the tile. Press the tile back in place. If you don't have the same adhesive, use bathtub caulking. Apply it to the back of the tile and press the tile into place. It must be flush with the surrounding tiles. Let it set thoroughly.

Regrout the joints surrounding the tile. Once the grout has set and cured (if the directions so specify), apply a silicone tile sealer.

An entire wall. If, on the other hand, you have an entire wall of loose tiles, you must start at the top and remove all the loose tiles. If the majority of them are loose, you probably are better off removing all of them. Prop the center tiles in place with sticks to keep the entire job from crashing down and causing some breakage. Use a wide chisel and hammer to tap the tiles away from the wall. Catch each tile as it comes off. Clean off dried adhesive from the tiles; repair the wall as needed with patching material (Chapter 2). In some cases it will be easier to add a new layer of backing rather than to patch a lot of holes. Follow repairs with a skim coating of adhesive or other primer as rec-

ommended by the tile manufacturer. Replace the tiles; let set; then regrout.

Replacing a Cracked Tile

It is difficult to remove a cracked tile because it is easy to damage surrounding, good tiles while you remove the cracked one. Scrape away the grout surrounding the tile; then, wearing safety glasses, use a metal chisel and hammer to break the tile into small pieces and to chip it out. Work from the center of the tile out toward the edges to avoid damaging any surrounding tiles. To remove the adhesive from the wall, use a flat wide chisel.

Butter the back of the new tile. Spread adhesive in the void in the wall and press in the new tile. If a ceramic accessory is broken, use a hammer to further break it off. Then use a chisel to remove it in the same manner as a tile.

Replacing Grout

Occasionally a tiled area will need to be regrouted. In this case, remove all old grouting using a sharp-pointed tool such as an awl — or create a tool out of a 10d nail and cardboard or a short piece of dowel.

Tools. This task requires a short piece of 1x3, 10d finishing nails, ceramic tile grout, whisk broom, vacuum cleaner, sponge, mixing container and a supply of clean, soft cloths.

Removing the old grout. To make a tool to dig the grout out of the joints, drive the 10d finishing nail through a piece of 1x3, near the end of the scrap. Scrape the grout from the joints. This takes lots of patience; the work goes very slowly. If the nail becomes bent, remove it and drive in another nail.

As you work, brush out the joints with

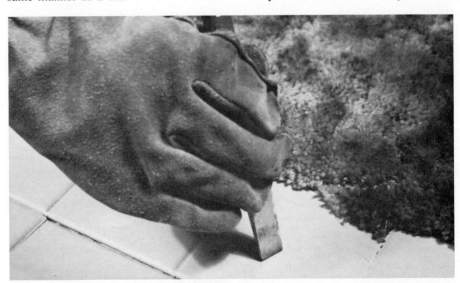

Wear safety glasses to remove a damaged tile that is still solidly adhered. Tap with a cold chisel and hammer to chip and break the tile loose. Work outward from the center.

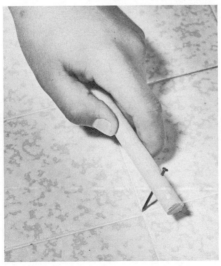

Use a nail jig to remove old tile grout. When one nail wears out, replace with another.

You also may use a sharp tool such as an awl or ice pick to remove grout from joints.

the whisk broom and vacuum away the debris. It is important to keep the work clean. If you do not, you will track the fine, powdered grout all over the house, and it is hard to remove.

Regrouting. When the joints are clear and you are satisfied with the job, mix up a small amount of grout. Spread this mixture over the tile, as discussed in Chapter 2.

RESILIENT TILE
Cleanup After Installation
Remove any spots of adhesive that may have been left on walls, woodwork or tile during the installation; follow the directions given on the adhesive label. In most instances this means removal with a damp cloth or, if the adhesive has dried, with fine steel wool. Use solvents only as recommended by the adhesive or tile manufacturer.

Do not wash or wax the floor for seven days after installation. This will give the tiles sufficient time to thoroughly bond to the subfloor. During this time, sweeping with a soft broom or cleaning with a damp cloth or mop is the only maintenance that should be carried out.

Light-Duty Cleaning
Modern vinyl asbestos or vinyl tiles, especially those with the nonwaxing feature, require very little maintenance. Normal maintenance usually involves nothing more than sweeping the floor daily to prevent loose dirt and grit from scratching the surface or becoming ''ground in.'' Wipe up spills immediately, before they become sticky or hard, to save the trouble of scraping off the substance later. If dirt accumulation is not handled by sweeping, mop with clear water. Use water sparingly; never flood the floor.

Thorough Cleaning
If you have given your floor daily care and kept it polished, a thorough cleaning two or three times a year will probably be all it needs, except in areas of heavy traffic and soiling, such as a kitchen or a hallway.

Cleaning the floor thoroughly not only eliminates dirt film and wax buildup, it also enables new wax to spread more evenly and smoothly, for a brighter shine. However, do not overclean — avoid cleaning too often or using too much water.

Avoid using strong soaps and scalding water. They can fade or discolor your floors or can make them hard and brittle. Cleaners containing caustics, harsh soaps and powders, or solvents such as gasoline, kerosene, naphtha, turpentine and benzene, as well as oil-base cleaners, can damage resilient tile floors and should not be used. Instead use a mild detergent or cleaner that contains no harmful solvents, harsh alkalis or abrasives. Try to use the cleaner recommended by the manufacturer of your floor tile.

Vacuum or sweep the floor just before you wash it. Dilute the cleaner following directions on the container and apply the solution with a clean mop or cloth. Allow the cleaner solution to remain on the floor for a few minutes to loosen ground-in dirt. Mop up the cleaning solution; then rinse the floor thoroughly with clear water to remove any residue. Dry with a clean, dry mop. Avoid flooding the floor with water.

Scuffs, Spots, Stains
To remove black scuff marks, rub them with a fine, No. 00 dry steel wool. For severe marks, apply a diluted solution of resilient tile cleaner to the steel wool; rub in, rinse and dry.

During washing, rub the hard-to-get-up dirt spots with No. 00 steel wool or a soft brush to help dissolve dirt film from the surface of the floor. Do not use steel wool on an embossed floor. Instead, rub the spot with a mild household cleaner on a damp cloth. Then rinse with clear water. Remove all stains and spots as quickly as possible to prevent permanent harm. The accompanying chart lists the more common stains and how to best remove them.

Waxing and Polishing
Depending on the type of tile and the methods recommended by your tile manufacturer, your tile floor may need some waxing in order to prolong the life and enhance the beauty of the floor. In other cases this job may be optional. In both situations, use only waxes that are easy to remove.

When to wax. A resilient tile floor is ready for waxing when it begins to look so dull from wet mopping and traffic that buffing does not restore its sheen. Apply the wax only after thoroughly cleaning the floor surface. If you choose, apply wax only to the traffic areas where the existing coating has become worn. Buff the floor first to help the fresh wax blend with the existing wax.

STAIN REMOVAL TECHNIQUES

Stain	Method for Removal
Alkali	1,3,9
Asphalt adhesive	1,4,7,8,9
Alcoholic beverages	1,3,9
Blood	1,7,8,9
Butter	4,5,9
Candle wax	4,7,8,9
Catsup	1,5,9 or 1,7,8,9
Cement (household)	4,7,8,9
Chewing gum	4,7,8,9
Cigarette burns	7,8,9
Cleansers	1,3,9 or 7,9
Coffee	1,3,9
Cosmetics	1,4,7,8,9
Detergents	1,3,9 or 7,9
Drain cleaners	1,3,9 or 7,9
Dry cleaning fluids	2,5,9
Dye	2,7,8,9
Eggs	1,3,9
Fats	1,4,7,8,9
Foodstuffs	1,4,7,8,9
Fruit juice	1,5,9
Furniture polish	1,4,7,8,9
Grass stains	7,8,9
Grease (all types)	1,4,7,8,9
Ice cream	1,5,9
Ink	2,5,9 or 2,7,8,9
Iodine	2,5,9 or 2,7,8,9
Lacquer	2,5,9 or 4,7,8,9
Medicine	2,6,9 or 2,7,8,9
Mercurochrome	2,6,9 or 2,7,8,9
Mildew	7,8,9
Milk	1,5,9
Mucilage	2,4,5,7,8,9
Mustard	1,5,9
Nail polish	2,5,9 or 4,7,8,9
Nail polish remover	2,5,9
Oil (all types)	1,5,9
Paint	2,5,9 or 4,7,8,9
Rubber heel marks	7,8,9
Rust stains	7,8,9 or 1
Shellac	7,8,9 or 6,9
Shoe polish	1,7,8,9
Soft drinks	1,3,9
Solvents	2,5,9
Strong soaps	1,3,9
Tar	1,4,7,8,9
Tea	1,3,9
Varnish	2,5,9 or 4,7,8,9

Key
(1) Remove or wipe up the spot or stain.
(2) If just spilled, blot the substance immediately, but do not rub. Let dry.
(3) Wash with a cloth that has been dampened.
(4) If the substance has dried, use a putty knife to remove it.
(5) Wash the area with a cloth dampened with liquid cleaner; rinse.
(6) Lightly rub, using a cloth to which alcohol has been applied; rinse.
(7) Dip No. 00 steel wool in liquid cleaner; rub; rinse.
(8) If the previous step is not sufficient, dust the area with a mild household cleanser. Rub with No. 00 steel wool dipped in liquid cleaner. Rinse well.
(9) Polish, once the floor has dried thoroughly.

What wax to use. Choose a wax product specified by your floor tile manufacturer, and one that can be removed without great effort. Hard-to-remove finishes soon form a thick, unsightly coating that can damage the floor. Do not use paste or liquid waxes that contain solvents such as kerosene, turpentine or naphtha.

How to wax. Put the wax in a shallow container. To prevent wax buildup, dip the wax applicator in the wax, press out any excess, and apply the wax with a damp (not wet) applicator. Spread the wax thinly and evenly, making long, straight strokes in one direction. Wait 30 minutes before walking on the floor and two hours before applying a second coat. For a higher gloss, buff when dry, using a clean, weighted cloth or a polishing machine. Use a soft fiber brush on the machine, not steel wool pads.

Two light coats of wax are better than one heavy coat. Although the surface of a heavy coat hardens, the polish underneath stays soft, enabling the finish to absorb ground-in dirt. Thin coats dry more thoroughly, protect the floor, are resistant, and are less slippery. Before waxing, check that no soap or cleaner is left on the floor. Waxing over a soap film reduces water resistance of the wax and may cause a spotted floor.

Achieving a gloss. For a high gloss, apply several light coats. After each coat dries, buff with a polishing machine or a weighted cloth. Frequent buffing, rather than frequent waxing, gives luster to your floor and prevents wax buildup.

Removing Old Wax Buildups

Use of too much wax produces areas where the wax film discolors after a number of waxings. Most waxes recommended today by tile manufacturers are water waxes that wash off with a diluted solution of resilient tile cleaner. However, to remove heavy buildup, use No. 00 steel wool dipped in a concentrated solution of tile cleaner.

Avoid harmful coatings such as shellac, varnish and plastic finishes, as well as multiple coatings of acrylic finishes that can permanently injure your floor. Do not use an oil mop. It will streak the wax and produce a sticky, dirt-catching film.

Protection from Indentation

All resilient floor tile is subject to indentation caused by heavy loads resting on small or uneven surfaces. Protect your floor by removing any small metal domes from furniture legs; try to substitute large, load-spreading furniture rests. The broad bases on the rests spread the weight over a larger area and prevent mars and dents. Choose rests that are flat and smooth, with round edges to prevent cutting the tile. For side chairs, small cabinets and other small pieces of furniture that are frequently moved, use glides with smooth, flat-base, rounded edges and a flexible pin to maintain flat contact with the floor. The size needed will depend on the weight to be carried. On heavy furniture that is not moved frequently, use composition furniture cups to prevent the legs from cutting into the floor.

Other chairs and movable furniture should have swiveling, ball-bearing rubber-tread casters or flat glides. Casters should have large-diameter wheels (about two inches) with soft rubber treads. Do not choose hard rubber casters with small diameters and crowned threads; these will mark resilient floors.

Instead of steel wool, apply resilient tile cleaner on a soft cloth to clean embossed tile.

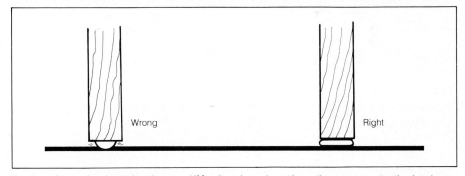

Resilient tile can be dented or damaged if furniture legs do not have the proper protective hardware. Small metal domes are especially destructive. Replace improper furniture supports with flat glides.

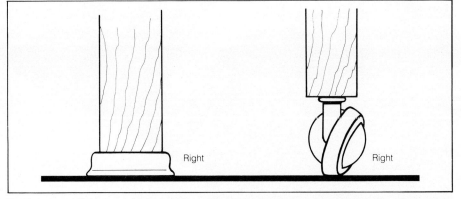

Furniture cups (left) cover the legs of heavy furniture pieces. Large-wheeled, soft-rubber casters (right) finish off chairs and other pieces that are moved often.

Use a knife or razor knife to make "sawdust" from a scrap piece of resilient tile. Then mix the residue with white glue. Press the mixture into small holes in resilient tile.

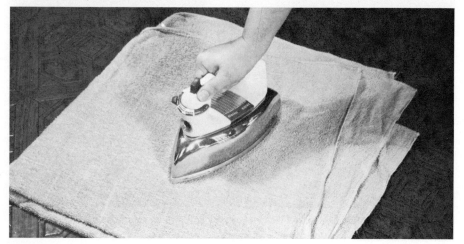

To loosen a damaged tile, heat it with an iron protected with a towel. Then use a chisel to cut and peel the tile from the floor. Make sure the new tile is flush with surrounding tiles.

Concealing Scratches

Remove light scratches by scrubbing with a lukewarm solution of resilient tile cleaner that is recommended by the manufacturer. Remove heavier scratches or cigarette burns by rubbing with No. 00 steel wool dipped in cleaner. In both cases, rinse, dry and polish.

Repairing Cuts and Gouges

If a resilient tile contains a severe cut, it may be best to replace the damaged tile.

Removing the old tile. Place a soft cloth between an iron and the tile and heat the tile. Then use a flat wide chisel to peel up the damaged tile. If the tile is old and brittle, you probably will have to chip it out. Be careful not to damage any of the surrounding tiles. Restrained, cautious use of a heat lamp also helps to soften old adhesive. Thoroughly clean all adhesive from the floor under the tile and from the edges of surrounding tiles.

Adding the new tile. If the tile is dry-backed, coat the back of a new tile with adhesive, press it in place and roll it securely. If using a self-stick tile, peel off the protective paper and press in place. In some instances you may need to utilize a small block of soft wood and a hammer to tap in the edges of the tile until they fit evenly with the surrounding tiles. Be careful not to bend or damage the new tile or the surrounding tiles.

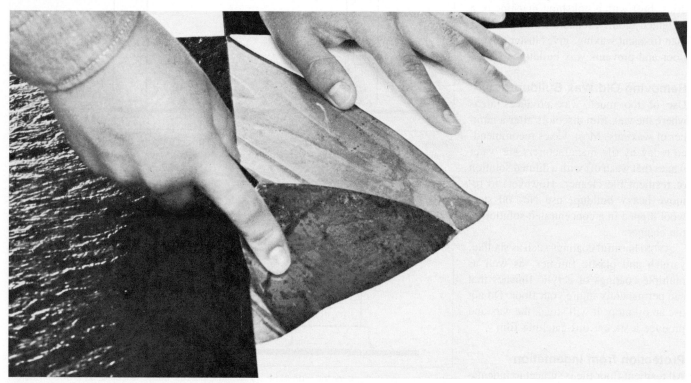

You may also heat tile with a heat lamp. Remove the tile with a scraper or putty knife.

MIRROR TILES

Clean mirror tiles in exactly the same manner as other household glass. They should be dusted daily with a soft cloth. To use a glass cleaner, apply the spray to the cloth, not the tiles. Do not use ordinary soap; it causes streaks. Work gently. Cloths can catch on the corners of the tile and actually crack, break or tear off a piece of tile. If the tiles are extremely soiled, wipe off the loose dirt with a soft cloth. Then use a special product or glass cleaner. Never use solutions that contain ammonia — it will remove the silver mirror backing.

Replacing a Broken Tile

If a tile becomes cracked or broken, it will have to be replaced. Use a sharp, wide chisel to get under the cracked or broken edge of the tile. Carefully pry it away from the wall or floor surface. Use leather gloves, and work carefully so you will not cut your hands on the sharp edges. Also wear safety glasses or goggles to protect your eyes. Be careful not to damage the surrounding tiles.

METAL TILES

Metal tiles should be cleaned with mild detergent and water. If they become darkened, use the appropriate metal cleaner. Since metal tiles do not break or crack, they rarely need to be replaced. However, they can occasionally become loosened from the mastic. They can also become dented, rusted, or corroded to the point that they must be replaced. In these cases, remove by prying up a corner with an ordinary kitchen knife. Clean away old mastic, apply new mastic to the back of a new tile, and simply press in place. In some cases the tiles may have been installed with double-faced tape on their back edges instead of adhesive. If so, re-install with double-faced tape.

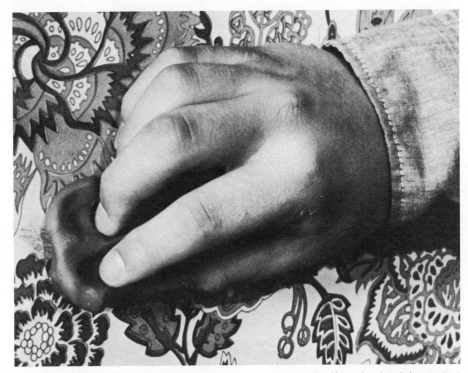

Dough-like wallpaper cleaner can wipe away much grime and dirt. Keep the dough in constant motion as you use it on the wallcovering, as it goes across the surface and as it comes off.

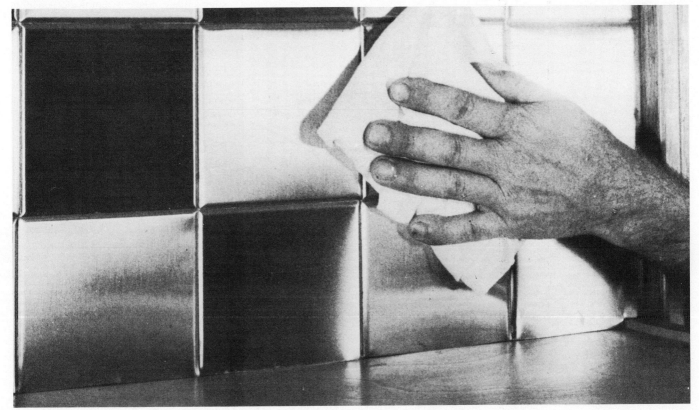

Clean metal tile with mild detergent. If this is not successful, use the correct metal cleaner or, if necessary, replace the tile.

Marble tile, which covers this fireplace surround, stains quite easily. At least once a month, clean with mild detergent and a soft cloth. Serious stains will probably require sanding.

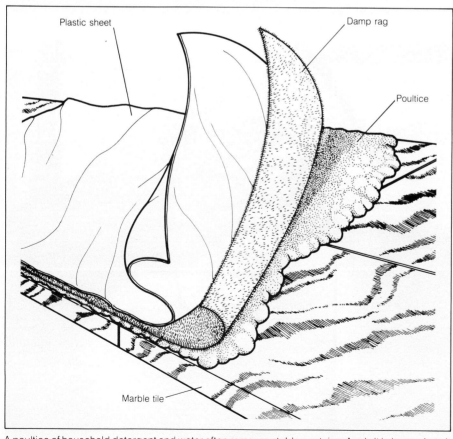

A poultice of household detergent and water often removes stubborn stains. Apply it in layers. Let sit overnight; remove the bag and let mixture dry. Scrape it away; clean and polish.

MARBLE TILE
Cleaning

Daily maintenance of polished marble tiles is best done with ordinary soft water and a soft cloth. Household detergent will help clean up more troublesome spots. To deal with very stubborn stains, you may wish to purchase a marble cleaning kit that contains the proper chemicals and instructions for specific stains.

Using a poultice. Ground-in grime can be removed by use of a poultice, and even some oil and grease stains can be removed in this manner. Use household detergent and a little water to make up a thick paste. Spread this over the surface of the marble in a coating about ¼ inch thick. Cover with a damp cloth; over this place a plastic sheet. Allow the poultice to sit covered for at least 24 hours. Then remove the plastic and the damp cloth and allow the material to dry in place for at least another 24 hours. Scrape away the poultice, flush with clean water and polish the marble surface with a soft dry cloth.

Organic stains on marble, such as tobacco, tea, coffee, or leached colors from flowers or textiles are best removed by bleaching. Make up a poultice by laying on the marble facial tissues soaked in a 20 percent solution of hydrogen peroxide. Cover the entire marble surface with the soggy mass. Place a damp cloth over it and cover this with a plastic sheet. Depending on how deep the stain is, it will require from one to 48 hours to remove it from the marble. Really stubborn oil stains are best removed using the tissue poultice but substitute detergent for the peroxide.

Scratches

Scratches can be removed by sanding with progressively finer grits of abrasive block.

The preliminary sanding. Start with 80 grit and work up through 320 grit. With moderate pressure, work back and forth, occasionally sprinkling the block with water to help reduce friction. If you prefer, do the preliminary sanding with the power finishing sander. As soon as you have removed the minor scratches stop and go on to the final polishing steps.

The final polishing. First, smooth the entire surface with a 600 grit abrasive disk or sander. Then apply a slurry mixture of rottenstone and water, with a felt pad on a power sander. After a few minutes of work, use a sponge and clean water to remove the slurry. Polish the marble with a soft cloth.

Remove small dull spots or scratches from a marble surface by using a tin dioxide or polishing powder. You can usually buy a small quantity of this material from monument or marble dealers. To bring up the polish, sprinkle some of the powder over the marble. Then dampen a medium-hard felt pad attached to a wood block and polish the stone.

Once you have polished the stone to suit, spray it with a protective wax spray that is especially formulated for marble.

Cracked or Broken Tiles

Cracked or broken marble tiles often can be repaired so they look almost like new. Assemble all the pieces on a flat, smooth surface to test how they fit together. Then use acetone to remove all dirt and grime from all edges. Purchase special marble-repair glue from a marble dealer, or use ordinary epoxy glue. With a small paint brush, cover the edges to be glued. Press the edges together and hold or clamp them for the amount of time specified by the glue manufacturer. Wipe away excess glue before it has time to harden.

A hole or broken corner in a marble tile requires another technique. Mix together marble dust (again, available from monument dealers) and a little polyester resin cement to form a paste. Pour it into the hole. To repair a broken corner, create a small wooden mold to fit. Cover the mold with wax paper and fill it with the paste. After overnight drying, remove the paper and the wooden form. Rub down the patch and surrounding marble, following the polishing steps mentioned above.

CARPET TILE

Routine cleaning of carpet tile consists of normal vacuuming, but when they become extremely dirty they can be cleaned with dry, carpet-cleaning powders. Do not use wet carpet cleaning machines because you stand a chance of loosening some of the adhesive on the tiles.

Replacing a tile is simple. Cut an "X" in the center of the tile and strip it out. Remove the old adhesive and then put in a new tile.

WOOD TILE

Day-to-day maintenance of wood tile, either parquet squares or planks, usually consists of nothing more than dust mop-ping, vacuuming or sweeping the floor with a soft broom.

Washing and Cleaning

Do not scrub a wood tile floor with water, although you should remove stains quickly, using a damp cloth. Most manufacturers of prefinished wood flooring products recommend only a light polishing with a good paste wax. Do not use a water-emulsion wax. Apply the wax about twice a year, according to manufacturer's directions. Buff thoroughly to bring out the natural coloring and sheen of the materials.

Repairs

Disguising scratches and marks. These can be concealed by applying wood

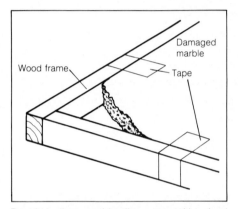

Repair broken marble tile corner with mixed polyester resin and marble dust placed in form.

Apply wood stain with a cotton swap to cover scratches and blemishes in wood tile.

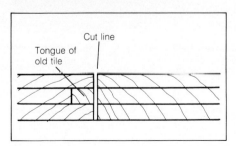

Do not cut into surrounding joints. Finish cutting through at the corners with a thin chisel. Chisel out the tongue of the old tile.

stain with a cotton swab. Fill deeper gouges with wood filler. Smooth with steel wool and buff. Use a good paste wax; then buff again.

Replacement. If a floor tile becomes damaged, you can remove it. Set the blade of a portable circular saw the thickness of the tile. Cut along the joint lines. Do not cut into adjoining joints. Complete the cut with a sharp chisel and pry out the old damaged tile. Remove all old mastic from under the tile. If the new tile is tongue-and-grooved, cut away the bottom lip on the tile's edges. Then apply mastic and press the tile in place. Tap the tile in, using a carpet-covered block of wood. The carpet strips act as a buffer to prevent scratches.

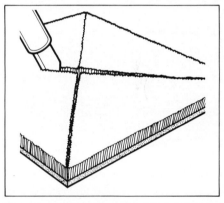

To remove a carpet tile, cut an "X" in the center with a utility knife; peel away.

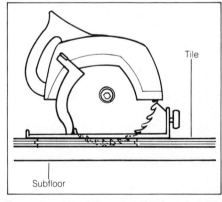

To remove a wood tile, use a circular saw set to equal the thickness of the tile.

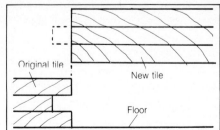

Remove the tongue and the bottom groove lip from the new tile. Apply mastic and set in place with a hammer and a covered wood block.

GLOSSARY

Apron   Trim or facing on the side or in front of a countertop or table edge.

Backer board   Fiberglass-coated, water-resistant wall covering or underlayment.

Backfill   Dirt inserted behind formwork for support once forms are set.

Backsplash   The wall area behind a countertop, sink or stove.

Base materials   Layers of gravel, sand, and field stones laid beneath a footing, patio, or on slab to provide protection from ground heave and to aid drainage.

Battens   Thin wood strips used to support ceramic tile and to ensure straight courses.

Bead   Quarter-round trim.

Beating block   A block of wood that is covered with carpet or other protective strips and used to seat tiles in adhesive.

Bleeding, concrete   Condition in poured concrete in which water rises to the surface of the pour.

Blind nail   Installation procedure for tongue-and-groove wood tile, in which the nails are driven at an angle through the tongue and back into the body of the tile and the floor.

Bond coat   A thin layer of adhesive applied over the primer or bare surface.

Brads   Finishing nails no longer than 1½ inch, they are used to secure molding or other trim while minimizing the visibility of the fasteners.

Bridging   Cross brace supports between joists or main structural lumber.

Bullnose   Finishing tile that has one rounded, smooth edge, and is suitable for finishing a course or row having exposed outer edges.

Butt-edged wood tiles   Tiles with flat edges along all sides.

Buttering   Applying adhesive to the back of a tile unit or a trim piece.

Carborundum stone   Used for polishing rough edges on cut ceramic tiles.

Chalkline   Working line created by snapping a chalk-covered string pulled tightly between two nails.

Cleats   Blocks (usually of 2x4s) used to support wood braces or members.

Closet bolts   Bolts that hold the toilet stool to the floor.

Contour gauge   A device consisting of small rods between two metal pieces, and used to copy shapes of features such as door moldings.

Control joints   A shallow groove installed in a concrete slab to contain cracking within a given area.

Course   A horizontal row of units or material, such as a course or row of tile or a course of base material (gravel, sand, stone).

Cove   A trim or finishing tile that creates a smooth joint between adjacent walls, a wall and a floor, or other surfaces.

Cross braces   Supports (usually 1x3s or 2x4s) running between structural members or components.

Cross lap joints   An interior joint resulting from matched sets of routed-out spaces; the overlapped wood faces meet for a flush surface.

Cure   The period of time concrete must be kept damp and allowed to set (or that grout must be left alone) in order for it to reach full strength.

Dado   A square-edged slot or groove cut into one piece of wood; the end of another piece of wood fits snugly inside the dado.

Darby A tool used to smooth the surface of a concrete pour after screeding.

Dressed lumber The actual size of stock lumber once its surface has been planed and smoothed.

Dressing joints Smoothing and shaping grout lines.

Dry-set mortar A cement-based adhesive.

Edge stiffener An edging of solid concrete designed to anchor a concrete slab in position and to reduce problems of frost heave and erosion.

Edger A tool for rounding off the perimeter edges of a concrete pour; the rounded edges prevent chipping and other damage.

Face-nail A nail driven from above through the top surface of the wood; a nail set can be used.

Feature strip A long, narrow resilient tile trim piece often interspersed in a resilient tile floor to provide contrast and design.

Float A long-handled tool used to smooth (darby) a concrete surface after screeding; requires two handlers.

Footing An enlargement at the bottom of or underneath a foundation, wall or pier, usually of concrete or concrete block, designed to support and distribute the load.

Forms Hollow structures usually made of 2x4s, 2x6s or other lumber, to hold, shape and support concrete until it cures.

Furring strip Strips of wood, usually long and narrow, used as facings or nailed to studs to support tiles or other surfacing materials.

Glass cutter A pencil-shaped metal tool at one end of which is a wheel-shaped device for scoring glass or tile.

Green concrete Concrete that has had insufficient curing time.

Grout A binder and sealer applied in the joints between ceramic tiles.

Half lap joints Two-piece joints in which half the thickness of each piece has been routed out and the two meeting wood faces create a flush surface.

Horizontal working line A level, horizontal line that acts as a guide for tile installation.

In-corner Trim tile for turning a right angle in an installation in which the ad-jacent wall is also tiled and faces the horizontal tile surface.

In-fill Extra earth added beneath a concrete base to compensate for the falling off of the ground surface or to create a desired drainage pitch.

Isolation joint Material inserted between a new concrete slab and an adjoining existing surface to allow for uneven responses to heat and cold.

Jack-on-jack Tile layout pattern in which tiles align vertically from course to course.

Laminated wood tiles Built of horizontal layers of wood; especially appropriate for damp areas.

Lath A wire mesh base found in plaster walls.

Layout stick A straight, narrow wood piece, 36 inches or longer; on which are drawn the tiles and their groutlines.

Lugs Insets attached to tiles to maintain even spacing for grout lines.

Mastic Adhesives made from organic substances.

Nail set A tool for driving nails just under the surface, after hammering the nail to within ¼ inch of the surface.

On-grade   At the same level with, or raised (no more than 6 to 8 inches) above the ground.

Open time   The amount of time adhesive can stay on a floor or wall before it dries out and no longer forms an effective bond.

Out corner   A trim tile used for turning a right-angle corner in an installation in which the adjacent wall is tiled and faces away from the horizontal tile surface.

Pipe strap   A soft metal band used to hold plumbing pipe to the wall studs.

Plumb line   A long string weighted at one end with a tear-drop-shaped plumb bob; used to determine true vertical lines.

Pot life   The maximum length of time that a mixed adhesive will stay flexible enough to spread and to create a good bond.

Prime coat   A sealer coat that keeps the subsurface from drawing the moisture out of the adhesive.

Rabbet   A rectangular recess cut along one edge of a piece of wood to match the width of a mating piece of wood.

Radiant stoves   Stoves that enclose a fire with a single layer of metal.

Reducing strip   A trim tile used to finish an edge of a tile installation so the new and old floor levels meet in a smooth joint.

Reinforcing bars   Rods, mini-trusses or metal ties which reach from one course to another through a concrete pour for greater stability and permanence.

Riser   The vertical face of the step structure.

Rubber float   A wide-bottomed squeegee used to apply grout.

Running bond   A tile pattern in which tiles in one course are staggered one-half the tile width from the tiles in the courses above and below.

Score   To scribe a line onto a surface, creating a very shallow groove (or a deep scratch).

Scratch coat   The initial rough mortar coat over a new concrete surface such as in swimming pools; as the initial levelling coat, it is not intended to hold tiles.

Screed   A straight 2x4 or 2x6 drawn across the top edges of a concrete form in order to scrape off excess and level the concrete.

Separation (concrete)   Caused by mishandling concrete; water separates from gravel and cement paste.

Shims   Thin, small pieces of wood or shingle used to raise furring strips or underlayments to a uniform level.

Sizing   Substance that seals the surface prior to wallpaper or other wall-covering; it usually is used on a newly constructed wall.

Skim coat   A very thin coat of adhesive applied before the final bonding adhesive coat.

Spacers   Individually inserted lugs that ensure evenly spaced grout lines.

Spackling compound   A powdery substance that mixes with water and is used to cover seams and nailholes in plaster and gypsum wallboard, or to repair plaster or wallboard. It dries to a very hard finish and is sanded smooth.

Spading   Pushing a shovel up and down at the corners and edges of the forms to eliminate air bubbles in a concrete pour.

Spline   A flat strip that fits into a groove or slot.

Striking joints   Shaping concave grout or mortar joints.

Stub wall   Mid-height wall framing or partition.

T-bolts   Bolts that connect the toilet stool to the floor.

Tamp   To pack down firmly with a series of taps or blows.

Thick-bed mortar   A thick layer of mortar (more than ½ inch) that is used for levelling.

Tile cutter   Special machine used to cut ceramic tile.

Tile nipper   A special pliers used to nibble away ⅛-inch bites of ceramic tile in order to create small, irregular or curved cuts.

Toe-nail   Nailing at an angle from one surface to another.

Tongue-and-groove wood tiles   Tiles cut with grooves on edges of two sides, and tongues on the others; the tongue of one tile fits into the groove of the next to create a strong joint.

Tread   The horizontal face of a step structure.

Trim tile   Specially formed tiles that are used in problem areas, such as corners, finishing rows, or around curved surfaces.

Underlayment   A level, smooth subfloor or base of plywood, tempered hardboard or particle board.

Vertical working lines   A working line based on plumb, true verticals; used as a guide for wall installation.

Wainscot   Surfacing reaching to chair-back height.

Water barrier   A polyethylene film (usually 4 mil thick) installed to prevent moisture condensation or penetration.

Weighted cloth   A polishing cloth that is applied to the end of a mop handle or other device designed to add pressure during buffing.

Wire mesh   Welded 10 gauge wire with mesh squares of 6x6 inch; used to strengthen the slab.

CONTRIBUTORS
ADDRESSES
PICTURE CREDITS

We wish to extend our thanks to the individuals, associations, and manufacturers who graciously provided information and photographs for this book. Specific credit for individual photos is given below, with the names and addresses of the contributors.

Grateful recognition must be given to American Olean Tile, 2583 Cannon Avenue, Lansdale, Pennsylvania, and the Tile Council of America/ Lis King, P.O. Box 503, Mahwah, New Jersey. Both were more than generous with information, assistance and art used throughout the ceramic tile chapters. We also wish to thank Marvin Greenfield of King of Tile, 6119 W. Capitol Drive, Milwaukee, Wisconsin, and Brian Jaschob of Color Tile, 5340 Washington Avenue, Racine, Wisconsin, for their advice and assistance during the preparation of this book.

Allmilmo Corporation c/o Haynes-Williams Incorporated 261 Madison Avenue, New York, New York 10016 *31, 64 top left.*

American Olean Tile 2583 Cannon Avenue, Lansdale, Pennsylvania 19446 *19 top right and bottom, 20 top left, 21 top, 24 right, 39 center, 48 left top and bottom, 50 top, 58, 61 top right, 63, 64 center left and right, 64 bottom, 65, 66, 67, 70 bottom left, 71 bottom right, 73 top left, 74 right, 81 bottom.*

Armstrong Cork Company Liberty Street, Lancaster, Pennsylvania 17604 *25 top, 94 lower, 99 bottom center, 100 top center, 100 center right, 102 bottom, 114, 116, 139 left.*

Azrock Floor Products P.O. Box 34030, San Antonio, Texas 78233 *96, 98 bottom right, 99 top left, 100 bottom right, 101 top.*

Michael Bliss, landscape architect, 221 Encinitas, California 92024 *22 bottom right.*

Barney Brainum-Shanker Steel Co. 70-32 83rd Street, Glendale, New York 11385.

Bruce Flooring 4255 LBJ Freeway, Dallas, Texas 75234 *26, 106, 138 right.*

Craig Buchanan, photographer, 490 2nd Street-Room 207, San Francisco, California 94107 *6, 9, 20 top right, 58 left, 105 bottom.*

California Redwood Association 1 Lombard Street, San Francisco, California 94111 *76 top.*

Cambridge Tile P.O. Box 15071, Cincinnati, Ohio 45215 *14 top right, 15 top left.*

Jane Cary 16 E. 96th St., New York, New York 10028 *69 left.*

Childcrest Distributing Inc. 6045 N. 55th Street, Milwaukee, Wisconsin 53218 *19 top left, 21 center right, 21 top.*

Country Floors 300 E. 61st Street, New York, New York 10021 *32.*

GAF Floor Products 140 West 51st Street, New York, New York 10020 *94 top, 138 left.*

Hoyne Industries Suite 825, East Tower, Rolling Meadows, Illinois 60008 *28, 119 bottom right, 120 top, 120 bottom left, 121 top.*

Kronos Products Corporation Louisville, Kentucky 40223 *58 right.*

Mike Leeds Designs Santa Cruz, California 95054 *30.*

William Manley, interior designer, 6062 N. Port Washington Road, Milwaukee, Wisconsin 53218 *2, 5, 14.*

Marco Tile Company Marco Macctioni, Rt. #2, Box 198 EE, Santa Fe, New Mexico 87501 *23.*

Marketing Support Inc. 233 N. Michigan Avenue, Chicago, Illinois 60601 *27 top left.*

Metalco Industries Inc. 258 Herricks Road, Mineola, New York 11501 *29.*

Mid-State Tile P.O. Box 627, Lexington, North Carolina 27292 *13 right, 22 bottom left.*

Monarch Tile P.O. Box 2041, San Angelo, Texas 76901 *11 bottom.*

David Morgan, playwright; area designed and built by Joseph Kaminsky, New York, New York, *107 top.*

W. F. Norman Sheet Metal Mfg. Co. Box 323, Nevada, Missouri 64772.

Richard V. Nunn Media Mark Productions Falls Church Inn, 6633 Arlington Blvd., Falls Church, Virginia 22045 *41, 42, 43 top left, 54 center and right second, 54 top, 87 center left, 108 top and center, 109 top and center, 131 center bottom, 134 top and bottom, 135 top.*

Portland Cement Association 5420 Old Orchard Road, Skokie, Illinois 60077 *84 center middle, 85 bottom right, 87 bottom, 88 center middle and bottom left, 89 left.*

Summitville Tile — Belden/Frenz/Lehman Inc. 1400 Keith Bldg., Cleveland, Ohio 44115 *16, 20 bottom right and left, 21 bottom.*

Sykes Flooring Products/Selz, Seabolt 221 N. LaSalle, Chicago, Illinois 60601 *25 bottom, 110 center and bottom.*

Tile Council of America/Lis King Box 503, Mahwah, New Jersey 07430 *8, 10 bottom, 13 left, 14 top left, 15 bottom right, 17 bottom, 18, 20 center left, 22 center, 51 left, 80 bottom left, 88 center bottom.*

David Ulrich & Neal DeLeo, Ulrich Inc. 100 Chestnut Street, Ridgewood, New Jersey 07450 *40.*

Waterford Stoves/Capitol Export Corp. 8825 Page Boulevard, St. Louis, Missouri 63114 *61 bottom.*

Wenczel Tile P.O. Box 5308, Trenton, New Jersey 08638, *11 top.*

Whittemore-Durgin Glass Co. P.O. Box 2065, Hanover, Masssachusetts 02339 *125, 127 bottom.*

Winburn Tile Company 1709 E. 9th St., Little Rock, Arkansas 72203 *15 top right.*

Wood Moulding and Millwork Producers P.O. Box 2578, Portland, Oregon 97225 *113 lower right.*

Tom Yee 114 East 25th Street, New York, New York 10010 *15 bottom left.*

LUMBER

Sizes: Metric cross-sections are so close to their nearest Imperial sizes, as noted below, that for most purposes they may be considered equivalents.
Lengths: Metric lengths are based on a 300mm module which is slightly shorter in length than an Imperial foot. It will therefore be important to check your requirements accurately to the nearest inch and consult the table below to find the metric length required.
Areas: The metric area is a square metre. Use the following conversion factors when converting from Imperial data: 100 sq. feet = 9.290 sq. metres.

METRIC SIZES SHOWN BESIDE NEAREST IMPERIAL EQUIVALENT

mm	Inches	mm	Inches
16 x 75	5/8 x 3	44 x 150	1¾ x 6
16 x 100	5/8 x 4	44 x 175	1¾ x 7
16 x 125	5/8 x 5	44 x 200	1¾ x 8
16 x 150	5/8 x 6	44 x 225	1¾ x 9
19 x 75	¾ x 3	44 x 250	1¾ x 10
19 x 100	¾ x 4	44 x 300	1¾ x 12
19 x 125	¾ x 5	50 x 75	2 x 3
19 x 150	¾ x 6	50 x 100	2 x 4
22 x 75	7/8 x 3	50 x 125	2 x 5
22 x 100	7/8 x 4	50 x 150	2 x 6
22 x 125	7/8 x 5	50 x 175	2 x 7
22 x 150	7/8 x 6	50 x 200	2 x 8
25 x 75	1 x 3	50 x 225	2 x 9
25 x 100	1 x 4	50 x 250	2 x 10
25 x 125	1 x 5	50 x 300	2 x 12
25 x 150	1 x 6	63 x 100	2½ x 4
25 x 175	1 x 7	63 x 125	2½ x 5
25 x 200	1 x 8	63 x 150	2½ x 6
25 x 225	1 x 9	63 x 175	2½ x 7
25 x 250	1 x 10	63 x 200	2½ x 8
25 x 300	1 x 12	63 x 225	2½ x 9
32 x 75	1¼ x 3	75 x 100	3 x 4
32 x 100	1¼ x 4	75 x 125	3 x 5
32 x 125	1¼ x 5	75 x 150	3 x 6
32 x 150	1¼ x 6	75 x 175	3 x 7
32 x 175	1¼ x 7	75 x 200	3 x 8
32 x 200	1¼ x 8	75 x 225	3 x 9
32 x 225	1¼ x 9	75 x 250	3 x 10
32 x 250	1¼ x 10	75 x 300	3 x 12
32 x 300	1¼ x 12	100 x 100	4 x 4
38 x 75	1½ x 3	100 x 150	4 x 6
38 x 100	1½ x 4	100 x 200	4 x 8
38 x 125	1½ x 5	100 x 250	4 x 10
38 x 150	1½ x 6	100 x 300	4 x 12
38 x 175	1½ x 7	150 x 150	6 x 6
38 x 200	1½ x 8	150 x 200	6 x 8
38 x 225	1½ x 9	150 x 300	6 x 12
44 x 75	1¾ x 3	200 x 200	8 x 8
44 x 100	1¾ x 4	250 x 250	10 x 10
44 x 125	1¾ x 5	300 x 300	12 x 12

METRIC LENGTHS

Lengths Metres	Equiv. Ft. & Inches
1.8m	5' 10⅞"
2.1m	6' 10⅝"
2.4m	7' 10½"
2.7m	8' 10¼"
3.0m	9' 10⅛"
3.3m	10' 9⅞"
3.6m	11' 9¾"
3.9m	12' 9½"
4.2m	13' 9⅜"
4.5m	14' 9⅓"
4.8m	15' 9"
5.1m	16' 8¾"
5.4m	17' 8⅝"
5.7m	18' 8⅜"
6.0m	19' 8¼"
6.3m	20' 8"
6.6m	21' 7⅞"
6.9m	22' 7⅝"
7.2m	23' 7½"
7.5m	24' 7¼"
7.8m	25' 7⅛"

All the dimensions are based on 1 inch = 25 mm.

NOMINAL SIZE (This is what you order.) Inches	ACTUAL SIZE (This is what you get.) Inches
1 x 1	¾ x ¾
1 x 2	¾ x 1½
1 x 3	¾ x 2½
1 x 4	¾ x 3½
1 x 6	¾ x 5½
1 x 8	¾ x 7¼
1 x 10	¾ x 9¼
1 x 12	¾ x 11¼
2 x 2	1¾ x 1¾
2 x 3	1½ x 2½
2 x 4	1½ x 3½
2 x 6	1½ x 5½
2 x 8	1½ x 7¼
2 x 10	1½ x 9¼
2 x 12	1½ x 11¼

WOOD SCREWS

SCREW GAUGE NO.	NOMINAL DIAMETER		LENGTH	
	Inch	mm	Inch	mm
0	0.060	1.52	3/16	4.8
1	0.070	1.78	¼	6.4
2	0.082	2.08	5/16	7.9
3	0.094	2.39	3/8	9.5
4	0.0108	2.74	7/16	11.1
5	0.122	3.10	½	12.7
6	0.136	3.45	5/8	15.9
7	0.150	3.81	¾	19.1
8	0.164	4.17	7/8	22.2
9	0.178	4.52	1	25.4
10	0.192	4.88	1¼	31.8
12	0.220	5.59	1½	38.1
14	0.248	6.30	1¾	44.5
16	0.276	7.01	2	50.8
18	0.304	7.72	2¼	57.2
20	0.332	8.43	2½	63.5
24	0.388	9.86	2¾	69.9
28	0.444	11.28	3	76.2
32	0.5	12.7	3¼	82.6
			3½	88.9
			4	101.6
			4½	114.3
			5	127.0
			6	152.4

Dimensions taken from BS1210; metric conversions are approximate.

BRICKS AND BLOCKS

Bricks

Standard metric brick measures 215 mm x 65 mm x 112.5. Metric brick can be used with older, standard brick by increasing the mortaring in the joints. The sizes are substantially the same, the metric brick being slightly smaller (3.6 mm less in length, 1.8 mm in width, and 1.2 mm in depth).

Concrete Block

Standard sizes

390 x 90 mm
390 x 190 mm
440 x 190 mm
440 x 215 mm
440 x 290 mm

Repair block for replacement of block in old installations is available in these sizes:
448 x 219 (including mortar joints)
397 x 194 (including mortar joints)

PIPE FITTINGS

Only fittings for use with copper pipe are affected by metrication: metric compression fittings are interchangeable with Imperial in some sizes, but require adaptors in others.

INTERCHANGEABLE SIZES		SIZES REQUIRING ADAPTORS	
mm	Inches	mm	Inches
12	3/8	22	¾
15	½	35	1¼
28	1	42	1½
54	2		

Metric capillary (soldered) fittings are not directly interchangeable with imperial sizes but adaptors are available. Pipe fittings which use screwed threads to make the joint remain unchanged. The British Standard Pipe (BSP) thread form has now been accepted internationally and its dimensions will not physically change. These screwed fittings are commonly used for joining iron or steel pipes, for connections on taps, basin and bath waste outlets and on boilers, radiators, pumps etc. Fittings for use with lead pipe are joined by soldering and for this purpose the metric and inch sizes are interchangeable.
(Information courtesy Metrication Board, Millbank Tower, Millbank, London SW1P 4QU)

NAILS

NUMBER PER POUND OR KILO

Size	Weight Unit	Common	Casing	Box	Finishing
2d	Pound	876	1010	1010	1351
	Kilo	1927	2222	2222	2972
3d	Pound	586	635	635	807
	Kilo	1289	1397	1397	1775
4d	Pound	316	473	473	548
	Kilo	695	1041	1041	1206
5d	Pound	271	406	406	500
	Kilo	596	893	893	1100
6d	Pound	181	236	236	309
	Kilo	398	591	519	680
7d	Pound	161	210	210	238
	Kilo	354	462	462	524
8d	Pound	106	145	145	189
	Kilo	233	319	319	416
9d	Pound	96	132	132	172
	Kilo	211	290	290	398
10d	Pound	69	94	94	121
	Kilo	152	207	207	266
12d	Pound	64	88	88	113
	Kilo	141	194	194	249
16d	Pound	49	71	71	90
	Kilo	108	156	156	198
20d	Pound	31	52	52	62
	Kilo	68	114	114	136
30d	Pound	24	46	46	
	Kilo	53	101	101	
40d	Pound	18	35	35	
	Kilo	37	77	77	
50d	Pound	14			
	Kilo	31			
60d	Pound	11			
	Kilo	24			

LENGTH AND DIAMETER IN INCHES AND CENTIMETERS

Size	Inches	Length Centimeters	Inches	Diameter Centimeters*
2d	1	2.5	.068	.17
3d	1.2	3.2	.102	.26
4d	1.4	3.8	.102	.26
5d	1.6	4.4	.102	.26
6d	2	5.1	.115	.29
7d	2.2	5.7	.115	.29
8d	2.4	6.4	.131	.33
9d	2.6	7.0	.131	.33
10d	3	7.6	.148	.38
12d	3.2	8.3	.148	.38
16d	3.4	8.9	.148	.38
20d	4	10.2	.203	.51
30d	4.4	11.4	.220	.58
40d	5	12.7	.238	.60
50d	5.4	14.0	.257	.66
60d	6	15.2	.277	.70

*Exact conversion

INDEX